BRITISH ADMIRALS
OF THE
EIGHTEENTH CENTURY

Tactics in Battle

JOHN CRESWELL

ARCHON BOOKS
1972

ISBN 0 208 012230

Published 1972 by George Allen & Unwin Ltd, London and
in the United States of America as an Archon Book by The
Shoe String Press, Inc., Hamden, Connecticut.

Printed in Great Britain

Preface

The era of fleet tactics, the period during which the major results in sea warfare were influenced by the manoeuvring in battle of rival fleets of big ships, lasted for something under two centuries. In the Anglo-Dutch wars of the seventeenth century fleets were too numerous and too heterogeneous for fully concerted manoeuvres. In the Pacific battles of 1942–4 there were still substantial numbers of the biggest ships that could be built, but by that time there was no visual contact between rival fleets other than in night actions between forces not of the first line: the principal fighting was done not with guns but with the aircraft which these great ships carried. In the twentieth century, therefore, the only important gunnery battles were those of Tsushima and Jutland. On the latter, brief as it was between the two main fleets, there has been a revival of interest in recent years, deriving largely from Professor Arthur Marder's detailed account (included in his extensive study of the naval aspects of the war of 1914–18) and this has been supplemented by the Navy Records Society's recent and forth-coming volumes of the Jellicoe and Beatty papers.

The fact that I had the privilege of commenting on the remarks on eighteenth-century tactics with which Professor Marder prefaced his account of Jellicoe's Grand Fleet Battle Orders turned my attention once more to the brief views on the subject of those earlier wars which I had included in an introductory study of naval warfare, published in 1936, a study which was largely based on the orthodox attitude of the early years of the present century. These doctrines were in effect the conclusions reached by historians at the end of the nineteenth and beginning of the twentieth century, and in those days Mahan was the most enlightening exponent of a convincing evaluation of sea power in general and naval strategy in particular as well as being the outstanding biographer of Nelson.

When it came to tactics, however, both Mahan and Corbett, the leading British theorist on naval warfare, seem to have been on less firm ground, in that they based their ideas on the assumption that the admirals of the eighteenth century were lacking in theoretical enterprise. Mahan's view was that they did not pay enough attention to the experience of land warfare which he assumed to be axiomatically applicable to battles at sea, despite the strong contrasts and conflicting requirements of their settings. At the same time Corbett's attitude was influenced in many respects by his assumption that the fighting instructions of the eighteenth century were Admiralty orders— which we now know they were not—and that in consequence they tended to cramp the initiative of fleet commanders.

One of the main conclusions that followed from these assumptions was that fighting a naval battle in what had been the usual way, line to line and ship *versus* ship, was a somewhat brainless way of handling the business and that it therefore behoved modern writers to suggest why things had gone wrong and how they should have been done better.

So thoroughly had this attitude towards sailing ship tactics been inculcated in the early years of the present century that as late as 1945, when Professor Michael Lewis, the leading naval historian of the time, asked my opinion on the tactical section of *The Navy of Britain* which he was then writing, I could only partially divest myself of the views on which my contemporaries and I had been brought up. But by then they no longer seemed to ring true. Lewis agreed that the abuse to which the fighting instructions had so often been subjected could not be fully justified and he amended his draft accordingly. But so deeply had the usual story become ingrained that no further alterations seemed to me practicable at that time. As a result it has been in my mind during the succeeding years, that a re-examination of these tactical problems of the eighteenth century (which in this case must be extended to 1805), free of any prior axioms and based solely on the history of the major battles, should enable one to arrive at a more balanced judgement and to decide in particular whether any planned procedure based on some theory other than forming a line parallel to the enemy would have resulted in more resounding victories. This I have now tried to do.

In arriving at the important fact that the mid-eighteenth-century fighting instructions, though printed by the Admiralty, were never issued 'By Command of Their Lordships' I am much indebted to the help of Miss V. Riley of the Naval Historical Library (Ministry of Defence) and Dr M. W. B. Sanderson, Librarian of the National Maritime Museum. Thanks are also due to the Society for Nautical Research for permission to reproduce the diagram showing the cross-section of the *Victory*.

Contents

Illustrations

The Toulon diagram is based on one in *The Navy in the War of 1739–48* by H. W. Richmond, and the Trafalgar diagram on the Report of the Admiralty Committee (1913). The remaining diagrams were compiled by the author from written sources and drawn fair by Northbourne Designs of Kinson, Bournemouth.

Chapter 1

ORIGINS OF THE LINE OF BATTLE

It has been said before now that of all the works of man's hands none has been more completely satisfying than the ship of the line of the eighteenth century. Under full sail she was of surpassing beauty and even when stripped of masts and yards her hull was so decorated with artistic carvings as to please the eye. But it was in so completely fulfilling her purpose within the physical limitations of the age that her greatest claim to respect lay. That purpose was to be both seaworthy and battleworthy in the highest degree. So well agreed in all European navies were the principal characteristics which these requirements enjoined that for a century and more there were no outstanding changes. Improvements there were both in hull design and in gunnery; and there seems to have been agreement that the extensive carving which beautified the ships of the late seventeenth and early eighteenth century was a shade too extravagant. But the essentials were unaltered.

If it was on the one hand in their appearance and their appropriateness that these ships excelled, they have also seldom been surpassed in the way they were handled: the combination of head and hand, of drill and muscle, that were needed to combat the elements and the enemy. Skilful sail handling and manoeuvring within the limitations imposed by wind and sea had to be combined with the strenuous drill needed to load and fire the cannon at such speed as would often be the decisive factor in a battle.

It is not to be supposed that all British ships of the line reached an ideal standard. English shipwrights were of a conservative turn of mind and were content to provide ships that were soundly built and did in fact fulfil their purpose. But they seldom looked beyond that, whereas the French, with more intellectual enterprise, were constantly effecting minor improvements. From this it resulted that a French ship captured was not merely an addition to the British fleet; she was often a pattern on which new British ships were at least partially modelled.

Nor, of course, were all British crews without blemish, particularly at the beginning of a war when most of the men were pressed and many of the officers lacked experience. But so constant was the seafaring once a war had started and, under the better admirals and captains, so frequently were the crews exercised at sail drill and gun drill that a high standard in ships of the line was the rule. It was these ships that were the backbone of a navy 'Whereon, under the good Providence of God, the safety, honour and welfare of our country do chiefly depend'. And as their name implied they were normally expected to fight in line of battle.

For two thousand years preceding the sixteenth century sea battles had been fought between oared galleys, and since all the offensive power of a galley—ram, missile weapons and boarding parties—was concentrated in her prow, the natural form of attack was in line abreast. Then came a change in warfare as drastic as had ever been seen, either ashore or afloat. Not only did sails succeed oars in providing the motive power in battle, but the guns, now powerful enough to batter an enemy into insensibility, were nearly all mounted on the broadside, unable to point more than a few degrees before or abaft the beam. From this it followed that any body of ships attacking in conjunction must be in line ahead or something like it.

At first there was no question of a sustained fighting posture. As compared with later days ships mounted more guns in relation to their size and crews, and there were therefore fewer men to man each gun. Consequently loading was a slow process and would have been even slower if the guns had been allowed to run back on recoil—for parties of men would then have had to go from gun to gun to run them out again. Because of this they were run out before the battle started and securely lashed in place, a procedure which would not have been practical in later years when improved, quicker burning gunpowder had increased the force of the recoil. After firing they were reloaded by men working outboard, and there the loaders would be exposed to the enemy's musketry fire if within range.[1] From this was derived a system of attacking in succession, each ship coming down from windward, firing her broadside, tacking, firing her other broadside, and then hauling to the wind to reload.

Little is known of the origin of these tactics. They may possibly have been employed in some of the encounters with the Spanish Armada,[2] but they were not definitely enjoined until Ralegh included them in the orders he issued in 1617 on his disastrous voyage to Guiana. Eight years later they were repeated and elaborated by Sir Edward Cecil, a distinguished soldier with no sea experience (ennobled as Viscount Wimbledon despite his failure), when he sailed on his shamefully mismanaged expedition to Cadiz.

As this method of attack took no cognizance of counter-action by the enemy it is difficult to visualize its probable result, but this is of only passing interest for in neither expedition was there any encounter with an enemy fleet at sea. And when, a generation later, the beginning of three wars with the Dutch saw the opening actions of as many and as hard fought naval battles as have ever been included in a span of twenty years, the loading of the broadside guns had been so much accelerated that there was no longer any thought of hauling out of action. The first indication of this is in the *Instructions for the better ordering of the Fleet in Fighting, issued by the Rt Hon. the Generals and Admirals of the Fleet* on 29 May 1653 over the signatures of Blake, Deane and Monck. In these it was enacted that

> As soon as they shall see the general engage, or make a signal by shooting off two guns and putting a red flag over the fore topmast-head, then each squadron shall take the best advantage they can to engage with the enemy next unto them; and in order thereto all the ships of every squadron

---

[1] L. G. C. Laughton, 'Gunnery, Frigates and the Line of Battle', in *Mariners Mirror*, vol. XIV (1928).

[2] *Fighting Instructions*, (Navy Records Society, 1905), pp. 27 ff.

shall endeavour to keep in a line with the chief unless the chief be maimed or otherwise disabled (which God forbid!) whereby the said ship that wears the flag should not come in to do the service which is requisite. Then every ship of the said squadron shall endeavour to keep in a line with the admiral or he that commands in chief next unto him, and nearest the enemy.[1]

In the same instructions it was also indicated that this line should normally be a line ahead, for the signal for forming the line ordered ships to come into the admiral's 'wake or grain', that is, astern or ahead of him.[2]

During the two succeeding wars it was made clear in writing, as it was probably already clear in practice, that the line ahead should normally be close-hauled, that is, as near to the wind as these ships could sail. This was partly because it was the constant endeavour to gain or retain the weather gage, but also because it was when close-hauled that ships could most readily regulate their speed, by backing or filling some of their sails, to the extent needed for keeping station.

It is hardly to be supposed that the vast fleets of the Dutch wars, as many as a hundred ships on each side in a great variety of sizes, could really achieve a continuous well-knit line. The fighting instructions laid down that 'In time of fight in reasonable weather, the commanders of his majesty's fleet shall endeavour to keep about the distance of half a cable's length (120 yards, a cable being then 120 fathoms) from one another'; but this is qualified by: 'but so as that according to the discretion of the commanders they vary the distance according as the weather shall be, or the occasion of succouring our own or assaulting the enemy's ships shall require'.[3] Under such instructions there must have been great irregularities in a

---

[1] *Fighting Instructions*, (Navy Records Society), p. 100.

[2] ibid., p. 101. The use of the word grain in this sense gradually died out during the eighteenth century.

[3] ibid., p. 127. One hundred and twenty fathoms was the regulation length of the hemp cable with which a ship anchored, and a cable, as a measure of distance, so continued into the nineteenth century. Diagrams in a new Signal Book of 1816, however, show a cable as a tenth of a mile, that is, one hundred fathoms, and this has been its meaning ever since.

line of a hundred ships but, despite that, it is on record that both our Dutch adversaries and the French observers who were present at some of the battles were much impressed by the appearance of the English line. It cannot have been manoeuvred with the precision of later days and captains must have looked mainly to their squadron commanders and subordinate flag officers as their rallying points, and for this a squadronal organization had now been firmly established. The fleet was composed of three squadrons flying red, white and blue ensigns respectively. Each squadron had its admiral, vice-admiral and rear-admiral and these nine were the only flag officers in the Navy List. The red squadron took the centre of the line and its admiral commanded in chief as Admiral of the Fleet. The white squadron was normally in the van and the blue squadron in the rear.

In later days, when a fleet was less numerous, there were seldom if ever as many as nine flag officers present in a battle; but on the other hand many more than nine were needed for the navy as a whole. This was achieved by commissioning more than one officer of each grade (with the exception of the Admiral of the Fleet) and the titles became merely indications of seniority, for example, a vice-admiral of the white was an officer of middling seniority; a rear-admiral of the blue was one of the most junior flag officers. The tripartite division of a fleet, however, into van, centre and rear with at least one flag officer in each remained throughout the era of sail, though at the end of the eighteenth century it was sometimes replaced temporarily by an organization in two 'grand divisions'.

It was from the strenuous and extensive experience of the Dutch wars that the basic conceptions of eighteenth-century tactics arose, but before the end of the seventeenth two more battles were to be fought. James II, one time Admiral of the Fleet and Lord High Admiral, was now an exile in France, and William of Orange and Mary Stuart reigned in his stead; and our former hard-fighting opponents, the Dutch, were now our allies against the attempts of Louis XIV to restore James to his throne. Both battles were one-sided and both were fought under orders which gave the commander-in-chief of the weaker fleet no option but to fight.

In 1690, with William fighting James in Ireland, Mary's Council of Nine insisted that Admiral Lord Torrington, commanding the Channel Fleet, should engage the French fleet under Tourville which was working up Channel along our south coast. What instructions for signalling and fighting he issued to his fleet does not appear but they may well have been founded on the by now well-known version issued by the Duke of York (now the exiled James II) in 1673—*his Instructions for the better ordering of His Majesty's fleet in fighting*.[1] It was at all events under the ideas there indicated that the battle was fought; a line against line action off Beachy Head in which Torrington, who was to windward with a north-east wind, endeavoured to stretch his line to an equal length with the French. In this, with only fifty-six ships against Tourville's eighty, he did not fully succeed. The Dutch van of the allied fleet had to fight against heavy odds and fought more impetuously than Torrington intended. The allies were clearly defeated and were only saved from complete destruction by anchoring when the tide made to the westward. The wind had now dropped and Tourville did not realize what had happened until his fleet was swept out of action on the west-going stream.

When, after dark, the tide turned again, the allied fleet weighed anchor and made the best of its way to the eastward. Aided by a fog on the following day Torrington was able to pursue his course undetected and found refuge in the mouth of the Thames.

Two years later the roles were reversed. This time it was Tourville who was ordered by his sovereign to give battle to the enemy; a mistaken order given in ignorance of the fact that the Dutch had already joined the English fleet, now commanded by Russell. An allied fleet of eighty-two ships now confronted Tourville's meagre forty-five. But the stage was set for James to invade England with an army comprising all the Irish regiments in the French service and about an equal number (ten thousand) of French troops—to be received, as he supposed, by an enthusiastic populace and replaced on the

[1] *Fighting Instructions*, (Navy Records Society), p. 152.

20

throne. In such circumstances it was clear to Tourville that his honour and his emphatic orders brooked no delay.[1]

On 19 May 1692, the two fleets met off Cape Barfleur, the north-eastern promontory of the Cotentin peninsula. Again the weaker fleet was to windward, this time with a south-westerly wind, and again both fleets formed their lines on the starboard tack, heading southward. The French bore down to attack and gave such a good account of themselves that they lost no ship that day, despite the inevitability of their rear being doubled on. At nightfall Tourville retreated to the westward with a light north-easterly wind, intending to make his escape through the Channel Islands. But by next morning he had made little progress and only about half his fleet succeeded in passing through the Race of Alderney on the west-going tide and taking shelter in St Malo. The remainder, caught by the returning flood stream, were swept back to the eastward where most of them took shelter in the small tidal harbour of La Hogue (Hougue) on the eastern side of the Cotentin. Here they were hauled close inshore, hard by the camp where James and his French-Irish army were waiting to embark. They were under the guns of some forts and the army's artillery, but such protection proved vain against an English fleet that had already tasted victory. In two fierce boat attacks during the nights of May 23rd and 24th, led by Rooke, Russell's second in command, all the warships and some of the transports were set on fire and destroyed. The French navy was severely crippled and twelve years were to elapse before the two fleets were again to face each other in battle.

It has already been mentioned that there were no outstanding changes in the design and equipment of line-of-battle ships during the eighteenth century but some general description of them as they were at the beginning of the century and their subsequent minor alterations may be worth noting. In the rig and handling of the sails there were gradual improvements,

[1] This is the generally accepted version, but Sir John Laughton gave it as his view that in the rather misty weather Tourville did not at first realize the weight of the odds against him. See the *Dictionary of National Biography*, 'Russell, Edward'.

but the fore and mainmasts continued to carry their courses (usually referred to as the foresail and mainsail), their topsails and topgallant sails; and the smaller mizzenmast also carried the upper sails, but in place of a course a boomed spanker was set on the lower mast, gradually superseding the lateen sail of the previous century. Under the bowsprit was spread a spritsail on its yard and prolonging the bowsprit was a jib-boom carrying a jib between its head and the fore topgallant mast. There were also staysails that could be set on the three topmast stays and of these the fore topmast staysail was the one most usually set, particularly after the sprit topsail, which had been carried on a small mast mounted on the bowsprit end, had gone out of fashion.

So rigged a ship of the line could keep her sails full so long as she was heading not less than six points from the wind.[1] If, say, the wind was from the north she could in this way be close-hauled on courses east-north-east or west-north-west. But it was only in exceptional circumstances that her close-hauled course could be made good through the water for she was affected by leeway, a very variable factor depending on the strength of the wind and the state of the sea as well as on the particular abilities of the ship. Leeway could easily be more than two points, in which case the ship would be failing to make any ground to windward. This did not, of course, affect the man-oeuvres of two rival fleets because they would be equally affected if both were close-hauled. But it was an important factor in strategical problems and navigational hazards, so much so that in the early part of the century it was thought inadvisable to keep three-decked ships at sea in the winter, their high sides naturally tending to increase their leeway in strong winds.

As regards the current classification of ships of the line by 'rates', the usage at the beginning of the century was slightly less logical in one respect than it was to become later. First-

---

[1] Only in the problems of nautical astronomy and open sea navigation were the 360 degrees of a circle employed by a seaman. All other matters—courses steered, direction of the wind, and bearings of other ships or of landfalls—were considered in terms of the thirty-two points of the compass. Each point was therefore $11\frac{1}{4}°$ and when greater exactitude was called for it was divided into quarter-points.

rates were ships of a hundred guns (occasionally more) and second-rates were those of ninety and up to ninety-eight. Both these rates carried the great majority of their guns on three decks. But in the third-rate, the eighties and seventies, the former were three-deckers and the latter had only two continuous gun decks. It was here that there was to be a change before long for the eighty-gun three-deckers went out of favour. The standard third-rate became a seventy-four, and when later a few eighties were found in the fleet, most of them captured from the French, they also were two-deckers. The third-rate also included a few sixty-fours.

The fourth-rates were sixties and fifties but it was not long before they ceased to be regarded as ships of the line despite the fact that they carried their guns on two decks. The fifth and sixth-rates were frigates and though some of the former in the early years were two-deckers, by the latter part of the century all frigates had only a single gun deck.

In the size of the guns carried there was no substantial change. Thirty-two pounders on the lower deck (though some of the first-rates originally mounted forty-two pounders there) and twenty-fours and eighteens on the deck or decks above, including what was sometimes called the main deck and sometimes the upper deck—though it was little exposed to the open air. The quarter-deck and poop covered the after half of the ship and the forecastle half the forward half. Only between the foremast and mainmast was there no continuous deck. There there was a gangway five feet wide at each side of the ship, connecting forecastle and quarter-deck, and amidships, between the gangways, were stowed the boats and the spare spars. With the additional deck space available light guns were mounted: ten or twelve on the quarter-deck and two or four on the forecastle. Towards the end of the century these light guns were often replaced by carronades, equally light but being very short they could be of a greater bore and thus able to fire a much heavier ball. Carronades found much favour when there were opportunities for really close action but their range was very short.

Though there was no general change in the size of the armament carried by each rate there was, on the other hand, a

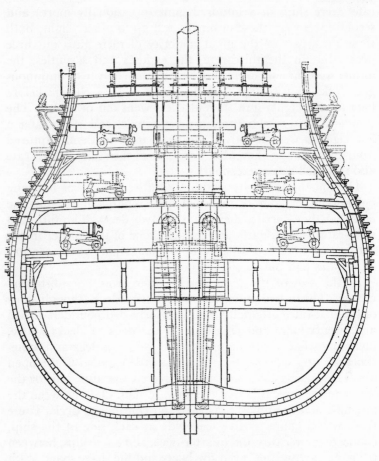

MIDSHIP SECTION H.M.S. *VICTORY,*
(LAUNCHED 1765)

10′		0		10′		20′		30′		40′

gradual increase in the size of the ships, probably with a view
to making them more seaworthy and perhaps to enable them
to carry more provisions and fresh water, the latter being the
main factor limiting their endurance. For example the *London*
of a hundred guns built in 1706 was of 1685 tons burthen and

the *Victory* with the same armament, launched in 1765, was of 2162 tons. And of the third-rates the *Cambridge* (eighty) of the year 1694 was 1194 tons, the *Bedford* (seventy) of 1698 was 1073 tons, whereas the seventy-fours of the latter half of the century were on the average about 1800 tons. These tons burthen, it may be noted, were much below the figures for displacement tonnage by which modern warships are measured. They were calculated by an elaborated formula based on various linear measurements. To arrive at an estimate of the displacement of a ship of the line, with her armament on board and fully provisioned and watered, between a half and two-thirds must be added to the burthen. It has been estimated, for example, that the *Victory*, 2162 burthen, had a displacement of about 3500 tons.

The eighteenth century increases in size only partially affected the complements of men. The first-rates carried about 800 throughout, but the average third-rate went up from about 500 to 600.

Beyond the general characteristics of ships of the line there was one important modification which not only increased the speed of every ship but tended, though with many exceptions, towards a more general uniformity of speed in a fleet as a whole. This was the introduction of copper sheathing. Since all other nations soon followed the British navy's example this did not give the latter a tactical advantage for very long. But it was a notable advance in the science of seafaring and the greatly lessened need for dry docking or careening (there were no dry-docks abroad) ensured that there was a greater proportion of ships fit for operations.

Ever since the seventeenth century and perhaps earlier some form of sheathing had been needed for ships in tropical waters to protect them against the shipworm, the teredo, which bored holes through the hull planking. This had been effected fairly satisfactorily by sheathing them underwater with specially treated felt secured by thin boarding outside it. But this did nothing to prevent the rapid growth of weeds in the tropics and the not much less rapid growth on the unsheathed ships in home waters. Then, early in the 1770s, it was found that sheets of copper in salt water would not only prevent the teredo boring its way into wood but that the salts formed on the surface of the copper would be continuously washed away by the movement of the ship. Consequently no weed could grow and the ship underwater would remain bright and smooth. Experiments were first made with small ships and were so successful that by 1778 it had been decreed that every ship should be coppered as soon as the necessary dry-docking could be arranged. Only one adverse factor made itself known soon afterwards: the iron bolts that held together many of the underwater timbers and some of the bottom planking (the rest of the planking was secured with wooden tree-nails) were found to be gradually eaten away by electrolytic action. The only remedy for this was to replace the iron bolts by copper ones and before long an order was given that all ships were to be copper-fastened below the waterline.

Chapter 2

TACTICS AT THE
OPENING OF THE EIGHTEENTH
CENTURY

When the rival fleets met off Cape Barfleur in 1692 the English fleet went into action with a set of instructions which was to be generally adopted by commanders-in-chief, scarcely altered though extensively supplemented, for the next hundred years. These were the 'Instructions made by the Right Honourable Edward Russell, admiral, in the year 1691, for the better ordering of the fleet in sailing by day and by night, and in fighting'. They were in several sections, and the articles of the sailing instructions, that is, those concerned with handling a fleet when not in touch with the enemy, were numbered separately from those of the fighting instructions. Whether these instructions were the same as, or similar to, the unrecorded ones which Torrington had used in the previous year is not known, but they clearly owed much to those which had been in force earlier in the century and many of the articles were in the same words. But the set as a whole had been modified by subsequent consideration of battle experience during the Dutch wars: modified, that is, from the principal previous instructions, those of the duke of York (later James II) in 1673.[1]

Experience seems to have suggested simplification and simplified they had been. The way in which a battle was to be fought had become generally understood and there were therefore fewer articles under that head. *Per contra* it was realized that more flag signals were needed: that it was inadvisable to rely too much on orders being sent by boat or passed by word of mouth as had so often happened in the past.

[1] *Fighting Instructions*, (Navy Records Society), p. 152.

27

The outcome of this was that in the thirty-two articles of the fighting section of Rooke's instructions of 1703 (slightly modified from the thirty articles of Russell's mentioned above) twenty-two were manoeuvring signals and, of the remaining ten, five dealt with the steps to be taken with regard to disabled ships and only five were concerned with what one might call tactical principles.

At some time after the War of the Spanish Succession had ended and George I had succeeded Queen Anne on the British throne these instructions of Rooke's were printed by the Admiralty, together with the twenty-six articles of his sailing instructions and several subsidiary sections, and the complete 34-page folio pamphlet was given the cover title 'Sailing and Fighting Instructions for His Majesty's Fleet'. Copies of this folio were thereafter available at the Admiralty for supply to newly appointed commanders-in-chief so that they might promulgate them to their ships—so avoiding the unnecessary labour of composing a new set.

Unfortunately Corbett, in dealing with the fighting section of these instructions when he edited the Navy Records Society's *Fighting Instructions* volume in 1905, sub-headed them 'The Permanent Instructions, 1703–1783', thus giving the impression that they were unalterable Admiralty orders which called for strict obedience. This view, based on a partial knowledge of the fighting instructions, had in fact already been stressed a decade or two earlier by Professor J. K. Laughton of London University and had been generally accepted by contemporary writers. We now know, however, that this was a mistake. Three years after Corbett had completed his task a long-forgotten chest of documents was discovered in the Royal United Service Institution and this was found to contain a voluminous collection of signal books and instructions, some printed and some in manuscript, mostly dating from the War of American Independence. These were used by Corbett as the main source for a further Navy Records Society volume, *Signals and Instructions, 1776–1794*, but he did not deviate therein from the previous impression that the 'Sailing and Fighting Instructions for His Majesty's Fleet' were Admiralty orders.

Recent examination of these documents has altered the

outlook, for the fact is that though there are now several copies of the mid-century instructions both in the Naval Historical Library (Ministry of Defence) and the National Maritime Museum there is no Admiralty authorization on any of them. Most of them are probably copies which were in the stock kept ready for issue, but two of them had been signed as orders to particular ships by the commanders-in-chief concerned— Byron in 1778 and Arbuthnot in 1779.[1]

However, despite the fact that responsibility for tactics rested on the admiral concerned, it was to be expected that the five articles which dealt with tactical principles should be looked on as embodying a common doctrine, for there was no reason for an admiral when hoisting his flag to spurn these useful instructions which the Admiralty had ready for him. Changes could come later with experience, in the form of minor amendments and additional instructions. Or the whole collection of instructions could be set aside locally. When in 1776 Howe introduced a new signal book of wider scope for use in his own fleet on the North American station, he referred to 'the general printed Signal Book', saying that it could be put aside unless they found themselves under the orders of a senior officer, and this book comprised none other than the thirty-two articles of the old fighting instructions supplemented by twenty-eight articles of additional fighting instructions which by that time had been printed—as well as the old sailing instructions which had also been supplemented. Some of the additional fighting instructions included signals for manoeuvres which might be needed when it was impossible to bring the enemy to action in the orthodox way, but the five articles of the old instructions mentioned above were still the only ones that dealt with basic tactical principles. Of these the most fundamental when considering the conduct of eighteenth-century battles was Russell's Article XVIII which became Article XIX of Rooke's and so con-

[1] As will be mentioned later, responsibility for bedrock instructions for ships in battle was transferred from commanders-in-chief to the Admiralty in 1799 and remained an Admiralty affair until 1914 when this duty was re-transferred to the commander-in-chief, Jellicoe, who had then to compile the Grand Fleet Battle Orders. These were followed by the Battle Instructions issued by Beatty in 1917 and his successors in command of the British navy's principal fleets.

tinued in the general printed instructions. This laid down: if the admiral and his fleet have the wind of the enemy, and they have stretched themselves in line of battle, the van of the admiral's fleet is to steer with the van of the enemy's and there to engage them.

This was the bedrock on which all actions between fleets willing to fight was to be based. It may be supposed that one fleet was sometimes somewhat less willing than the other, but that the fleet to leeward was seldom so unwilling as to turn tail and thus risk losing its slowest ships and perhaps its honour. It would normally be prepared to stand and fight, each ship gaining in that posture some advantage over his attacker who would usually have to present his virtually unarmed bows to his enemy before coming to close action .

Article XIX cannot be said to be explicit as to how the fleet was to be manoeuvred when it had stretched itself in line of battle 'there to engage them', but this had been well understood during the Dutch wars. In Blake's instructions of 1653, already quoted, it was laid down that 'As soon as they shall see the general engage, or make a signal by shooting off two guns and putting a red flag over the fore topmast head, then each squadron shall take the best advantage they can to engage the enemy next unto them'. A red flag at the fore it remained in the printed instructions, Article XIII. 'As soon as the admiral shall hoist a red flag on the flagstaff at the fore topmast-head, every ship in the fleet is to use their utmost endeavour to engage the enemy, in the order the admiral has prescribed unto them.' In the meanwhile there had been a comment with regard to bearing down on the enemy in the instructions given by Lord Dartmouth, who had been appointed by James II to parry William's invasion. This was included in the instruction for approaching to windward of the enemy on opposite courses and then tacking together: 'Note that they are not to bear down all at once, but to observe the working of the admiral and to bring to as often as he thinks fit, the better to bring his fleet to fight in good order; and at last only to lask[1] away when they come near within shot towards the enemy as much as may be, and not bringing their heads to bear against the enemy's broadsides'.

[1] To sail with the wind on the quarter.

This was obviously sensible provided the enemy line stood on with a fair spread of sail and your own line had tacked at just the right moment to meet this contingency, even though lasking would have involved a very slow approach if you were to keep your broadside in action. But if, as was often the practice, the fleet to leeward awaited attack with its headsails aback (in later days its main topsails to the mast) a perpendicular attack might be inevitable. *Per contra*, if you delayed tacking to allow for this and the enemy stood on, close-hauled under full sail, your van might miss its mark and either be doubled on or lose the weather gage.

Fleet tacking too late if enemy stands on under full sail

Fleet tacking too early if enemy backs some of his sails

ENEMY

Positions for attacking from the weather gage

Whether or not for these reasons there was no further appearance of this note in subsequent instructions for this manoeuvre, though the main instruction had its place in Russell's and in the subsequent printed instructions. There, in Article XVII, the fleet is to tack when 'our rear [is] abreast the enemy's van'.

There is in fact no trace of detailed orders about movements immediately prior to opening fire until one comes to a memorandum issued by Hawke in 1756 at the beginning of the Seven Years War:

When sailing in line of battle one ship ahead of another, and I would have the ship that leads with either the starboard or larboard tacks aboard to lead down to the enemy, I will hoist a Dutch jack under my flag at the mizzen topmast head and fire two guns. Then every ship in the squadron is to steer for the ship of the enemy that from the disposition of the two squadrons it must be her lot to engage, notwithstanding I shall keep the signal for the line ahead flying, making or shortening sail in such proportion as to preserve the distance assigned by the signal for the line, in order that the whole squadron as soon as possible may come into action at the same time.[1]

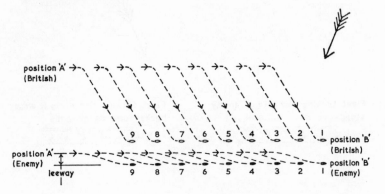

Hawke's manoeuvre for attacking from the weather gage.

In the following year the 'Dutch jack under my flag at the mizzen' became 'the Union flag at the main top-gallant-mast head'[2] and so remained until after the War of American Independence, as did also the wording of this article virtually intact in the various editions of additional fighting instructions.

This discussion of the mode of joining battle has taken us

[1] *Fighting Instructions*, (Navy Records Society), p. 217. The use of the verb 'lead' here may tend to confuse modern readers. To 'lead down' seems naturally to mean that one ship leads and others follow astern of her. But that is evidently not the case here and one assumes it means that the other ships are not to put their helms up until the leading ship is seen to be starting to turn.

[2] *Signals and Instructions, 1776–94* (Navy Records Society), appendix A.

ahead of the introduction of the generally accepted fighting instructions to which we must now return. And here we come to a conflict of opinion between those who shaped these instructions and adhered to them as the basis of their practice for the next hundred years on the one hand and, on the other, the commentators who examined them at the end of the nineteenth century and the beginning of the twentieth. In this conflict two main elements can be distinguished. One arose, as has already been shown, from Corbett's misguidedly labelling the printed instructions as the permanent instructions, leading to the assumption that they were Admiralty orders deterring admirals from using their initiative. That despite this he did not altogether condemn them is shown by his comments in his original volume, and this brings one to the other major influence on tactical commentators, Mahan's already-published condemnation of the accepted tactical doctrine of the eighteenth century. On this point Corbett wrote of 'those stereotyped Fighting Instructions to which, as all modern writers seem agreed, was due the alleged decadence of naval tactics in the eighteenth century'. This idea he mildly confuted when criticizing Mahan's indictment of them as a caricature of systematized tactics, which Corbett says 'may be taken as well representing the current judgment'. He goes on to say: 'we may well doubt this judgment does not require modification. We may doubt, that is, whether Russell's orders, so far from being a caricature of what had gone before were not rather a sagacious attempt to secure that increase of manoeuvring power and squadronal control which had been found essential for any real advance in tactics'.[1]

Corbett's protests, however, were of little avail and his view was deflected later by the feeling that there should have been some follow-up to Nelson's planned, but only partially implemented, tactics in October 1805. Like other writers of his time, therefore, he seems to have felt unable to give support to the single, close-hauled line of battle which the men of the eighteenth century and the first third of the nineteenth looked on as the essential basis of their art, and to have accepted what he had described as 'the current judgment'. This was the

[1] *Fighting Instructions* (Navy Records Society), p. 176.

hardening opinion that the fighting instructions were a dead hand and that the line of battle was a fetish. There was no dead hand and no fetish, but there were some inescapable facts of which the battle-tried and not unintelligent seamen of those days were well aware. There was no dead hand because there was nothing to prevent an admiral issuing his own additional instructions, sometimes in such terms as 'Notwithstanding the general Printed Fighting Instructions'. And there was no fetish, for surely such a term cannot be applied to a system approved by successive generations of naval officers over a period of nearly 150 years, in the later decades of which every admiral had experience of at least two previous wars. The instructions included in the Signal Book of 1799, which replaced the tactical aspects of the former printed fighting instructions, put as much, or rather more, stress on the importance of the line as the normal method of attack as did Russell's of 1691. And after all the lessons of the eighteenth century and Napoleonic wars had been digested responsible opinion was still the same. Almost the last tactical treatise published in the days of sail (1834) was the first full translation of Hoste's work of more than a century earlier, with comments by the translator emphasizing once more the same basic principles.

What worried the latter-day critics of the line of battle is not far to seek. The line to line engagement seemed a dull affair. Could not more inspiration be injected into naval tactics? The great captains of land warfare had never been content with anything so commonplace. Could not the principles of tactics be learned from them?

The most emphatic as well as the most influential thinker on these lines was Captain Alfred Thayer Mahan, USN, and here one may reasonably detect some ingrained bias. His father Denis Hart Mahan was from 1830 to 1871 the admired Professor of Civil and Military Engineering and the Art of War at West Point, and the younger Mahan is reported to have said in later life that his first interest in strategy had been aroused by listening to his father's lectures, which may well be supposed to have included tactical as well as strategical aspects.[1]

Probably even more influential however were the facts that

[1] Dupuy and Dupuy, *Military Heritage of America* (New York, 1956), p. 194.

34

the first book he read about war on a grand scale was Sir William Napier's *History of the War in the Peninsula and in the South of France*, and that when, a few years later, he was summoned by Commodore Stephen B. Luce, the founder of the U.S. Naval War College, to assist him as a lecturer on naval history and modern tactics, he was much influenced, as also was Luce, by his intense study of the works of Jomini, the Swiss soldier and writer who had served in Napoleon's armies. One of Jomini's four principal maxims was 'to manoeuvre so as to engage fractions of the hostile army with the bulk of one's forces', and this maxim Mahan assumed to be as applicable to battles at sea as it undoubtedly was to battles on land. When, therefore, he came to write his illuminating lectures on naval history and strategy with their concomitant remarks on tactics, and to develop from these lectures *The Influence of Sea Power upon History*, this had its effect in his scathing criticisms of Rooke's tactics at the battle of Malaga (1704)[1] and his fulminations against the British tactical system at the time of the battles of Toulon (1744) and Minorca[2] in which he writes of the 'erroneous underlying general plans contravening all sound military precedent', and says that the highest and most authoritative conception of a fleet action (as expounded at Byng's court martial) was 'contrary to universal military teaching'. This attitude he maintained to his last book on the subject (*Naval Strategy*, 1912) in which he wrote: 'I am always much in favour of enforcing military analogies'. And although this book was concerned almost entirely with strategy he follows the foregoing statement soon afterwards by writing: 'The rule (of concentration) applies to the limited field of tactics, as well as the broader of strategy'.[3]

If lessons were to be sought in land warfare there were certainly plenty of examples. For every ten naval battles recorded in history there must have been five or more times that number of battles on land which had been argued over time and again and from which some general principles of tactics had been derived. The primary requirement on land, as had been pointed out by others besides Jomini, was to concentrate a major

---

[1] op. cit., p. 211.   [2] *Types of Naval Officers*, chap. I, *passim*.
[3] op. cit., p. 45.

35

portion of your forces on a weaker part of the enemy *while preventing him from striking a similar blow at you on some other part of the field of battle*. Supposing the two armies were numerically equal, therefore, a minor part of your forces must contain a numerically superior part of the enemy, that is, this larger enemy force must in some way or other be held in place while its comrades were being defeated elsewhere.

This was the prime need when the opposing armies were on the same level of drill and weapon power, but it was not quite the first step in battle wisdom. From the days when the legions of Rome overcame more numerous hordes of barbarians, drill and discipline had often been all that was needed. The brave but undisciplined barbarians struck piecemeal at a close-knit force and so presented their enemies with concentrations against them. In more civilized battles drill and discipline were so well understood as to be less worthy of remark. But they could only be forgotten at peril, and in naval warfare they were still emphasized after the wide and continuous experience of the eighteenth century. In the 'Instructions for the conduct of a fleet . . . when engaged with an enemy', printed in the *Signal Book for Ships of War, 1799*, Article II states: 'The chief purposes for which a fleet is formed in line of battle are: that the ships may be able to assist and support each other in action; that they may not be exposed to the fire of the enemy's ships greater in number than themselves; and that every ship may be able to fire on the enemy without risk of firing into the ships of her own fleet'. And in Nelson's *Plan of Attack* issued to his fleet off Toulon in 1803 there is: 'The great object is for us to support each other'.

This in itself called for great skill in the handling of fleets, but it certainly lacked scope for such tactical manoeuvres as had been the hallmark of so many of the great captains on land. It was tempting, therefore, for later commentators to view strict adherence to the line as lacking in imagination and to clutch at such a fortuitous incident as Rodney's passing through the French line at the battle of The Saints as a remarkable stride in the tactical art. But none of the latter-day writers could suggest any improvements that would have withstood the test of battle. All they could offer was Nelson's memorandum of October 1805; a plan which rested on exceptional factors, among which his own personality was outstanding, and which was never fully executed. This was realized at the time and the single line of battle was retained as the basic formation; but because anything that Nelson had said became sacrosanct little attention was paid to the views of his contemporaries by writers sixty or seventy years later and the men of those days were written off as unimaginative reactionaries.[1]

As already indicated, the basis of tactical skill in land battles was the concentration of a major portion of your forces on a weaker part of the enemy while preventing him from striking you a similar blow elsewhere. To bring about such an achievement there were three physical factors that could be called to one's aid, sometimes separately and sometimes in conjunction. One was the strength that could be contributed to a defensive position by the nature of the ground or by field fortifications, a strength that could be used by part of your army to resist a much larger force of the enemy. A second factor was the concealment which might be afforded by the lie of the land which, combined with the mobility conferred by good march drill, might enable you to bring a major force to a decisive point unknown to the enemy. A third was the fact that any army deployed in line of battle was more vulnerable on its flanks than on its front; if a flank could be enveloped the whole line might be rolled up.

None of these factors had any significance in a battle at sea. The opposing fleets were in full view of each other, and to hold back any of one's own (to 'refuse' one part of your line, as the army term was) would have been to play into the hands of the enemy. Though the bow and stern of a ship, her flanks from the gunnery aspect, might suffer crippling damage from the raking fire of a single antagonist, there was no question of a flank being rolled up—for the assailants' broadside could not be moved sideways. Nor was there any way of adding to the defensive strength of part of one's fleet so as to contain a stronger part of the enemy's fleet. In these respects, therefore, there was clearly nothing to be gained from the experience of armies.[2]

[1] See Corbett, in *Fighting Instructions*, pp. 335 ff.
[1] Despite this, the urge to quote precedents from classic land battles when

There was, however, one other practice in land battles, almost universally approved, which was not in itself dependent on physical factors. In civilized warfare it was unusual for the commander-in-chief to commit all his troops at the outset. Either by organizing a reserve as a separate body, or by calling on some of the troops of the main line of battle that were not yet engaged, he retained forces under his hand until the climacteric moment arrived. Here, it might be thought, was a practice which might be of value at sea as well as on land. But with the numbers of ships on each side clearly visible there could be no hanging back at the outset, and it was only by a superior fleet that such an idea could be entertained. In fact it was never entertained with the same aim in view as made it so important on land. In the latter half of the eighteenth century there was a signal in the additional fighting instructions, for use when the British fleet was more numerous than the enemy, ordering the smaller, surplus ships to quit the line and 'hold themselves in readiness to assist any ship that may be disabled or hard pressed'.[1] But it was seldom used. Byng used it for his one surplus ship in his ill-starred battle off Minorca; and at Malaga fifty years earlier, before any signal had been established for the purpose, Rooke, in his written Order of Battle, stationed two of the smallest of his fifty-three ships of the line to windward of the centre—whence they were in fact able to come down to him and give some much needed help when he was hard pressed. But there is no other recorded instance of this practice.

When all was said, therefore, it was clear that there was nothing to be learned from the tactics of land battles. Navies must develop their own methods from their own, dissimilar conditions. Unless you had more ships than the enemy and could concentrate on his van or rear, perhaps by doubling, there could be no soundly planned concentration on an enemy's

discussing sea warfare has survived in at least one instance until modern times. In 1944 I read a translation of a captured Japanese dissertation on the employment of aircraft carriers which started with an account of Hannibal's double envelopment of the Roman army at Cannae (216 BC). Whether the Japanese profited by Hannibal's example, I cannot say.

[1] *Signals and Instructions* (Navy Records Society), p. 226.

well-conducted line. A concentration might come one's way, but only if, in Jervis's expressive words, the commander-in-chief of the enemy 'bitches it so as to misconduct his line'.[1] It was here that the real essentials of naval tactics lay, the well-drilled line of battle and such flexibility as would enable advantage to be taken of any opportunities the enemy might offer. The latter note was well struck in Collingwood's remarks in a letter written four years before Trafalgar in which he appraises the genius of Nelson, his admired friend of nearly thirty years standing. In this he says: 'Without much previous preparation or plan he has the faculty of discovering advantages as they arise, and the good judgement to turn them to his use. An enemy that commits a false step in his view is ruined, and it comes on him with an impetuosity that gives him no time to recover'.[2] At that time Collingwood could not have cited any example of his hero's genius in this respect when commanding a fleet fighting an enemy under way, but it clearly emphasizes his, and probably Nelson's, view of the most eminent characteristic of a successful commander-in-chief in battle.

That the whole fleet should be in line of battle was, of course, on the assumption that the enemy was in some similar formation, either to leeward and standing to fight or else plying to windward to retain the weather gage. That any instruction were needed for engaging an enemy who was intent on escaping to leeward without giving battle had not occurred to the men of the seventeenth century, for nothing of the sort had ever happened. But once the enemy was beaten and flying the orders were clear. No ships were to pursue any small number of the enemy till the main body was disabled or run (Article XXI); but (Article XXVI): 'If the enemy be put to run, and the admiral thinks it convenient the whole fleet shall follow them, he will make all the sail he can after the enemy, and fire two guns out of his forechase; then every ship in the fleet is to use

[1] Jervis to Jackson (1778). Quoted by Hannay in *Letters of Sir Samuel Hood* (Navy Records Society), p. viii. The full letter is in Tucker, *Memoirs of the Earl of St Vincent*, save only that it is bowdlerized by the omission of 'bitches it'.

[2] Collingwood to Dr Alexander Carlyle, 24 August 1801, *The Private Correspondence of Admiral Lord Collingwood* (Navy Records Society).

his best endeavour to come up with the enemy and lay them onboard'.[1]

Nearly half the eighteenth century was to pass before the need arose to prescribe tactics for fighting a flying enemy who had not yet been engaged.

---

[1] In the course of this chapter, four out of five basic tactical articles in the printed fighting instructions have been mentioned: XVII, when to windward of the enemy on opposite courses; XIX, when to windward of the enemy on parallel courses; XXI and XXVI, mentioned above. The fifth was XX: Every commander is to take care that his guns are not fired till he is sure he can reach the enemy on a point-blank; and by no means to suffer his guns to be fired over any of our own ships.

Chapter 3

HOSTE'S *NAVAL EVOLUTIONS*

During most of the eighteenth century the British navy's approach to the tactical art had little in it that was theoretical. Admirals were content with stating some simple dispositions by which it was hoped to defeat the enemy and providing signals to effect them, signals which were steadily added to as experience showed the need for increased flexibility. But until near the end of the century there was no attempt to propound a comprehensive theory of tactics or to discuss mathematically the complications of manoeuvring a fleet under sail, complications which were often increased by shifts of the wind. One commentator there was, however, at the end of the seventeenth century who set out his views on some aspects and this he did in the form of Observations which were included in a richly bound manuscript copy of the Duke of York's instructions of 1673.[1] Corbett surmised that the author might have been Dartmouth or Torrington but at the same time gave reasons against both of these ascriptions. Carr Laughton assigned the manuscript to 1689 'by internal evidence' and put forward the view that, as none of the suggestions had any subsequent effect, 'it may perhaps be inferred that he was either a man of comparatively junior rank, who never got a chance of pushing his ideas, or that he died soon after completing the volume'.[2]

Since there is no evidence that these Observations had any contemporary effect, they cannot be said to have contributed to the development of British tactics. But they include one point that is of interest in the light of much later developments. During the somewhat confused battles of the Dutch wars it sometimes happened that some squadrons passed through the

[1] *Fighting Instructions* (Navy Records Society), pp. 152 ff.
[2] *Royal United Service Institution Journal* (1923), p. 376.

enemy's formations. From this was derived Article III of the 1673 instructions which laid down that if the enemy was to windward the English fleet was to stand close to the wind

> And if the van of his majesty's fleet find they have the wake of any considerable part of them, they are to tack and stand in, and strive to divide the enemy's body; and that squadron that shall pass first, being got to windward, is to bear down on those ships to leeward of them; and the middle squadron is to keep her wind and observe the motions of the enemy's van, which the last squadron is to second; and both of these squadrons are to do their untmost to assist or relieve the first squadron that divided the enemy's fleet.

On this the Observation is:

> Unless you can outstretch their headmost ships there is hazard in breaking through the enemy's line, and it commonly brings such disorders in the line of battle that it may be rather omitted unless the enemy press you near a lee shore. For if, according to this instruction, when you have got the wind you are to press the enemy, then those ships that are on each side of them shall receive more than equal damages from each other's shot if near, and in case the enemy but observed the seventh instruction[1]—that is, to tack with equal numbers with you—then is your fleet divided and not the enemy's.

Whether or not they were influenced by the author of these Observations, his views in this respect seem to have been shared by Russell and Rooke, for it is only on that surmise that one can account for the omission of any reference to passing through the enemy's line in the fighting instructions they adopted.

If the English approached tactics mainly on a practical basis, it was a different matter with the more intellectual French. No doubt in their view this difficult art deserved a clear statement of its principles and an exact exposition of the way in which they should be put into effect. And before the end of the seventeenth century a writer appeared who proved himself eminently

---

[1] This was evidently the old Instruction VII (*Fighting Instructions*, p. 156) which became No. XI in the manuscript. It refers to tacking with an equal number of ships if part of the enemy tacks.

successful in providing just such a book as was needed. Paul l'Hoste (usually referred to as Hoste) was a Jesuit mathematician, born in 1652, who in 1697 published his *Treatise on Naval Evolutions*.[1] His qualification for this task was twelve years' service at sea under three admirals of whom the last was Tourville, the most renowned flag-officer in the history of France. He was with Tourville at the battles of Beachy Head and Cape Barfleur, and of Tourville he says that he 'has communicated to me his ideas, and ordered me to compose a Treatise on a subject which, I think, has not yet been treated of'.

The greater part of this book deals, as the title says, with evolutions, that is the intricate matter of handling a fleet under sail, and of these he says in his preface that 'the Naval Evolutions are so simple, and without presuming any knowledge of geometry, that a little application, with practice, will suffice to render their use familiar to the dullest comprehension'. Anyone who studies this book today, lavishly illustrated with diagrams as it is, can only conclude that the comprehension of French naval officers at that time must have been of a very high order. But no doubt the operative words were 'with practice'.

The intricacies that are the hardest to comprehend, however, are mostly confined to three of the book's six 'parts', those which deal with changing the dispositions of the several columns in which a fleet may be sailing, either because of a shift of wind or in a change of circumstances with regard to a possible encounter with an enemy. The chapters that contain Hoste's ideas on battle tactics, given in the first and fifth 'parts', are more straightforward.

The first 'part', entitled *On Forming the Orders*, deals with the order of battle, five different orders of sailing, and the order of retreat. Of these the order of battle is discussed at the greatest length, with conclusions that in no way differ from British practice. The need for the line ahead to be close-hauled in normal circumstances is reasoned in some detail and strong emphasis laid on it. A corollary of this is his insistence that a fleet, when manoeuvring to engage, should be in one or other

[1] The most important sections of his book were translated into English by Lieutenant Charles O'Bryen, RN in 1762, and the whole work by Captain J. D. Boswall, RN in 1834. My quotations are from the latter.

of the 'lines of bearing', either starboard or larboard, whatever its course. The starboard line of bearing was such that ships would be in line ahead when they hauled to the wind on the starboard tack, and similarly when on the larboard line of bearing. With the general assumption that ships close-hauled were standing six points from the wind, it followed that a fleet formed on the starboard line of bearing but standing close-hauled on the larboard tack would be in a bow-and-quarter line.

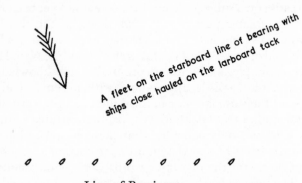

Line of Bearing

Hoste's assumption regarding the order of battle is that the fleets will fight ship against ship on parallel courses; but curiously, as it may seem, neither here nor in later chapters is there any discussion about how the fleet with the weather gage is to be manoeuvred immediately prior to opening fire. This seems to be taken for granted, as it was in Article XIX of Rooke's fighting instructions until supplemented by an additional instruction half a century later. It seems curious also that when citing such points as favour the lee gage if the weather gage cannot be attained (notably that in blowing weather an enemy to windward will be unable to keep his lower deck guns in action without the danger of shipping more water than the pumps can cope with), he makes no mention of the disadvantages imposed on an attacking fleet coming down before the wind by being exposed to the enemy's broadside, unable to reply until ships haul the wind in close action. This seems to be assumed as an inevitable factor which must be set off against the advantage to the weather fleet of being able to choose its moment of attack.

There is, however, an interesting sidelight on this matter in another French work published more than sixty years later, soon after the end of the Seven Years War, as a textbook for the Cadets of the Academy at Brest.[1] In his introduction the author remarks:

> I am afraid we already rest too well satisfied (through long habitual prejudice) that bravery alone will amply supply every other deficiency on the day of battle: on the contrary, if we give ourselves time to weigh things properly, we shall find, from the recent experience we have had with our neighbours, how greatly we are deceived, especially when we trust so much to the impetuosity of our first fire we so generally rely on, though often found to our cost so ineffectual and indecisive: whereas the enemy, by skilfully waiting till the impatient ardour of our first fire, we so much boast of, gradually subsides, gain the advantage of conquering us in the end, which a steady and well timed, as well as an unremitting fire never fail to procure them.

It may have been this, at least in part, that gave the British fleet confidence in facing the theoretical disadvantages of attacking end-on.

The object of all Hoste's five orders of sailing is to keep the fleet so formed that it can be most readily drawn into line of battle on whichever tack is likely to be most advantageous for engaging the enemy. The simplest order is a single line on either the starboard or the larboard line of bearing. This, however, is too extended for a big fleet unless battle is imminent, and the more favoured orders were those in either six or three columns. It was when so formed that the more complicated evolutions were called for.

At this time the British navy had not yet adopted anything so elaborate. When cruising, ships grouped themselves loosely on the quarters of their squadronal admirals. But later in the eighteenth century commanders-in-chief promulgated orders

[1] *Naval Tactics, or a Treatise on Evolutions and Signals,* by the Vicomte de Morogues (1763), translated into English by a Sea-Officer in 1767.

of sailing which were assumed when there was any likelihood of encountering an enemy fleet. These were usually in the three squadrons, though later still they were sometimes in the two 'grand divisions' into which the order of battle was divided in addition to the van, centre and rear. Whatever the order of sailing, however, the aim was the same as that set out by Hoste: to facilitate forming single line on either the starboard or the larboard line of bearing, whichever seemed best for an expected encounter.

These were important matters, but it is in the fifth 'part' of the book that the main tactical interest lies. This is entitled *On the Movements of a Fleet without Touching the Orders* and deals with fleets manoeuvring in sight of one another and when in action, and to illustrate these movements accounts are given of the relevant phases of battles of the previous thirty years. As Hoste says in his preface to this Part,

It is in this that the art of war at sea properly consists. I feel that I have not the necessary lights to give rules on a subject of so much importance, and do not propose to give precepts for Admirals of fleets, but content myself with proposing to them examples, because in matters so vast as these scarce anything can be decided in theory; it is the genius of a hero, possessing professional talent and experience, that is necessary to constitute a great Admiral. I wish only to place here, in a few words, some general reflections, on which I count much more than on my own ideas; some things will be found on which I have determined nothing, having solely proposed the reasons for and against in different plans that may be adopted, for in effect there are some things so doubtful, that they can only be decided on circumstances, arising out of particular cases.

Here there are chapters on gaining the weather gage; on disputing the wind with the enemy; on avoiding engagement; and on forcing an enemy to engage. It is assumed that the fleets are equal in speed and in weatherliness, and on this assumption it is clear that the fleet to windward cannot be forced to engage nor can that to leeward avoid an engagement for long if the wind remains steady. But winds are not always steady and fleets must be so manoeuvred as to be ready to take advantage of any shift, matters on which some general guidance is given but which evidently need much judgment and dexterity.

All this is discussed for engagements between fleets of equal numbers, but there follow chapters on the situation if one fleet is more numerous than the other, the only situation that, in the opinion of the time, made possible a planned concentration on part of the enemy. These are: 'to double on the enemy' and 'to prevent being doubled'. The arguments before and against doubling on the van or the rear are set out in detail with the conclusion that despite the dissent of some experienced officers, it is always best to double on the rear.

After this there is a short chapter: 'to receive the enemy when bearing down', which does no more than enjoin the leeward fleet to be in good order. And finally one on 'to break through the enemy's line'. Here his view is that 'this manoeuvre is equally delicate and bold', but he comes to conclusions which are very similar to those of the commentator on the Duke of York's instructions quoted above. Hoste does not think that the manoeuvre is greatly to be feared by the enemy, and that it should not be attempted unless to avoid a greater evil or if the enemy leaves a great spaces in the centre of his line; or if it is necessary to extricate some ships that have been cut off.

It is noticeable here that there is no mention of any difficulty in passing through an enemy's line to windward if one were in a position to do so, which may seem surprising if the enemy ships were only a cable apart and moving ahead. One can only surmise that this arose from the relatively loose formations of the great fleets of the Dutch war battles, despite their general success in keeping the squadrons in some sort of line. On the occasion in later years on which this manoeuvre was attempted against a well-ordered fleet—by Howe on 29 May 1794—the leading ship 'made four attempts to break the enemy's line but could not effect it. Their rear being so compact left no possibility of sailing ahead of any of their ships, particularly from the shattered state of our ship who barely steered'. Eventually Howe himself, tenth in the line, went through between the fourth and fifth ships from the French rear. His next astern was unable to follow him through in line ahead as intended but succeeded in passing between the second and third ships from the rear.[1]

In one general aspect Hoste's book has an interest in addition to its tactical details. He considers at some length an Order of Retreat and one chapter is headed 'To Avoid an Engagement'. To include these matters is logical and they are soundly dealt with, but the interest lies in the fact that there is no mention or suggestion of such things in any of the British instructions. Is it perhaps reasonable to detect here a difference in outlook of the two services that had a continuous effect throughout the eighteenth century. In 1791 Paul Jones, founder of the American navy, in a long and clearly argued letter to his friend the comte de Kersaint (an admiral who had taken up Revolutionary politics which brought him to the guillotine two years later), wrote: 'In general I may say that it has been the policy of French admirals in the past to neutralize the power of their adversaries, if possible, by grand manoeuvres rather than to destroy it by grand attack'. Later on he says firmly but politely: 'The French tactical system partakes of the chivalry of the French people. On the wave as on the field of honour they wish, as it were, to wound with the delicate and polished rapier, rather than to kill the enemy with the clumsy—you may say brutal—pistol. I frankly confess that my fibre is not fine enough to realize that conception'.[2]

In other words, confidence in their personal bravery seemed to them to justify an over-logical conception of strategy and tactics that was 'calculated to subordinate immediate or instant opportunities to ulterior if not distant objects', as Paul Jones put it.

Averse to such niceties, the British were in no doubt that any opportunity of attacking an enemy fleet, unless overwhelmingly superior, should be seized, despite the fact that an attacking fleet coming down wind was at a disadvantage until the ships could again haul to the wind and bring their broadsides to bear. This disadvantage could well be, and usually was, outweighed by the zest that goes with offensive action and which is one of the reasons, perhaps the main reason, for the over-

[1] *Logs of Great Sea Fights* (Navy Records Society), vol. I, pp. 68, 73.
[2] Buell, *Paul Jones*, vol. II, pp. 297, 302.

whelming respect in which that attitude is held by most writers on the art of war. If considerations of morale are left out of account, it may be that defensive action better serves the purposes of strategy than does attack; but the well-instanced fact is that a prolonged defensive attitude puts a heavier strain on morale than human nature in the mass is likely to be able to bear.

So it may have been with the French. They held their heads well up, confident in their personal standing, but when put to the test their leaning towards a defensive attitude sometimes led to an uncomprehended loss of morale which weighed eventually against their fighting strength.

Chapter 4

THE BATTLES OF
MALAGA AND TOULON

At the opening of the eighteenth century the French had a logical and sound exposition of tactics available to them and in the English navy there was a simple code of signals, embodied in sailing instructions and fighting instructions, based on much the same principles as their enemy's. From this it might be supposed that the subject offered little theoretical scope for expansion. The rest must be left, as Hoste said, to 'the genius of a hero possessing professional talent and experience'. And such to a large extent was the situation. It was to the possession or lack of such genius that the results of battles between fleets of sailing ships largely depended—on that and on the speed, accuracy and doggedness with which the crews served their guns. There were, however, two aspects which deserved further study by the British navy. One, which had not arisen in the seventeenth century, was the possibility that the enemy might wish to avoid action or break it off prematurely, either because he was in inferior force or because he had some ulterior motive. The other, in Jervis's words, was that the commander-in-chief of the enemy might 'bitch it so as to misconduct his line'. Both for these reasons and for general improvements in fleet handling there was a call for adding to and rationalizing the signal books, an object which was finally achieved, as already mentioned, at the end of the century.

On neither of these counts, however, was there a need for any modification in the established tactics for nearly half a century. During that period there were only two actions in which a large British fleet was concerned: that off Malaga in 1704 against a French fleet of equal strength, and forty years later the battle off Toulon against a Spanish squadron supported by and under the orders of a French squadron. In the first there was neither shyness nor misconduct on the part of either fleet: in the second the enemy stood to fight, though not very wholeheartedly, and such shortcomings as there were in the handling of his combined fleet were counterbalanced by misconduct on the Britishside, misconduct that was more personal than tactical.

The battle of Malaga, was, to the men of those days, a famous fight in which there was nothing for shame and little for introspection. The French gave only one doubtful opening for tactical concentration, and the English and Dutch allies fought them with a vigour and endurance which led to heavy casualties on both sides.

Of the strategical setting one need only mention the events that brought the French on the scene. In the spring of 1704 Sir George Rooke, the hero of La Hogue, now aged fifty-four and considered the most eminent admiral in the English navy despite the failure of his and the Duke of Ormonde's attack on Cadiz two years previously, entered the Mediterranean with an Anglo-Dutch fleet. From the Straits of Gibraltar he sailed to Barcelona where it was hoped that on his arrival the town and the whole province of Catalonia would declare for the Archduke Charles, claiming the Spanish throne as Charles III. In this Rooke was disappointed, the governor of Barcelona maintaining his allegiance to the French claimant, Philip V, the king in possession. Rooke then made sail towards Toulon, to reconnoitre, and beyond that to get in touch with the Duke of Savoy if it was found that the French were attacking Nice or Villefranche.

Meanwhile the French Atlantic fleet, commanded by the 26-year-old comte de Toulouse, the much prized son of Louis XIV by Mme de Montespan, had left Brest bound for the Mediterranean, and this force was sighted by Rooke as it beat up for Toulon. It was, however, already to windward of him and his attempts to bring it to action were unsuccessful. The resultant concentration of the Brest and Toulon fleets made Rooke much inferior in number of ships of the line and he therefore returned to the Straits of Gibraltar where he was joined by reinforcements from England under Sir Clowdisley Shovell. With no possibility of pursuing any extensive land operations on the Spanish coast because no troops were available, he decided, on July 17th, to attempt the capture of Gibraltar which was at this time very weakly garrisoned and its land approaches were so restricted that it could be isolated from the rest of Spain.

Five days later the marines of the fleet were disembarked on the neck of the flat land joining the Rock to the mainland and the governor was summoned to surrender. On his refusal a squadron of sixteen English and six Dutch ships of the line and three bomb vessels, under Rear-Admiral George Byng, warped inshore, and on the following morning they opened fire on the western defences of the town and their extension to the southward to the base of the New Mole. These defences were soon overpowered and parties of seamen were landed to take possession. With the town now surrounded the governor capitulated and next morning the marines marched in from the northward.

With Gibraltar captured Rooke now had a fairly good anchorage to which he could resort, and with this under his lee he had to decide what more he could do. A further thrust at Barcelona would have been most welcome to the Archduke Charles, but in consultation with his council of war he decided that it was now too late in the year to penetrate so far into the Mediterranean. He would therefore remain in the vicinity of the Straits until the approach of the season of winter gales in the Atlantic made it time to take the bulk of his heavy ships home. The Rock was secure, at least for the time being, and was being put into better shape for defence by the loan of carpenters and quarter-gunners from the fleet. But some reaction from the French was naturally to be expected and in what strength the junction of the Brest and Toulon fleets had put them was not fully known. The fleet therefore watered intermittently on the Moroccan coast when the weather permitted and on August 8th, with most of their water complete, the main body stood to the northward about ten miles to the eastward of the Straits' mouth, the wind being light and easterly.

Meanwhile the combined French fleet under Toulouse, comprising fifty ships of the line together with frigates, fireships and twenty-four galleys, had visited Barcelona expecting to meet the English there, only to be greeted by the discouraging news that Gibraltar had been lost. With this there was an urgent appeal from Madrid that the fleet should do what it could to assist in the siege and recapture of the fortress, now to be attempted by the bodies of troops converging on it. Toulouse therefore sailed coastwise to the south-westward. Early in August he had reached the vicinity of Malaga.

It was on August 9th that the first touch was gained between the two fleets. At daylight a look-out frigate to the windward (eastward) reported enemy ships further to the eastward and for the first time in this war the two main fleets were in contact.

Substantial fleets they were, and to all appearances they were as evenly matched as would call for hard fighting if either side was to prove itself superior to its adversary. In ships of the line Rooke could pit thirty-nine English and twelve Dutch against Toulouse's fifty, augmented by twenty-four galleys. In the Mediterranean the latter were still looked on with some respect as fighting ships, though in fact their only employment in the coming battle was as tugs, ready in the light airs that prevailed to tow badly damaged ships out of action or to help in dressing a disordered line. A thorough evaluation of the fifty French against the Allied fifty-one is virtually impossible to arrive at because of the variety not only of their sizes but of their armaments, the French carrying in general heavier guns than the equivalent English and Dutch ships. In size the allies varied between ninety-gun three-deckers and fifty-gun two-deckers; the French between 104-gun three-deckers and fifty-four-gun two-deckers—with one fifty. For the eventual battle Rooke decided to hold two of his fifties in reserve, on the disengaged side with the frigates and fireships, and of the two lines of battle it can reasonably be said that the difference in potential strength was unimportant except for the fact that the allies were to be handicapped in a prolonged battle because they were short of the ammunition that had been expended in bombarding Gibraltar. They would also have suffered from a shortage of men but for the fact that as soon as the French were sighted more than half of the marines that had been landed to garrison the fortress were quickly brought back to the fleet by all the small ships available.

This first contact between the opponents, however, was not immediately followed by a battle. Rooke worked to windward (eastward) hoping the French would come down to fight, but the sound of their signal guns, which was soon the only intimation of their presence, became fainter and fainter and it was thought Toulouse had no stomach for a battle. His ships were so recently out of port, and therefore so much cleaner than the allies, that he had no difficulty in gaining ground to windward. But in fact it was not to avoid action but to pick up his galleys that he was making off. They had been left at Malaga, some sixty miles from Gibraltar, and having collected them and completed his ships with water he again stood to the southwestward.

And so it happened that after three days of fruitless searching and a consequent decision by Rooke and his council of war to go back to the Straits' mouth, it was against their expectations that the French were sighted to the north-westward heading westerly. The allies formed a line of battle and, so formed, made sail to intercept them. Early next morning, Sunday, August 13th, they found the enemy to be some ten miles to the westward (leeward), forming their line with heads to the southward, or on the larboard tack.

As to the exact formation of the French line there is no conclusive information. It seems that despite Hoste's, and presumably Tourville's, strongly held views to the contrary the general trend of the line was with the wind abeam. But there are doubts as to its straightness, and the most modern authority on the battle (Carr Laughton in a lecture given at the Royal United Service Institution, 16 December 1922) was of the opinion that the van (white and blue) squadron was on the larboard line of bearing, that is tending, though not steering, towards the English van. He also suggested that the rear may have been similarly formed towards the Dutch squadron, that is on the starboard line of bearing or something like it, thus giving the impression noted in some of the English ships that the whole fleet was in a crescent formation. Whether such an elaborate formation was intended cannot be confirmed, but

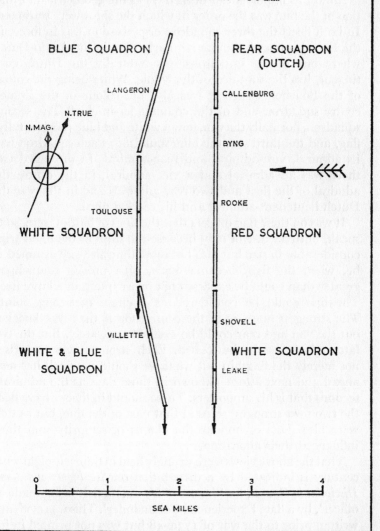

THE BATTLE OF MALAGA
August 13th 1704

CONJECTURAL SITUATION AT 9·30a.m.

BLUE SQUADRON

REAR SQUADRON
(DUTCH)

LANGERON

CALLENBURG

N.TRUE

N.MAG.

BYNG

ROOKE

TOULOUSE

WHITE SQUADRON

RED SQUADRON

SHOVELL

VILLETTE

WHITE & BLUE
SQUADRON

WHITE SQUADRON

LEAKE

0   1   2   3   4

SEA MILES

if it was it was presumably at the instance of Toulouse's chief of staff, the 44-year-old d'Estrées, son of the admiral who had commanded the French squadron allied to the English fleet in the Third Dutch War and already, like his father, a Marshal of France.

Almost as important in those days as the geometrical formation of the line was the order in which the ships were stationed. In both fleets the three squadron organization was in force, in the French somewhat more regularly than in the Anglo-Dutch where one of the squadrons was naturally the Dutch contingent, less than a third of the whole. White being the colour of the Bourbon ensign it was also the colour of the French centre squadron and of the commander-in-chief. The second squadron, normally the van, flew a white and blue (horizontally) flag, and the third was the blue squadron. Each squadron had its admiral, vice-admiral and rear-admiral. In the allied van there was an admiral and a vice-admiral, in the centre the admiral of the fleet and two rear-admirals and in the rear the Dutch lieutenant-admiral and his rear-admiral.

It was on these flag officers that the lines of battles were, so to speak, buttressed. Not only because the ships of the line varied considerably in size but also because admirals were assumed to be, when the fight became fierce, of a proven staunchness greater than could be expected of every captain in a large fleet. The line could be considered as a chain of strong points. The strongest must be in the centre, for if that was knocked out the van and rear could be assailed separately. But the two latter also must be buttressed. Each strong point comprised not merely the flagship but what we should now call her next ahead and next astern—known in those days as the admiral's seconds that is his supporters. These should in theory have been the two next strongest ships in that part of the line, but as they were also posts of honour the claims of seniority sometimes influenced their allocation.

That the above views were strongly held in the early eighteenth century is indicated by a dissertation on *Sea Fights and Naval Discipline in General*, for 'the use of his son on first being made an officer', by a 'late Experienced Commander'. This was evidently written prior to the war of 1739–48 but was not printed in full until 1767 when it was included in a volume containing the *Naval Tactics* of Vicomte de Morogues, translated by a Sea-Officer. The latter was probably the Lieutenant Christopher O'Bryen who had translated part of Hoste five years earlier, and the 'Experienced Commander' was almost certainly an elder Christopher O'Bryen, whether father or uncle, who was present at the battle of Malaga as a midshipman in the *Orford*, Captain (later Admiral of the Fleet Sir John) Norris, and who later commanded a ship of the line in the Sicilian operations of 1718–20 under the elder Byng. Unfortunately there is no similar work of this period with which to compare his views but they are well set out and give the impression of being sound and generally accepted.

Both fleets having formed their lines, Rooke stood down before the wind until he had closed to a mile. There, at about 9 a.m., he stayed for a time, for the French, lying with their headsails to the mast, were nearly stationary, and he could only attack bows-on instead of edging down as he would have preferred. This aspect of affairs, however, was soon altered by the French van, under Villette, admiral of the white and blue, setting their mainsails and hauling to the wind with the intention, so it seemed, of concentrating on the leading ships of the English van. This was soon frustrated by Shovell's squadron also making sail, though with the result that a gap appeared between the English van and centre. The French centre then set their mainsails with the apparent aim of making for this gap, and this determined Rooke to fall to, about 10.30 a.m., without further delay. The gap was soon closed and the battle gradually became general. Hard fighting resulted in some disablement of ships and what in those days were adjudged considerable casualties—in general about 15 killed and 40 wounded (many of whom would probably die) in each ship, though in Rooke's flagship and his second astern there was a total of 72 killed and 187 wounded out of a combined complement of 1400.[1] What

---

[1] Since there has sometimes been a tendency to imply that Malaga was not a really hard fought battle, it is interesting to compare the casualties with those suffered a hundred years later at Trafalgar. At Malaga the average casualties of the 41 English ships engaged were 17 killed and 40 wounded. At Trafalgar the average for the 27 British ships was 17 killed and 46

the French casualties were is uncertain. They stated only 1500 killed and wounded against an Anglo-Dutch total of 2700, but their proportionate loss of officers seems to have been higher. Toulouse himself was slightly wounded and four of his personal staff were either killed or wounded.

During the course of the afternoon the English van squadron had forced their opponents to leeward (an advantage completed by a heavy explosion in the after part of Villette's flagship) and Vice-Admiral Sir John Leake, who was near the head of the line, sent his flag captain to Shovell, urging that they should pursue. With this Shovell did not agree. Many of his ships were by this time incapable of concerted movement and it was clear that Rooke in the centre was being hard pressed. The two fifties in reserve had been called in to help him but they could not compensate for the number (eventually seven including his second ahead) who had run out of ammunition and quitted the line in consequence. The fleet as a whole was short of the ammunition expended in bombarding Gibraltar and although there had been some distribution thereafter to the ships that had bombarded, there were evidently some ships whose rate of fire had been too much for their reduced outfits. It was in these circumstances that, now there was no longer any pressure on the van, Shovell and the ships astern of him made a stern board (that is sailed stern first under backed topsails: a difficult manoeuvre) towards his commander-in-chief to give closer support to the embattled centre. And so as the afternoon wore on, the fleets fought each other to a virtual standstill.

Leake's suggestion that the van squadron should endeavour to complete the destruction of the French van, now seemingly admitting defeat, raises a point of perennial interest in fleet tactics which can be traced in some sort even down to the days of Jutland—not in the events of that battle but in some of the subsequent criticisms. How far is it justifiable to jeopardize the cohesion of the fleet as a whole with the aim of defeating on part of the enemy's? How are the sometimes conflicting claims of cohesion and diversity to be balanced?

wounded. At the later battle, however, the ships of the line were bigger, with an average complement of 610 as against 450 for those at Malaga.

In Rooke's instructions (and in all fighting instruction since 1665) the answer is quite clear. Article XXI says: 'None of the ships of the fleet shall pursue any small number of the enemy's ships till the main body be disabled or run'. But the question arises whether the French van squadron was a 'small number'. In Leake's view it was more substantial than that and he believed that if the whole English van squadron drove them further to the leeward the French centre would have to relinquish its destructive action and go to leeward too. That is as may be, but it is clear that Shovell, who could see more of what was happening in the centre than Leake, did not agree. Leake was probably the most able and reliable admiral that this war produced. His whole conduct in this and the previous war had been and was to continue, without blemish, and he was never bedevilled by the political motives and intrigues that so often afflicted his contemporaries. But whether he was right on this occasion no one can say with assurance.

Fifty years later there were two instances of Article XXI being suspended, as will be mentioned in due course, but on each occasion it was soon reintroduced and the 'Instructions for the conduct of the fleet preparatory to their engaging, and when engaged, with an enemy' in the Signal Book of 1799, which superseded the former fighting instructions, go back to principles of a century earlier though rather more wordily. Article XV stated:

No ship is to separate from the main body of the fleet, in time of action, to pursue any small number of the enemy's ships that have been beaten out of the line, unless the commander-in-chief, or some other flag officer, be among them; but the ships which have disabled their opponents, or forced them to quit the line, are to assist any ship of the fleet appearing to be much pressed, and to continue their attack till the main body of the enemy be broken or disabled; unless by signal, or particular instruction, they should be directed to act otherwise.

This would certainly have given the scope needed to justify Leake's contention, for Villette, second-in-command of the fleet, and his vice and rear admirals were among the ships that had been driven out of the line. But decision on this point must always have been a matter of nice judgment. To Leake it seemed obvious that they should complete the disablement of the French van. To Shovell it may have appeared equally obvious that he could not desert his hard-pressed commander-in-chief while the outcome of the battle in the centre was still in doubt. Probably Shovell was right, in view of Rooke's troubles in the centre, as Leake's biographer seems partially to have admitted. As the matter is fundamental to the tactics of this time and was still important, though perhaps somewhat less so, in later years when fleets were smaller and rather more uniform in composition, these views merit quotation in full.

The French, having resolved to fight, drew up their line of battle in the best manner; making themselves strongest in the centre. Contrariwise the Confederates were, in proportion, stronger in the van, and weak in the centre; whereby, though we beat their van, our centre maintained the fight with difficulty. And this was doubtless a great error in the English Admiral (unless he had made better use of our advantage in the van) for it is well known, and sufficiently proved in this battle, that the whole success in a manner depends on the strength of the centre. For had the enemy's centre, instead of their van, been beaten, their whole line would have been broken and they must have suffered a total defeat; whereas their centre remaining firm, though their van was broken, they did not in the least suffer by it. For this reason the French always made a strong centre, and therefore Sir George Rooke should have done the like; whereas he himself was in the smallest and worst Second Rate in the English Navy, in fact no better than an 80-gun Third Rate for though she had 90 guns they were no larger than those of a Third Rate. Notwithstanding he might be certain, in case of action, to engage the best First Rate of France. This may be an instance indeed of courage; but of great imprudence from the ill effects which might follow to himself and the public service.[1]

[1] *The Life of Admiral Sir John Leake*, by Stephen Martin-Leake (Navy Records Society), vol. I, p. 177.

This seems, however, an unjustifiably harsh criticism of Rooke. He had no first-rates and only five second-rates. Of the other four, two were the flagship of Shovell and Leake, one was Rooke's second astern and one was Shovell's second ahead. Martin-Leake (Leake's nephew by marriage, the son of his flag captain, and his eventual heir) may have been right in stigmatizing the *Royal Catherine* as the smallest and worst second-rate in the navy, but when one peruses the respective orders of battle of the two fleets it does not seem that the English centre as a whole was notably weaker than the French. It was not Rooke's fault that his opponent, Toulouse, was flying his flag in a 104-gun first-rate and had a hundred-gun ship and an eighty-eight as his seconds. But it emphasizes the current view that the centre must be strong and that the commander-in-chief should be in the centre.

That night both fleets, having fought to a standstill, lay by to repair damage. In the Anglo-Dutch fleet it was not only battle damage that worried them but the fact that they were now almost destitute of ammunition. By the morning a shift of wind to the westward had given the French the weather gage, but they were not yet ready to attack, even if willing. Both fleets continued to repair damage aloft and with the allies there was a further equalization of such powder and shot as remained. Rooke and his council of war then decided that they were no longer fit to offer battle and must return to Gibraltar for further repair and perhaps to assist in the defence of the fortress against the Spanish army now steadily approaching. They would not court action, but if the French stood in their path they must burst their way through as best they could. Rooke, was, however, prepared to bluff, and on the following day when, during the afternoon, the wind changed to the eastward once more, he moved towards the enemy, now some fifteen miles north-west. Darkness intervened, however, before he had gone far, and next morning there were no French ships to be seen. Toulouse had decided that there was nothing more worth doing and was retracing his steps towards Toulon. This was not yet known to Rooke, but whether the French had gone to the westward or the eastward it was apparent that the way to

Gibraltar was now open and the allies put up their helms and steered for the Straits' mouth.[1]

Further news soon made it clear that the enemy had not gone to the westward and were in fact returning to Toulon. On August 20th, therefore, the whole fleet anchored in Gibraltar Bay and arrangements for the coming winter were put in train. All the marines, sixty heavy guns and sixty seamen gunners were landed to reinforce the garrison of the fortress, soon to be heavily besieged and stoutly defended under the resolute command of Prince George of Hesse-Darmstadt. The ships under Rooke and Shovell then sailed for England, either direct or via Lisbon for further repairs, leaving Leake with eleven of the line and some frigates to remain in Spanish waters for the winter with Lisbon as their base.

The battle of Malaga, though it could not be acclaimed a victory for the English fleet and its Dutch allies, left no cause for shame or recriminations. With the encounter off Toulon forty years later it was a different matter. Though a few ships

[1] Because steering orders changed with the disuse of sails and even more drastically in the present century, a note on the subject seems worth while. The helm is, of course, the tiller, even when out of sight or, as in steamship days, sometimes imaginary; and the top of the steering wheel always moves the opposite way to the tiller. To put the helm up (i.e. to windward) is to turn the wheel to leeward, and therefore the rudder to leeward, resulting in the ship's head paying off to leeward. The converse is to put the helm down, i.e. to bring the ships' head to the wind. The matter was further confused in the old days because the expression 'to bear up' was sometimes used to mean to put the helm up, and at the same time there was the expression 'to bear down' on an enemy. So it could be said of a fleet having the weather gage that it 'bore up, and bore down on the enemy'! When sailing before the wind, and even at other times, the orders could be 'port the helm' or 'starboard the helm', 'port' (origin unknown) having been used in a verbal sense for more than a century, to make sure there was no doubt in this vital matter. It was also used later in the expression 'to alter course to port'. But in every other respect the adjective was "larboard" throughout the eighteenth century.

Helm orders continued in the British navy until about 1930, i.e. 'port your helm' meant that the wheel and the ship's head turned to starboard. The change over to rudder, as opposed to helm, orders was temporarily a time of some anxiety for captains and officers of the watch—lest in a moment of crisis the mind should revert to its long established habits.

fought stoutly, if in some disarray, the battle was followed by the heaviest crop of courts martial that have ever sullied a British naval action.

In 1739 Britain had gone to war with Spain on questions of transatlantic trade and it was primarily to West Indian waters that her initial efforts were directed. But in the following year the European scene was transformed by the death of the Emperor Charles VI (in the previous war an unsuccessful ally of Britain as claimant to the Spanish throne) leaving no male heir to the Habsburg dominions. His daughter, Maria Theresa, was accepted as queen of Hungary, but agreements that she should inherit all the Austrian lands, which had been pledged to her father by the other continental powers, were quickly forgotten. From north, west and south she was heavily assailed, the latter attack being that of a Spanish army aimed at conquering the various Austrian duchies in northern Italy. As Britain had declared her support for the hard-pressed queen, here was another sphere of activity for the British navy. The best routes to Italy for Spanish reinforcements and supplies, indeed the only routes if Piedmont continued to stand in the way, were be sea, and to throttle these every effort must be made.

Curiously, though France as well as Spain was attacking Maria Theresa, there was as yet no war between Britain and France. In 1743 George II commanded in person at the battle of Dettingen but he did so not as king of England but as commander of Hanoverian troops acting as auxiliaries to the Austrian army, a contingent in which there were also some British regiments. But in the Mediterranean there were as yet no Anglo-French hostilities. Toulon had been thrown open to the Spanish fleet as an advanced base and there was clearly the possibility of a junction of the French and Spanish fleets at sea which would call for action against the whole body. But until that happened French warships and French shipping were not to be molested.

It was in 1742 that Admiral Thomas Mathews was sent to the Mediterranean to shoulder the far-from-easy task of frustrating Spanish expeditions while at the same time being ready to face the more serious challenge of a combined Bourbon fleet. Such a force, emerging at its selected moment, might well be more numerous than a sea-scarred British fleet which, if it was to continue seaworthy, would usually be reduced below its full strength by the absence of ships careening at Minorca. Mathews was now sixty-five years old. Though he had been promoted to post captain at the age of twenty-seven and had thereafter held commands at sea until 1712, he had then gone ashore to look after his estates in south Wales. Six years later he returned to the sea for two years in command of the *Kent* in Sir George Byng's Mediterranean fleet which destroyed the Spanish fleet off Cape Passaro (though there was no declaration of war between England and Spain) and supported the Austrian army from 1718 to 1720 in its campaigns against the Spanish army in Sicily. During this period Mathews was sometimes the senior officer of a small force guarding the southern entrance to the Straits of Messina.

This commission was followed soon afterwards by two years as commodore of a squadron intended to suppress piracy in the East Indies—in which its success was negligible. That employment came to an end in 1724 when he again retired to his estates, apparently for good. But twelve years later, perhaps because of the need of more money to rebuild his house and enlarge his lands, he returned to naval affairs in the civilian post of Commissioner of Chatham Dockyard. There he continued until 1742 when he was summoned to take his place once more on the active list, a place determined by the date of his first commission as post captain which now gave him the rank of admiral.

That he had the basic ability needed for his strategic task there seems little doubt, but whether he had the physique to stand up to the strains it imposed may well be queried. Not only had he to command the fleet but he had also to co-operate with the Duke of Savoy (who was now also king of Sardinia) in the defence of his Piedmontese dominions, for Savoy after some hesitations had now thrown in his lot with the Austrians. What was needed Mathews saw clearly, but he also felt increasingly that he was being denied the means to meet all his requirements and his querulous correspondence with the Admiralty became more and more embittered. In fact before eighteen months had elapsed he had reported himself not fit enough to carry on and was looking forward to his supersession. But while he could not consider himself physically incapacitated and there was no relief in sight he continued to fly his flag.

Perhaps all might have gone well if he had had a second-in-command of compatible personality and one who would have been prepared to put up with the downright and tactless manners of his chief. For such a role, however, Richard Lestock was not well suited. He was three years junior to Mathews in age and seniority but his seagoing and fighting experience had been more extensive, particularly of late years. As a lieutenant he had served in Shovell's flagship at the battle of Malaga, and from 1718 to 1720 he had been George Byng's flag captain during the Sicilian operations. And he had served in the West Indies in peace and during the present war, leading a division of Vernon's fleet in the attack on Cartagena. But he had also, unfortunately, held the appointment of senior officer afloat in the Medway from 1734 to 1738 and for the last two years of this period Mathews, as already noted, had been Commisioner of Chatham Dockyard. In that post Mathews had no authority over ships in commision but these two officers, almost contemporaries, must often have come in contact, and for some reason not explained Mathews had come to the conclusion that Lestock was not fit for an important sea command. He said later that this was because his health would not stand up to it, and Lestock did in fact die three years after the coming battle. But there may well have been more to it than that, and the auspices for a harmonious command, now that they were once more thrown together, were evidently not promising. They were perhaps rendered even more unpromising by the fact that Lestock had been in command of the station for several months after the breakdown in health of the previous commander-in-chief and he had probably hoped that his temporary command would have been made permanent.

As it was, things went badly from the start; from the arrival of Mathews in the fleet, then anchored off Villefranche, when he treated Lestock with some rudeness in front of some British and Piedmontese officers. He then sent him off with such ships as were available to keep watch on Toulon, where there was as yet no sign of activity. Mathews himself remained at Villefranche for the time being to deal with Piedmontese affairs, and thereafter he was so taken up with the problems of the various Italian powers that his flagship was often away from the fleet. So neither Lestock nor the rear-admiral (Rowley) nor their captains saw much of their commander-in-chief. When they did there was never any question of their being consulted, or given any guidance, on tactical affairs, and they were sometimes treated in so blunt and outspoken a manner as could not have endeared their chief to them.

It was not until January 1744, more than eighteen months after Mathews's arrival on the station, that there were at last some indications of movement in Toulon. The situation as regards the French fleet was still anomalous but it was at least clear that if the Spanish fleet came out with the French in company the combined fleet must be brought to action without distinction of nationality.

This in fact was what the French expected. They kept up the makebelieve of not declaring war, but the orders given to the French admiral, de Court, in January enjoined a junction with the Spanish squadron under Navarro and a simultaneous egress from Toulon under de Court's command. He was then, in an assumed superiority (numbers of ships, full crews and cleaness of bottoms), 'to seek out the British ships under Admiral Mathews and attack them with his combined fleet, either off Hyères islands or wherever else they may be found'.[1] But to maintain the political fiction he was told that: 'His Majesty wishes his ships to be employed only as auxiliaries to the Spanish squadron in this expedition, and desires M. de Court when he is within range of the English ships—if they do not commence the action—to cause them to be attacked by the Spanish ships, which should engage them in such a manner that it cannot afterwards be said that hostile acts have been committed by His Majesty's ships before a declaration of war.'[2]

It should perhaps be remarked here that de Court was seventy-eight years of age, an all-time record for an admiral commanding a fleet in battle, one supposes. He had been Toulouse's flag captain in the *Foudroyant* at Malaga forty

[1] Richmond, *The Navy in the War of 1739-48*, vol. II, p. 257.
[2] ibid., p. 258.

years earlier and was said to be still full of vigour. In fact he had another eight years to live. It was only just a record, however, for there was nearly a clash between British and French forces in the Channel during this same month, only frustrated by a gale which blew the French fleet to the westward. There the British fleet was commanded by Sir John Norris, Admiral of the Fleet, said to have been born about 1660. If so he must have been a very remarkable octogenarian. The curious policy of sending an admiral to sea at so advanced an age as that, however, was never repeated in the British navy, though there were sometimes commanders-in-chief who would nowadays be judged too old for the post.[1]

The first movement of the Franco-Spanish fleet was on the afternoon of February 8th when Mathews's look-out frigate reported the French making sail to clear the harbour. The British fleet was then moored in Hyères roads, some twenty miles south-eastward along the coast from Toulon, and the signal was at once made to unmoor, that is to ride at single anchor. The allied fleet had not the superiority in numbers that de Court's orders had envisaged, for Mathews had just been reinforced by two ships of the line and was to be joined by three more before he went into action. But this was not to be just yet, for only the French ships, forming the van, got clear of the land that day, the Spaniards anchoring for the night outside the harbour.

It was in this situation that during the evening Lestock visited his commander-in-chief in the *Namur* to ask Mathews whether he had any orders for him—a justifiable query, it would seem, when two great fleets, each of twenty-eight sail of the line, were about to join battle. To this Mathews replied that he had not and that he wished him a good evening. It is not difficult to surmise what Lestock's feelings must have been.

Next morning the Spaniards again made sail and the combined fleet stood to the southward. The British weighed anchor and started to beat out of Hyères roads with the wind at southwest. But it was only a light breeze and what with that

---

[1] The authority for Norris's age is Laughton in the *Dictionary of National Biography*, but he notes that is a conjecture, for there are no records of his birth or boyhood.

and a strong east-going current they failed to clear the islands surrounding them. At 4 p.m. the fleet again anchored and so remained until daylight (February 10th) when a west-north-west wind made conditions more favourable and a fresh start was made.

Soon, however, there was further frustration for the breeze died away, to be succeeded by calms and light airs; but many ships hoisted out their boats to tow them and the whole fleet did in fact clear the islands by midday and then stood to the southward in a necessarily confused order. This was gradually straightened out as a steadier breeze, this time from the eastward, made itself felt. The fleet was now forming with Rowley's division in the van, as was the prescribed order of battle when on the larboard tack, and with Lestock in the rear. The latter had originally, with the westerly wind, expected to lead, since the fleet would then have been on the starboard tack, and in heaving-to to let the van and centre pass him he seems to have overdone things to the extent of letting the centre get several miles ahead of him before he made full sail.

Meanwhile the Franco-Spanish fleet had stood towards the British with the westerly wind which they still held for several hours, but when the east wind reached them they formed their line of battle on the larboard tack, heading to the southward. Their intention was to give battle, but Mathews feared that de Court's aim was to allow the Spanish squadron to return to a Spanish port and then disengage, and he knew he must do all he could to prevent this. He therefore made the signal for the line of battle abreast and steered towards the enemy.

This led to further separation of the rear squadron from the centre, Lestock, so it is said carrying only easy sail so as to let the ships of his squadron sort themselves out into the prescribed order of battle. Though the signal for the line abreast was flying from about 3 p.m. to dark he was by that time still several miles to the north-eastward. There was, however, no question in those days of a deliberate night battle, even with the weather so clear and unclouded that Mathews said he could still see the enemy plainly even after the moon had set. He therefore made the night signal for the fleet to bring-to, assuming, so it seems, that Lestock would bring his squadron into the prescribed position in the line of battle before coming to a halt.

But Lestock thought differently, evidently determined to abide only by the letter of the law in any orders given by his strict and uncongenial commander-in-chief. In the latter's sailing instructions (as in Rooke's) the night signal to bring-to specified that ships to windward were to bring-to first, those to leeward following the motions successively—an obviously sea-manlike precaution to prevent collisions if ships were in close order or the night was dark or stormy. Lestock, therefore, being to windward of the centre squadron at once hove-to. It seems that from now onward he was determined, in the modern idiom, to 'work to rule', that phrase of unpleasant repute. That this resolution was not derived from any inherent opposition to flexibility in a naval battle is made remarkably clear by an incident of two years earlier, when he was temporarily com-mander-in-chief and was exercising the line of battle. One division had been slow in taking up its station and he had reprimanded the captains for not leaving their divisional commander and joining the line. One of them replied that it was his duty to keep in company with his own flag officer. This view Lestock controverted, concluding by telling him that the divisional commander had no power to stop a captain leaving his division to join the battle.[1] In his present state of exaspera-tion with Mathews all such sentiments were forgotten. On this evening of February 10th there was not at the moment any question of joining battle, but from now onwards his determina-tion to work to rule was firmly held however much it might conflict with his natural inclinations, and in defending himself at his subsequent court martial the jots and tittles of the printed instructions were firmly stressed.

Lestock having brought-to his division on the larboard tack, that is with their heads in the south-eastern quarter, then left the deck and turned in without leaving any orders with his flag captain or officer of the watch. Perhaps one should remind oneself here that both these admirals, of sixty-five and sixty-two years of age, were in indifferent health. Mathews suffered

[1] Richmond, vol. II, p. 19.

from the gravel, a sometimes very painful urinary affliction common in those days, and Lestock was much troubled by gout.

Next morning, February 11th, at daylight Lestock's division was found to be seven or eight miles from the rest of the fleet, some three or four miles more than on the previous evening. He therefore made sail to close, what time Mathews was ordering the line of battle abreast so as to get nearer the enemy. What had caused this extended separation is not clear but Lestock put it down to a more drastic shift of wind from east to north in his position than had affected the rest of the fleet and this had made his hove-to ships lie up more to port, that is to the eastward.[1] To this he added that the currents were stronger the closer you were to the shore, as he was, compared with the centre division. However that may be, it would clearly be many hours before the rear division could come into line. This was the more so because the easterly breeze was very light and there was a heavy swell from the southward. And beyond that was the fact that few ships had been careened recently; the majority were foul and sailed heavily. This had a further influence in that all the enemy ships were clean and sailed, many witnesses said later, 'three feet to our one.' (One went so far as to say 'six feet to our one'.) All exaggerations, of course, but a factor of importance.

Having got a few miles closer to the enemy in line abreast Mathews then signalled the line of battle ahead, steering to the southward on a course intended to bring him parallel to the allies and, in the words of the nineteenth article of the fighting instructions, to have the van of his fleet steering with the van of the enemy 'there to engage them'. Had the sixteen French ships in the van and centre hove-to to await attack, as was the normal practice with equal fleets, this would eventually have been possible, slow as Lestock's approach was evidently going to be. Whether this could have been hastened without Lestock detaching his cleanest ships remained a disputed point in the virulent subsequent discussions and courts martial. Probably not much if at all. On two occasions Mathews sent a lieutenant

[1] It seems that the wind had been somewhat to the south of east when the fleet hove-to in the evening and that it had backed to the north-eastward during the night, but not as drastically as Lestock averred.

by boat to Lestock but exactly what passed and what sail Lestock was carrying remained in dispute.

Nor, again, is it by any means certain that Mathews could have joined his fleet van to van even if Lestock had been closer at hand. What influenced de Court's decisions at this time does not appear from his report or his log. Perhaps his instructions not to fire the first shot were in his mind, but however that may be it is evident that he was loth to let the British come abreast of him. Whenever they appeared to be doing so he made more sail, and with his 'three feet to our one' had no difficulty in retaining his lead. To the British there was the suspicion that he might be aiming to double the van, a possibility to be guarded again even though in theory this could have resulted in the doubling of his rear had Lestock been closed up, a manoeuvre usually considered the more effective of the two. But whatever his intention may have been he continued to keep his squadrons well forward even though this resulted in the twelve Spanish ships astern of him, less disciplined in keeping station, becoming strung out.

By this time, about noon, Mathews was becoming worried, not only from the purely tactical point of view but on two strategical aspects. He feared that the enemy might lead him more and more to the south-westward and thus leave the route for reinforcements from Spain to Italy wide open; and he knew that a French squadron from Brest was on its way to the Mediterranean and that if it joined de Court before the present encounter had been determined he would be in numerical inferiority.

Something, he felt, must be done and he therefore hailed his second astern, the *Marlborough*, and arranged that the two of them, both ninety-gun ships, should assail Navarro's flagship, the *Real Felipe* (usually referred to as the *Real*), mounting 114 guns and the biggest ship then afloat. Who was to be the chief assailant and who was the support was not entirely clear but Mathews's own account at his court martial two years later was: 'In the situation I made the signal to engage and edged down athwart the *Real*'s fore-foot.'

It was with Mathews edging down that the fighting began and in this small fraction of the line it was fiercely contested.

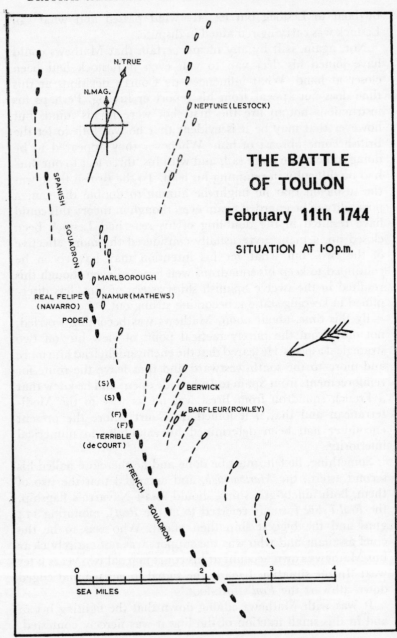

N. TRUE

N. MAG.

NEPTUNE (LESTOCK)

SPANISH SQUADRON

THE BATTLE
OF TOULON

February 11th 1744

SITUATION AT 1·0 p.m.

MARLBOROUGH

REAL FELIPE (NAVARRO)
NAMUR (MATHEWS)

PODER

(S)
(S)
(F)
(F)
TERRIBLE
(de COURT)

BERWICK

BARFLEUR (ROWLEY)

FRENCH SQUADRON

0   1   2   3   4

SEA MILES

Before long the *Namur* had to haul ahead to avoid becoming entangled with the *Marlborough* who was creeping up on the *Reals*'s larboard quarter, all within pistol shot and, it must be remembered, with only a light breeze and a heavy swell. Mathews could then no longer bring his broadside to bear but the *Marlborough* fought on, eventually losing all her masts. Her captain, the gallant Cornewall, one of the most promising officers of his time, was already dead, having had both his legs shot off early in the action. But the *Real* had also been heavily hammered and had now fallen to leeward.

Elsewhere there was little to boast about on either side. Mathews's second ahead had soon driven her opposite number out of the line, and Navarro's second astern had fallen to leeward of her admiral where she was sheltered. But the five ships astern of the *Marlborough* made little or no attempt to support that ship or to attack the next ships in the Spanish line within their reach. The third and fourth ships of the Spanish squadron, that is the two ships ahead of Navarro's second ahead, were engaged by their British opposite numbers to some effect. (The two leading Spaniards were well ahead with the French.) The fourth Spaniard, the *Poder*, was in fact so heavily assailed that she hauled down her colours some three hours later to the *Berwick* (Captain Hawke) who had broken away from the van squadron to finish her off.

Meanwhile the problem presented to Rowley and the van squadron was a difficult one with no clear solution. He had ten of the line to oppose de Court's eighteen—his sixteen French ships and the two Spaniards who had joined him from astern. As his commander-in-chief was engaging Rowley must do the same, but where should he place his unequal line, supposing his faster enemy should let him engage where he wanted to? Partly, perhaps, from the old, almost feudal, feeling that admiral should engage admiral and perhaps partly because he was in a ninety-gun ship (the *Barfleur*) with eighty-gun seconds ahead and astern, he decided to attack de Court, flying his flag in the *Terrible* (seventy-four) with only fifty-gun seconds; a considerable disparity even though the French carried heavier metal, gun for gun, than the British. This he could easily do, for the *Terrible* was thirteenth ship in the French line whereas the *Barfleur* was only sixth in the British. The action round the flagships and the ships astern of them though sharp was not in general closely contested, while the ships in the van, that is the four ships ahead of the *Barfleur*'s second ahead, kept close to the wind and out of range of the French line. They were so greatly outnumbered that they could easily have been doubled on, and though the captains of the three leading ships were among the many subsequently court martialled for not doing their utmost to take, burn, sink or otherwise destroy the ships of the enemy and were convicted of disobeying various articles of the commander-in-chief's fighting instructions and cashiered, they were all later restored to their rank. They had certainly taken up the best disposition for dissuading the enemy from doubling had he had it in mind, and in fact de Court had earlier made a signal for his van to tack in succession. But for some unexplained reason his three leading ships, having come round on to the starboard tack for a few minutes, had then resumed their southerly course on the larboard tack.

The battle, partial as it was, had now been in progress for three or four hours, but apart from Hawke's final assault on the *Poder*, it was only close to the Spanish flagship that it had been fought nearly to a finish. The *Real* still had her masts standing but had now born away to leeward. Her chief assailant, the *Marlborough*, was dismasted. The single British fireship in this neighbourhood had been told to attack the *Real* but this seemingly dangerous form of offensive action had failed as it was destined always to fail throughout the eighteenth century, despite the hopes derived from some successes in the Dutch wars when many fireships were included in the fleets of both adversaries. The spectacular burning of the *Royal James*, flagship of Lord Sandwich, second-in-command at the battle of Sole Bay in 1672, with the loss of most of her complement including the admiral, seems to have left such a lasting impression on men's minds that fireships were continued in service, though in lesser numbers, for another century and more. On this occasion the fireship was ill supported by the gun-shy captains astern of the *Marlborough* and Mathews's last-minute move to cover her with the *Namur* was unavailing. Fired on by the Spanish ships she eventually blew up while still short of her target.

It was at about this time that de Court, seeing his Spanish allies in considerable confusion and their flagship in much trouble, felt he must go to their rescue. Tacking his whole fleet together he headed north-west to cover the *Real*. Rowley and the British van conformed to this movement, necessarily leaving the surrendered *Poder* to the enemy; and so did Mathews with the somewhat disorganized centre, intent on keeping the weather gage. A few of Lestock's leading ships had engaged the rear Spaniards at long and ineffectual range and then his squadron tacked to the northward and became the leading division. Both fleets then lay-to for the night, repairing damage to the small minority of ships that had been in close action. The *Namur* had been so knocked about by the *Real* that Mathews shifted his flag to the *Russell* (eighty).

Next morning the Franco-Spanish fleet was in sight of the British, making off to the westward but somewhat further away than it had been in the evening. Mathews followed as best he could but his fleet soon became unduly strung out, and from now on such eagerness as there was to renew the battle seems to have shifted from him to Lestock whose squadron had taken the lead. After lying-by the next evening for part of the night, as had also the enemy, and then continuing the chase for a few hours the following morning (February 13th), he decided to abandon this project. He recalled Lestock and as it was now blowing too strongly from the north-east for the ships with crippled masts and spars to ply to windward, the whole fleet hove-to.

This move was not justified by events. Mathews's reasons for his decision were firstly that it was important to regain his station on the route from Spain to Italy, thus assisting the Duke of Savoy in defence of Villefranche and, second, that he feared the Brest squadron might join de Court and that the British would then, assuming the Spaniards were still with the French, be in a marked numerical inferiority. In the event the weather was such that he was unable to regain a position off Toulon and he therefore retired to Minorca. And as for the strength of the enemy, the Brest force never came into the picture, several Spanish ships soon parted company, and even the remainder, in company with the *Real* whose masts were still standing but so injured aloft that she was now in tow, had left de Court and were making the best of their way to Cartagena.

The British arrival at Minorca was marked by the start of an acrimonious correspondence between Mathews and Lestock, soon to be published as a pamphlet, presumably on information supplied by the latter.[1] Mathews demanded replies to a series of questions couched in terms of reprimand which in those days of punctilio must have sounded even ruder than they do today. Lestock's replies were coldly correct but naturally made no admission of wrongdoing. This phase ended with Lestock being ordered to haul down his flag—to which he replied that nothing could give him more pleasure. He was then sent home in a fifty-gun ship on convoy escort duty.

Mathews followed him home soon afterwards on the grounds of ill health, and then began an intense battle of words—in pamphlets, in Parliament and in courts martial. The whole affair was investigated at great length in the House of Commons and at the end of this Lestock was allowed to recapitulate the evidence at the bar of the House. Courts martial followed. Eleven captains were summoned for trial, one of whom, Norris, son of the Admiral of the Fleet, disgraced his family by absconding. Many were cashiered though some, as already noted, were later restored to the list. Then in the spring of 1746 after much delay for the collection of witnesses came Lestock's trial on charges 'in behalf of the Crown', based on Mathews's official report.

The court comprised two rear-admirals and fourteen captains, the junior rear-admiral being John Byng, unworthy son of an eminent father. It has sometimes been said that their acquittal of Lestock on all seven charges in the indictment had a political background, and the fact that the judgments on some of the items appear contradictory seems to show that the court was determined to acquit the vice-admiral. But one feels there must have been more to it than that. There is little doubt that Lestock did much to suborn witnesses, chiefly masters and junior officers, while preparing his defence and that several ships' logs were tampered with, making it easier to find technical

[1] *Original Letters and Papers between Adm—l M—ws and V. Adm—l L—K* (London, 1744).

excuses for his conduct. And there is no doubt that if his heart had been in it he would have continued under sail on the evening before the battle and come reasonably close to the rest of the fleet during this fine moonlight night before he brought-to with his division. But here the printed instructions were definite—so useful when they can be quoted in defence, for even the Devil can cite scripture. As already noted, the night signal for bringing-to printed in the sailing instructions (four lights in the fore shrouds and the firing of eight guns) included the injunction that the ships to windward were to bring-to first. This was quite unnecessary here, but what with the printed word, signed by Mathews, and much conflicting evidence as to the position of Lestock's division relative to the commander-in-chief it would hardly have been possible for the court to agree that the charge of his bringing-to too soon was proved.

Beyond that, there seems to have been an undercurrent of opinion that Mathews himself had not fought hard enough against the *Real* once he had made sail ahead to keep clear of the *Marlborough*. Nor had he done anything to see that the shirkers of his own division astern of the *Marlborough* gave her the support she needed. Instead he had simply blamed Lestock for not being nearer at hand.

Lestock's acquittal was followed during the summer and autumn of 1746 by a court martial on Mathews himself on a series of fifteen articles drawn up by the Attorney-General, the court comprising nineteen officers, admirals and senior captains. Each article was investigated in great detail. He was unanimously exonerated from the charge of engaging in battle before Lestock's division had joined him, but it was agreed by eleven votes to eight that he endangered his fleet by bearing down on the Spanish admiral, leaving only his van division opposed to the more powerful French van and centre. In several of the first nine articles of accusation there were references to his breach of the nineteenth article of the fighting instructions which he had signed ('the van of the admiral's fleet is to steer with the van of the enemy') but it was accepted by the majority of the court that if the French made sail ahead, as they did, he could not have managed it.

Had these been the only charges he might well have been acquitted, but it was when the later parts of the battle were considered that the tide turned against him. There was much argument about his actions after leaving the *Marlborough* to fight a virtually single-handed battle against the *Real* and after the French had tacked to the north-westward to relieve the Spanish flagship—when the British fleet kept to windward, leaving the captured *Poder* to be recaptured and apparently risking the dismasted *Marlborough*. Further articles dealt with the half-heartedness of his pursuit on the following days when, as we now know, the allies were much separated and the *Real* was so damaged aloft as to be in tow. A pursuit if pressed with vigour might well have resulted in a resounding victory. On not chasing vigorously on the day after the battle he was unanimously condemned by the court, but on whether he should have pursued on the following day when the enemy was nearly out of sight there was much difference of opinion, eleven members considering that he should have continued and eight that he was justified in breaking off. On the final, comprehensive article of the accusations—'That the said Thomas Mathews was guilty of notorious breaches of duty . . . before and during the engagement of His Majesty's fleet with the combined fleets of France and Spain . . . and was a principle cause of the miscarriage'—it was agreed that he was, and that he should be cashiered.

The sentence does not seem to have worried Mathews unduly. He was notably self-opinionated. If others thought him wrong that was their look-out and it did not follow that he should in any way feel abashed. In his defence he had expressed his point of view clearly and logically. On one item he agreed that it was possible that he might have made an error of judgment but was firmly of the opinion that he had done no such thing. On the strategical aspects his view that he should regain the Franco-Italian coast before risking a battle in which he supposed the Brest reinforcements would have joined his enemies was logical but in fact misguided. Had he taken the traditional British course of engaging any enemy fleet that was not obviously too powerful and of letting the eventual outcome look after itself the battle might have assumed a very different

THE BATTLES OF MALAGA AND TOULON

aspect. But it seems clear now that however sound he may have been in the strategical and political aspects of his command of the Mediterranean station he lacked the abilities and personality rightly expected of the commander-in-chief of a fleet in battle. He neither endeared himself to the fleet as a whole nor took any steps to call the delinquent ships of his own division to order. There cannot of course be any justification for Lestock 'working to rule', but the provocation to do nothing more than he need in support of a chief who had done less than nothing to inspire loyalty must have been very strong. Presumably Lestock's gout did not improve his temper. He had to be helped up and down ladders and he died three years later from 'gout in the stomach'—whatever that may have been in modern terms.

It has sometimes been implied that one result of this battle was to increase the rigid respect in which, so it was said, the printed fighting instructions were held. But of this there is no evidence. Naturally the courts martial examined the diverse movements of ships and squadrons in the light of such printed instructions as seemed to be applicable. But in one of the accusations against Mathews (Article VI) to the effect that he attacked with an unequal distribution of force 'contrary to discipline, in breach of his duty, the Fighting Instructions, and to the great danger of his Majesty's fleet', the court decided by fourteen votes to five that the charge was not proved— though, as noted above, they had already agreed that the distribution of force was unequal. Rooke's fighting instructions remained, as they had a right to remain, the pattern on which tactics were to be based where practicable, but there was no question of their imposing an unjustified rigidity on an admiral whose appraisal of a situation saw that more flexibility was called for. What were still lacking at this date were the means of signalling more than a very limited number of tactical movements. Orders for anything that needed further explanation had to be sent by boat and this might often be inconvenient or even impossible, however stalwart the boats' crews. Fortunately before the end of this war there were two battles in the Bay of Biscay which, though not between numerically equal fleets, were hard enough fought to show that there was nothing hidebound in the ideas of Anson and Hawke. They also showed that there was no reluctance to issue additional fighting instructions when needed and from then on an increasing body of additional signals was built up by admirals commanding-in-chief on the various stations. Many of these signals and the instructions they conveyed became common form and some sets were printed by the Admiralty, not as instructions from their Lordships but for convenience of commanders-in-chief who could modify them in manuscript as they saw fit.

Chapter 5

THE BEGINNING OF ADDITIONAL INSTRUCTIONS AND THE TWO BATTLES OF FINISTERRE

Precisely when a substantial body of Additional Fighting Instructions generally adopted by admirals commanding-in-chief made its first appearance is uncertain, but it seems that much had been achieved in that direction before the War of the Austrian Succession ended in 1748. Writing of that war (c. 1913, though not published till 1920) Captain H. W. Richmond, as he then was, included in an appendix a set of fifteen articles issued by Hawke in manuscript in September 1747 when commanding the Western Squadron. In Richmond's view, however, it was unlikely that these additional instructions originated with Hawke and in fact they were probably inherited from either Martin or Anson or Warren, his consecutive predecessors in this command from 1746 onwards. That they endured through the subsequent peace can be seen from the set issued by Boscawen in 1755 when he was sent across the Atlantic to intercept French reinforcements to Canada, even though war had not yet been declared. This set included thirteen of the fifteen articles of Hawke's instructions (omitting only one about fireships and one about readiness for action), but the articles were not numbered and are interspersed among what would normally be classed as sailing instructions, aimed at finding the French squadron he had been sent to stop. It is of interest as tending to confirm Richmond's surmise about the origin of the Hawke instructions that Boscawen had served under Anson in the spring of 1747 and had no doubt received instructions from him, but he had not been with Hawke in September.[1]

[1] Boscawen's Additional Fighting Instructions of 1755 are in *The Barrington*

81

These instructions, or something very like them with later additions, were in force throughout the Seven Years War and it happens that the earliest printed set extant was also a Boscawen one, dated 1759 when he was commanding in the Mediterranean. It seems certain, however, that there were other printed sets in these years, made available by the Admiralty, which were issued by Anson and Hawke to the Western Squadron in 1758 and 1759 if not earlier. For this the authority is the journal of a commodore who, in May 1757, was about to sail for the Leeward Islands station. He noted that on May 28th he issued to his captains 'The Sailing and Fighting Instructions, with the printed Additional Signals and further Additional Signals'.[1]

It might seem reasonable to suppose that these additional instructions were based on the successful fighting experiences of 1747 on the outskirts of the Bay of Biscay (usually known as the battles of Finisterre) against weaker French forces, or at least on Anson's in May of that year, were it not that this is contradicted by their probably earlier date of origin. It is all the more strange, therefore, that as will be mentioned later the one wholly new manoeuvre which they include and which might, one would have thought, have been useful in the two actions now to be described was not in fact ordered in either.

In the first of these battles (May 3rd) Anson, with fourteen ships in his line of battle (the two smallest being of fifty guns), had intercepted French convoys outward-bound to Canada and India with escorts which together gave their senior officer, La Jonquière, six warships in his line (the smallest a forty-six). Three of the East Indiamen joined him in his battle against heavy odds but they were only of thirty, thirty and twenty guns respectively, so could not be expected to achieve much.

When first sighted the French bore south-west with the wind north-north-east and Anson chased towards them in loose formation. A nearer approach showed that the French war-

Papers, vol. I (Navy Records Society) p. 131. They were not given to Barrington till August, when he joined Boscawen at Halifax, but it can be presumed that they were identical with those that had been issued to the squadron with which Boscawen sailed from England in April.

[1] Corbett, England in the Seven Years War, vol. II, p. 64n.

ships had formed a line of battle ahead with their heads to the north-westward to allow the convoy to escape south-westerly. Anson then began to close his squadron into a line of battle abreast and soon afterwards changed this to line ahead on the starboard tack, that is roughly parallel to the French though still more than a mile from them. Because of the poor sailing of some of the British ships it was nearly two hours before all were in station, during which time his flagship was hove-to as were the French. He then made the signal to lead large[1] so as to close the enemy. On this Rear-Admiral Warren, his second-in-command who was with the van division, bore away in chase without waiting to follow the leading ship. For this he was at once called to order, Anson not favouring the idea of a haphazard attack on a well-formed line, even one so much weaker than his own, despite the fact that he had called Warren to within speaking distance while the line was being formed and that it is generally believed that the latter had then advocated an immediate attack in chase.

The French, however, having stood their ground long enough to give their convoy a good start, now put their helms up and made away in a body, and in these circumstances Anson once more made the signal for a general chase without any stipulations as to the order in which his fleet should engage. His leading ships were soon in action but were heavily hammered by the more concentrated French rear. It was not long, though, before his superior numbers began to take effect, and despite the stout resistance put up by the enemy all had been forced to surrender within two hours of opening fire. Later five merchant ships and three frigates were captured by three of the line, a frigate and a sloop which Anson had detached as soon as the main action was over.

There were no tactical lessons to be derived from this battle except the evident one that a stronger fleet, if it fought hard, could beat a much weaker one whatever the order in which it

[1] To sail 'large' was to sail with the wind near or abaft the beam, as distinct from sailing 'by' the wind, i.e. close-hauled. Hence the expression 'taking her (or things) by and large', meaning on all points of sailing—an expression in common use nowadays though no doubt with its nautical origin often unrealized.

attacked. But it is interesting to note that this was the first time mention is made of a signal (that is of a flag signal) ordering a general chase. The general printed fighting instructions included a signal for a particular squadron to give chase: 'If the admiral would have any particular flagship, and his squadron or division, to give chase to the enemy, he will make the same signal that is appointed for that flagship's tacking with his squadron or division and weathering the enemy.' But for general chase there was only Article XXVI, already mentioned (p. 39), which dealt with the situation when the enemy had been put to the run in the course of a battle: '. . . he will make all sail he can himself after the enemy and fire two guns out of his fore-chase.' In the folio of printed sailing and fighting instructions, also, there were signals for particular ships to chase to windward or to leeward (in the sailing instructions), with further signals for chasing in either of the four quarters of the compass on a supplementary page in the folio; but none of these referred to the fleet as a whole. Early in the next war, however, in fact before the official declaration, Boscawen inserted in the orders he gave to his squadron: 'And if I would have all the ships chace (sic) I will hoist the Chaceing Flag in the Mizzen Shrouds, and a Pendant at the Mizzen Peek (sic)'.[1] And so it remained for the next two wars. It may well be, therefore, that this signal was already in use in 1747.

Hawke's battle of October 14th of that year had much in common with Anson's. He had fifteen ships (twelve of sixty guns or more plus two fifties and a forty-four) as against the eight of l'Étanduère's squadron, one of which was a fifty but most of the remainder were larger and more heavily gunned than the British. He was not, however, in such an advantageous position, for when he was close-hauled on the larboard tack with the wind at south-south-east his enemy was right ahead of him and the numerous French merchant ships, bound for the West Indies, were still further away to the south-westward. It was on the escort that Hawke decided to concentrate, sailing close-hauled so as to be sure of fetching them—for l'Étanduère was also keeping close to the wind and forming his line ahead under easy sail. The British fleet, in open order

---

[1] *The Barrington Papers*, vol. I, p. 128.

and somewhat scattered at daylight when the enemy had first been sighted, had since then been closing fairly rapidly—the cleanest ships, that is—Hawke having ordered a general chase.

The French admiral, now realizing that his convoy was not going to be molested, ordered it to sail about four points free, that is about west instead of south-west. This gave the merchant ships some additional speed and they soon gained ground and no longer came into the picture. (After the battle was over Hawke sent a sloop to Barbados to tell the Leeward Islands squadron of the approaching convoy and some ships were captured before they reached their destinations; but in fact knowledge of the convoy's sailing which had already reached the Admiralty had been sent straight to the West Indies and had given an earlier warning.)

By 10 a.m. Hawke was four miles or less from l'Étenduère and he then, as Anson had done, hoisted the signal for the line of battle ahead, intending to be well concentrated before joining action. This was a slow process, however, for several ships had been too long out of dock to sail well and had dropped astern. As time passed, with his line only partially formed, he naturally became impatient and by 11 a.m. he would wait no longer. Hauling down the union flag from the mizzen peak (the signal for the line of battle ahead) he again hoisted that for the general chase and with all ships under full sail he once more stood on.

Thereafter he made no more signals except 'to speak with the captains' of two or three ships, achieved by their closing him and conversing through speaking-trumpets. No doubt some instructions were passed in this way but there is no record of them. The rest was hard fighting as the British ships gradually overhauled the French. The rear French ships naturally had the worst time of it, but the leading British were hard pressed as they came up with fresh Frenchmen successively. Hawke himself in his 66-gun *Devonshire* eventually reached his post of honour for engaging l'Étanduère's 80-gun *Tonnant* on her lee side, but he had not been able to make as much ground to windward as he would have liked to and so was denied the close action at which he aimed.

Further disappointment was to follow when he opened fire on her with his larboard guns on their extreme forward bearing.

On their recoil the breechings of all the lower deck guns broke and he had to forge ahead to give time for reeving new ones. It seems that there was a fresh breeze and presumably he was carrying a fair spread of sail and standing as close to the wind as he could so as to come up with the enemy's line. The *Devonshire* may therefore have had a pronounced heel to the disengaged side and the guns would be recoiling down hill. (But curiously the same fault is said to have been experienced, at least partially, in the *Namur* in 1744 when Mathews 'edged down' to engage the *Real*, and in that case he was firing to leeward.)[1]

It seems strange that there was no contemporary suggestion for putting this matter right or even any attempt to explain it, for it was on the handling of the guns, particularly the heaviest, in the lower tier, that success or failure in battle usually depended. The only subsequent comment in this case seems to have been that of Mahan who put forward the view that 'the breaking of the Breechings was no doubt accelerated by the undue elevation necessitated by the extreme range' (*Types of Naval Officers*, p. 91). But evidently Mahan had not been blessed with the education in applied mechanics given to naval officers brought up in the twentieth century. The retarding force on a gun's recoil, until it was finally checked by the breeching, was supplied by the friction between the wooden wheels (known as trucks) and their axles, which were fixed to the carriage. The greater the elevation of the gun the greater would be the down thrust on the carriage. This would naturally increase friction between axles and wheels and so the braking effect. Other things being equal, therefore, high elevation would put less strain on the breechings than firing with the gun parallel to the deck.

What seems a possible answer to this conumdrum can reasonably be derived from some correspondence of thirty-four years later. At that time Sir Charles Douglas was commanding the three-decker *Duke* and was pressing his views on the Comptroller, Sir Charles Middleton, as to various improve-

[1] Laughton (editor) in *The Barham Papers* (Navy Records Society) vol. I, p. 271 n. There is, however, no mention of this in Richmond's detailed description of the battle in his *War of 1739-48*.

ments in gunnery which he was innovating.[1] His chief aim was to increase the arc of training of the broadside guns, and one of his main proposals was the removal of such of the 'standards' as got in the way of the recoil when firing obliquely. These standards were inverted knees which were bolted to the frame timbers above the deck and to the beams below it, where it seems some of them did not do any good. Some were removed in the *Duke*, and later in some other ships, and this enabled the guns to extend their arcs of training perhaps to three points before the beam—to the astonishment of the French in the battle of the Saints, according to Douglas, for they found themselves being heavily fired on by British ships on bearings where they thought themselves quite safe.[2] Douglas had also advocated, and carried out in the *Duke*, the incorporation of steel springs in the breechings because of the restricted room for recoil when on extreme bearings, whether or not the standards had been removed. From this it seems reasonable to suppose that there was a greater strain on the breechings when firing obliquely than when firing on the beam. This may have arisen in the former case either because it was necessary to shorten the breechings or because of the unequal length of the two parts when the gun was trained round, which allowed less elasticity to the shorter leg. The breeching was not, of course, seized to the gun but passed through an eye which was part of the gun casting, but it could hardly be expected to render through this eye when subjected to the sudden jerk of the recoil. It is interesting to note from Hawke's despatch that he says of this trouble, 'the breechings of all our lower-deck guns broke and the guns flew fore-and-aft'. What caused the latter movement is not clear, nor whether it was the muzzle or the breech that was pointing forward, but it is clear that the unequal action of the breeching as it took the strain before it broke had slewed the gun round.

No more, however, of this serious failure, putting the flagship out of action for more than an hour[3], is recorded at the time. A resounding victory can be relied on to distract attention

[1] *The Barham Papers*, vol. I, pp. 268–84.
[2] See also the Note on Gunnery at the end of this chapter.
[3] Mackay, *Admiral Hawke*, pp. 79, 82.

from material shortcomings, and six ships of the line captured or out of action put it in that class.[1]

It might well have been hoped that annihilation would be complete, but in fact the eighty-gun French flagship, being disabled aloft though with her stoutly built hull still sound, had made off to leeward about 5 p.m. accompanied by a seventy-four to support her. Though l'Étanduère had stood his ground courageously until his convoy had made a good offing he had presumably realized by now that the remaining ships of his squadron had been so battered that they must inevitably strike their colours before long and that he was therefore justified in making for Brest. Hawke had signalled to three of his sixty-gun ships to follow the French admiral and his consort but his signal had not been seen. Rodney, however, the 28-year-old captain of the *Eagle* (sixty), coming up from astern where he had been heavily engaged, saw what had happened and chased with all the sail he could carry and he was followed by a sixty-four and a sixty. He came up with the French ships about 7 p.m. and engaged them single-handed for half and hour before his supporters arrived, but thereafter the two latter were much damaged and the chase had to be abandoned.

From these actions in the Bay of Biscay, Anson's and Hawke's, two points arise which are of general tactical interest. It has already been said that Hawke had issued a set of Additional Fighting Instructions in September and that there is a strong probability that these had already been promulgated previously. One of these instruction, a double one, which remained in the signal books throughout the next two wars is worth quoting in full.

[1] My suggestion here that this matter was just shrugged off may well be unjustified. In a private letter of 23 December 1747 to Anson, Augustus Keppel, who had been one of Anson's midshipmen in the circumnavigation and was now a post captain aged twenty-two, includes among other matters: 'We meet today to consult about the breechings of the great guns. Many things will be mentioned in the ordnance way now we are about it.' (T. Keppel, *The Life of Augustus Viscount Keppel*, vol. I, p. 128.) 'We' seems to imply the flag officers and captains present (at Portsmouth) but, alas, there is no further mention of the subject.

IX. And if I would chase with the whole squadron and would have a certain number of my ships that are nearest the enemy draw into a line of battle ahead of me in order to engage the ships in their rear endeavouring at the same time to get up to their van till the rest of the ships in my squadron can come up with them, I will hoist a white flag with a red cross on the flagstaff on the main top mast head and fire the number of guns as follows:
When I would have

Five ships }	draw into a line ahead of	{ 1 gun
Seven ships }	each other I will fire	{ 3 guns.

X. Then the ships are immediately to form the line without any regard to seniority, or the general form delivered, but according to their distances from the enemy viz: The headmost and nearest ship to the enemy is to lead and the sternmost bring up the rear, that no time maybe lost in the pursuit; and all the rest of the ships are to form and strengthen that line as soon as they can come up with them without regard to my general form for the order of battle.

These instructions read as if they were tailor-made for both Hawke's and Anson's battles. But as already mentioned (p. 82) they were not used. Hawke was to use them twelve years later under the far more hazardous conditions of his chase into Quiberon Bay, but then, as he said in his despatch, he was under the necessity 'of running all risks to break this strong force of the enemy'. There was no such necessity in 1747 but it does seem remarkable that these two distinguished admirals should have consumed so much time in concentrating against evidently inferior forces even though they seemed to have the whole day ahead of them.

The conventional explanation in the late nineteenth century would have been that they were held in the straitjacket of the printed fighting instructions, but we now know (p. 29 above) that there was no such straitjacket, and that such an explanation, in these instances, would be entirely unconvincing. Though this was Anson's first experience of anything more than a single ship action and it was not tactics but his indomitable perseverence in this voyage round the world that had brought him to his present position, he was now a Lord Commissioner of the Admiralty and unlikely to have any hesitation in making whatever tactical moves he thought best. He had already shown his independence of mind in another respect three years earlier when he had returned a commission as rear-admiral sent him by the Admiralty, because the Board had refused to confirm a temporary commission he had given his second-in-command during his circumnavigation. In his covering letter enclosing the returned commission he had remarked: 'It has ever been my opinion that a person trusted with command may and ought to exceed his orders and dispense with the common rules of proceeding, when extraordinary occasions require it'. And in the next war he was to make one of the most drastic alterations to the principles included in the old instructions to which they were ever subjected—an alteration which was later to be cancelled, as will be told in due course.

On the handling of his squadron on the present occasion Richmond's view was: 'He was a man who set great store by accuracy of movements and what was called "discipline" in a fleet, meaning what we should now (1913) term good station keeping. After months of practising his fleet in bearing up and attacking in good order, he may well have been determined that his attack should be orderly, his squadron well in hand, and its effect as conclusive as possible'.[1]

As for Hawke, it was known from his conduct off Toulon three years earlier that he was a hard fighter who had no scruple about hauling out of the line to capture an enemy ship (which contravened the fighting instructions) even at such risk that he was later forced to abandon his prize. And now, in 1747, his hesitation to attack before forming line-of battle was briefer than Anson's. It was also more understandable considering that he had to attack to leeward with the probability of longer time intervals between successive ships coming into action.

As a postscript to the general question of discipline in the line of battle, Hawke's behaviour in the battle of Toulon, cited

[1] Richmond, *The Navy in the War of 1739-48*, vol. III, p. 90.

above, brings forward a further interesting point which shows that even in the eighteenth century there was at least one writer, background unknown, who was ready to make an unjustified mock of the current fighting instructions. Hawke's first biographer notes that those reading about the Toulon battle 'will find successive compilers copying from one another the absolute error that Hawke, although he was the only captain to take a ship, was tried by court-martial for breaking the (British) line, broke and immediately reinstated'. This statement 'probably first appeared in the *Gentlemen's Magazine* for 1760. Here Hawke is said to have been "broke for his bravery and restored by the King". . . the story may be disposed of henceforward. The officers just mentioned were the only ones accused or tried, and our narrative has shown that no charge of any kind could have arisen out of Hawke's conduct in the battle'.[1]

A NOTE ON SOME ASPECTS OF EIGHTEENTH CENTURY GUNNERY

The limits of the arcs of training within which the broadside guns of a line-of-battle ship could be fired were evidently important factors in tactical problems, particularly in a British fleet which was so often concerned with attacking from the weather gage. It seems curious, therefore, that so little information on the matter is on record, and that what there is is sometimes unconvincing and sometimes conflicting. Sir Charles Douglas, who has been quoted above, was enthusiastic about various improvements in gunnery in which he had been concerned, but his letters read as if he was inclined to brag about his achievements. He did state emphatically, however, that when commanding the *Duke* he had no hesitation about firing his lower deck guns three points before the beam even though that entailed firing them without their being fully run out, relying on the incorporation of steel springs in the breechings to prevent them parting. And he alleged that ships which

---

[1] Burrows, *The Life of Edward, Lord Hawke*, p. 162. Montagu Burrows was a retired captain, RN, who was Chichele Professor of Modern History at Oxford when, in 1883, he wrote Hawke's life.

had had their standards removed could engage an enemy who was nearly four points before the beam or thereabouts. Also in Hawke's battle, just related, it seems certain that the guns of his flagship must have been trained well forward when he opened fire on his opposite number or they would not have ended up fore-and-aft after breaking their breechings.

On the other hand Sir Humphrey Senhouse, who had studied the tactics of Trafalgar (he had been there as a lieutenant) and had written a Memorandum on the subject about twenty years later, stated that: 'At a distance of one mile five ships at half-cable's length apart might direct their broadsides effectively against the head of the division (in a line ahead, approaching at right-angles) for seven minutes, supposing the rate of sailing to have been four miles an hour'. This could have been done by the leading and rear ships of the five training their guns only eighteen degrees (less than two points) aft and forward respectively at the conclusion of the seven minutes period which would have brought the range down to about nine hundred yards. And when Clerk of Eldin, the Scottish laird with no sea experience, was propounding his views on how a fleet should attack from to windward, to wit that the approach should never be at right angles to the enemy's line, he assumed that the guns of the fleet to leeward would be fixed on the beam bearing and that any concentration of fire on a ship heading towards them would necessarily entail some of these ships yawing to bring their sights on.

Fortunately, however, though there is no longer a line-of-battle ship afloat, there is one, H.M.S. *Victory*, in Portsmouth Dockyard with guns aboard and restored in all respects to her condition in 1805. Whether she was built with 'standards' when she was launched in 1765 is not known, but if so they were removed subsequently. Her present commanding officer was therefore appealed to for a solution of this query and has returned the following helpful answer: 'I have not been asked this particular question before and cannot find a recorded answer to it. However by practical measurement I am convinced that 20 degrees either side of the beam is a realistic figure. If the gun is pointed further round than this (*a*) the outboard carriage wheel touches the ship's side and (*b*) the gun barrel is too close to the ship's side and would cause burning.' In view of this it has been assumed throughout this book that, despite Douglas, the normal arc of fire of a broadside was from something under two points before the beam to the same amount abaft it. There would, of course, have been some slight modifications of these figures for two or three guns at the extreme ends of a gun deck owing to the curvature of the ship's side, but these would have been less than 10 degrees each way.

Ranges and elevations. The description of ranges in the eighteenth century was naturally in general terms. The usual meaning of 'gun-shot' was the maximum effective range, which for 32, 24 and 18 pounders was assumed to be about 2000 yards. This was attained by elevating the guns 7 degrees (Simmons, *Sea Gunner's Vade-Mecum*, quoted in Falconer, *Marine Dictionary*). 'Musket-shot' as a description of range implied about 300 yards, and 'pistol shot' 50 yards. 'Point-blank' implied that the guns were horizontal but was used rather loosely. Simmons gives the range of the above-mentioned guns as 1000 yards at 2 degrees elevation which seems as near point-blank as one could need, but if the guns were double-shotted, as they often were, particularly for the first broadside, the 1000 yards would be reduced to 500.

Firing. The normal method of firing a gun was to fill the touch-hole (also known as the vent) with priming powder from a horn and put some more powder in the pan at the top of the hole. When the captain of the gun ordered 'fire' a slow match was applied to this and the flame of the powder ran through the touch-hole to the base of the charge. Towards the end of the century, however, it was found that greater reliability and greater accuracy of the moment of discharge could be insured by using a goose-quill tube, charged with a special composition of powder, in the touch-hole and igniting it with a flint-lock fixed to the gun and fired by pulling a lanyard.

Chapter 6

BYNG AT MINORCA

When John Byng, admiral of the Blue, was executed by a firing squad on the quarterdeck of a ship of the line in March 1757, it was generally understood, one supposes, that the refusal of George II to grant a reprieve of the capital sentence imposed by a court martial was not in reality on the score of his conduct in battle. Though this was lamentably inadequate there was no precedent for inflicting a death sentence for mere stupidity. The basic essence of his crime was his pusillanimous retreat to Gibraltar, leaving the garrison of Minorca to its fate. On the latter score, however, there was no Article of War on which he could have been brought to book and he had therefore to be tried on the charge that 'he did not do his utmost to take or destroy every ship which it shall be his duty to engage, and assist and relieve all and every of His Majesty's ships which it shall be his duty to assist and relieve'. This naturally resulted in a very thorough investigation by the court martial into the handling of his fleet in battle with the French fleet which was supporting the army of invasion, and it brought into prominence the tactical questions involved.

The bickering of transatlantic hostilities in 1755 had been succeeded throughout the following winter by speculation as to what offensive action the French were likely to take in Europe. One move which seemed probable was an expedition to capture Minorca where, at Port Mahon, Britain had a valuable dockyard. It was to Minorca, therefore, that Byng was despatched in April 1756, with ten ships of the line to reinforce the small, peace-time squadron already in the Mediterranean.

Pausing at Gibraltar for some discussions with the governor and a council of war, the tone of which boded ill for the fate of Minorca, Byng sailed on and made his landfall on May 19th. Somewhat curiously the formal declaration of war by England on France had only been made the previous day, but by this time a French army of about 15,000 men had already been a month in the island and had driven the garrison into St Philip's Castle, a well-constructed fortification at the mouth of Port Mahon. There they were secure for the time being but were somewhat short in numbers, in particular of officers from this station who had been on leave in England. These were now with Byng, ready to return to their posts as soon as a way could be found to land them at St Philip's without undue risk. Arrangements to this effect were unfortunately muddled and had to be set aside when, during the afternoon, a French fleet was sighted and Byng shaped his course towards it. The wind soon failed, however, and at nightfall the two forces were still a long way apart.

Daybreak on May 20th came in with misty weather and it was not till 9 a.m. that the two fleets were in sight of each other. At that time, according to the log of Byng's flagship, the *Ramillies*, the French bore south-east by east from him, distant about twelve miles. All ships were ordered to close the admiral and at 10 a.m. he made sail to the south-eastward while forming line of battle ahead. At this time the wind was light and variable, but by 11 a.m. it had settled at south-south-west enabling the British line to steer south-east, that is close-hauled (six points from the wind) on the starboard tack.

Meanwhile the French fleet also was shaping course to close its enemy and everything pointed to an evenly and well contested battle. Byng had thirteen ships of the line, including two fifties; his opponent, the Marquis de la Galissonière, an officer with a reputation for enterprise and professional competence, had twelve of the line, which also included two fifties. But with the French guns in general heavier than their British counterparts there was no appreciable difference in strength on the material side. To equalize the lines later, just before engaging, Byng ordered one of his fifties to haul out to windward of his division as as reserve, but as this division never came effectively into action this did not in the event affect the situation.

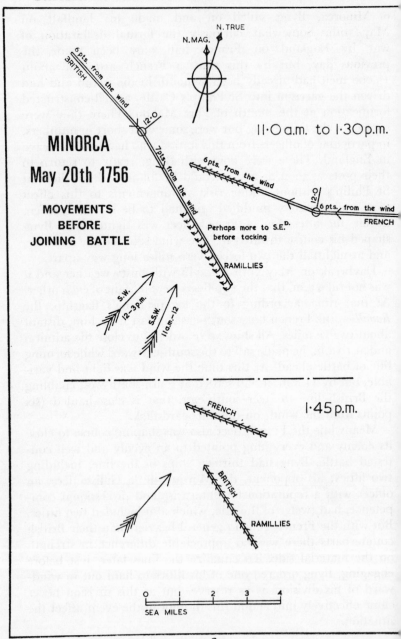

N. TRUE

N. MAG.

MINORCA
May 20th 1756

MOVEMENTS
BEFORE
JOINING BATTLE

6 pts. from the wind

BRITISH

12·0

7 pts. from the wind

11·0 a.m. to 1·30 p.m.

6 pts. from the wind

6 pts. from the wind

12·0

FRENCH

Perhaps more to S.E.ᴰ
before tacking

RAMILLIES

S.W.
12–3 p.m.

S.S.W.
11 a.m.–12

FRENCH

1·45 p.m.

BRITISH

RAMILLIES

0   1   2   3   4
SEA MILES

The French line was also close-hauled but on the larboard tack, that is to say that with the south-south-west wind they were steering west. Each fleet, therefore, was striving to attain the weather gage so as to give it the initiative for the next manoeuvre, and as things then were it could not be predicted which would achieve its object. The respective vans might have met at a point and in that case it would have been a matter of which could out-face the other. It should perhaps be noted here that though the respective lines were heading south-east and west they would not have been making good those courses. Leeway to the probable extent of between one and two points would have been affecting them, but with both lines close-hauled the leeway would have been about the same for each. It would not therefore have affected their relative positions and movements.

The matter of a possible collision between the two vans did not, however, eventuate, for about noon the wind veered from south-south-west to south-west. This threw the French ships aback, and by the time they had filled on the new course forced on them (west-north-west) it was clear that the British could easily pass to windward.

This being the situation Byng realized that he should now follow the sage advice of the seventeenth article of the fighting instructions. This laid down that 'If the admiral see the enemy's fleet standing towards him and he has the wind of them, the van of his fleet is to make sail till they come the length of the enemy's rear and our rear abreast the enemy's van; then he that is in the rear of our fleet is to tack first, every ship one after another as fast as they can, throughout the line'. This seems plain enough but some common sense was needed in its application and this Byng failed to supply. If the fleet to windward was to be so formed as to be immediately ready for battle after it had tacked it should be parallel to the enemy fleet to leeward, and this had in fact been stated in the Duke of York's instructions of 1673 but had not been included in Russell's, perhaps because it seemed obvious. On this occasion both fleets had been striving for the weather gage and had been close-hauled, six points from the wind, on opposite tacks. If the weather fleet maintained its course and tacked in succession from the rear, that is virtually tacking together, keeping the line on the same slant (for the signal for the line of battle ahead was kept flying), the two fleets would not be parallel but at an angle of four points. This was not what was wanted and once the two vans had passed each other there was clearly no reason why the head of the British line should not alter course to port, followed by the remainder, to bring the whole line parallel to the French—who would presumably continue close-hauled if, as seemed likely, they were ready to give battle. This could have been ordered by Byng by using the signal for altering course in succession, introduced ten years earlier in the Additional Fighting Instructions. Alternatively he could merely have altered the course of his flagship, which was fourth in the line while on the starboard (eastward) tack, and either have left it to the three ships ahead of him to conform or emphasized the need of this by hoisting a blue flag at the mizzen peak (Article VI of the fighting instructions) which would have ordered them to get in his 'grain'.[1]

But he did none of these things. The angle between the two lines was not the four points mentioned above because, after the shift of wind from south-south-west to south-west, it was obvious that he need not stand as close as possible to the wind in order to weather his enemy. He was therefore steering seven points from the wind instead of six. But even so the angle between the lines would be three points after he had tacked and in that case the new van would obviously be in close action long before Byng's division, now in the rear, would come within effective range. If Lord Dartmouth's instructions of 1688, now only a memory, had been in force there would have been further possibility of rectifiying the situation, for in these, on the subject of the same manoeuvre, it had been said: 'The whole line is to tack, every ship in his own place, and to

[1] In the most recent account of this battle (Pope, *At 12 Mr Byng Was Shot* (London, 1962), it is stated that when the shift of wind allowed Byng to pass to windward of the French he steered his fleet parallel to his enemy's new course, in the opposite direction—as he should have done. But no authority is given for this statement and it conflicts with the *Ramillies* log and all other accounts, including a diagram in the work quoted. All these show battle being joined between a French close-hauled line and a British line which had the wind abeam or somewhat abaft it.

bear down on them as nigh as they can without endangering the loss of wind—note that they are not to bear down all at once, but to observe the working of the admiral and to bring to as often as he thinks fit, the better to bring his fleet to fight in good order'. But the letter of this order was extinct and the spirit seems to have been outside Byng's grasp.

One further point called for some thinking before the British fleet altered to the course on which it was intended to engage. When his van came abreast of, though at a distance from, the French rear, Byng had the Fighting Instructions in his hand open at the seventeenth article and his secretary remarked that according to that article the fleet should now tack. To this Byng replied that he would hold on beyond the enemy's rear before he tacked, so as to give an opportunity to every ship to lead slanting down to the one she was to engage, and they would not be so liable to be raked by the enemy's shot. This mode of attack, also, had been implied in Dartmouth's instructions of seventy years earlier, but as already discussed (p. 31 above) its success depended on the enemy doing what you expected him to—and in that respect you might easily be disappointed. Beyond that there was the question of what course the attacking ships should steer so as to be able to fire their broadside guns as they approached.

Here one of the limitations was how far before the beam the guns could be trained. On this there is no direct evidence, but judging by such knowledge as is now available, summarized at the end of the previous chapter, one would suppose that not more than two points before the beam was the limit at this time. If that was so a ship might possibly steer up to four points inwards on her opponent provided each was two points before the beam of the other *and they were sailing at the same speed*, that is closing on a steady bearing. But as the situation was here it was not only the individual ships that would have been steering what Byng supposed were suitable courses for his plan of action. The whole British line would be on the same slant, and approaching in that way the rear could not come into action until long after the van was fully engaged. That was one major miscalculation, but even more important was his decision to hold on, past the French fleet, before tacking.

There could then no longer be any question of each ship approaching her opponent on a steady bearing with her guns in action, for it would now be necessary to overtake the enemy, that is to sail much faster, and this would throw the line of sight from each ship to the ship she was due to engage much further ahead, beyond the forward limit of bearing of her guns. It was presumably in this connection that the court martial came down on Byng so explicitly for not tacking as directed in Article XVII—'our rear abreast the enemy's van'. And sailing, as he did, in the wrong direction before tacking he was not only delaying action but widening the lateral distance from the enemy's track.

These considerations did not seem to worry Byng at the time, and at 1.30 p.m. he made the signal for the rear of the fleet to tack first—the Union flag at the mizzen topmast head. This implied that the rear ship should tack at once and the rest in succession from the rear, a manoeuvre not unlike the German *Gefechtskehrtwendung* of 1914–18, designed to ensure that ships of what would now be the van were not overtaken or hampered by those that should now be astern of them.[1] Unlike the celerity with which such a movement could be achieved under steam, however, tacking a ship of the line took some time and if each ship waited for 'mainsail haul' in the ship astern of her before putting her helm down (say, five minutes) the distance between ships would have been increased and the whole line would have become too extended for engaging a close-knit enemy. Because of this Rooke had altered the original Article XVII by adding: 'And if the admiral would have the whole fleet tack together, the sooner to put them in a posture for engaging the enemy, he will hoist the Union flag on the flagstaffs at the fore and mizzen mast heads and fire a

[1] The wording of this signal in the printed instructions contained an error which must hold a record in misprints in that it persisted for a century. There were two articles for tacking: ' . . . the van of the fleet to tack first . . .', and ' . . . the rear of the fleet to tack first . . .', and these were clearly stated in the Duke of York's Instructions (1673). In Russell's, however, the second had become: ' . . . the rear-admiral of the fleet to tack first . . .', and so it remained in print until these instructions were superseded at the end of the eighteenth century, though some admirals (Arbuthnot, 1779; Rodney, 1782) crossed out 'admiral' in the copies they issued.

gun.' This Byng did as soon as the rear ship, the *Defiance*, started to tack.

The immediately subsequent events and particularly what went on inside Byng's head are not easy to understand. La Galissonière, seeing the British line on his weather quarter and at a rather curious angle relative to his, not unnaturally supposed that Byng might be attempting to concentrate on his rear. He therefore threw all aback, and thereafter though he maintained his close-hauled line ahead he was making only very little headway. It followed that the *Defiance*, now leading the British line, was no longer closing the leading Frenchman laterally on a steady bearing, as she would have been supposing that the French had held on as they were going and that the moment of tacking had been rightly judged by Byng for implementing his ideas. She was in fact forging ahead. This worried Byng. According to Corbett, 'he expected to see . . . the *Defiance* . . . bear up immediately to engage the leading ship of the French. This he believed to be the recognized thing to do under Article XIX'.[1] The latter was the basic article about engaging van to van. Why he should have expected the *Defiance* to do any such thing on her own initiative is incomprehensible. It had always been generally understood that ships when in line of battle to windward of the enemy should not open fire until the admiral made the signal for battle (a red flag at the main topmast head), and this had been emphasized by Mathews at some time previous to the battle off Toulon by an addition to the article (XIII) which was subsequently incorporated.[2] As Byng had sat on the Mathews court martial one might have supposed that he would have understood this.

To make matters worse Byng now signalled to the *Defiance* to lead one point to starboard, presuming that this would persuade her to engage her opposite number. One notes that if she had done so she would probably have been forced to forfeit the benefit of firing her broadside as she closed, the ostensible aim of Byng's manoeuvre, for her enemy which she

---

[1] *England in the Seven Years War*, vol. I, p. 119.
[2] *Fighting Instructions* (Navy Records Society), p. 190 n.

was already overtaking would now have been well before her beam.

Here there is one more incomprehensible point. There were two articles in the Additional Fighting Instructions for the leading ship to alter course: V, To lead more to starboard; VI, To lead more to port. Only the latter terminates with: 'And every ship of the squadron is to get into his wake as fast as possible'; but this obviously applies also to the former which was the one used here. And yet at Byng's court martial his flag captain informed the court that as a result of this signal ships were now on the bow-and-quarter of each other. It would have been excellent if they had been and if the line had been parallel to the enemy. But in fact the signal for the line of battle ahead was still flying and the rear ships, Byng's division, were still a long way to windward of their opposite numbers in the French line.

Then, as there was still no firing between the leading ships, Byng at last made the signal to engage. There was then no hesitation in the van and there was soon a fierce action between the six leading ships on each side with Rear-Admiral Temple West, commanding the leading division, flying the signal for closer action. Now was the time for Byng's division to bear down in what would have been something like the bow-and-quarter line that his flag captain mentioned at the court martial. But it did not do so, for the signal for the line of battle ahead was not hauled down, the admiral apparently fearing, though with no justification, that he would not be properly supported. He seems to have thought in a muddle-headed way that it was because Mathews bore down on the *Real* with his line in somewhat irregular order that he was subsequently cashiered, which as already shown (p. 77 above) was not the case. He therefore continued to approach on his previous course.

This he did without overtaking his van because there had been a pile-up in the centre. The *Intrepid*, sixth in the line, had lost her fore topmast while closely engaged with her opposite number, and what with this and the battle smoke which prevented the ships astern from seeing just what was happening, the latter were compelled to throw all aback and sort themselves out. The result was that these ships, including Byng's *Ramillies* never came into effective action. Some of them fired away some ammunition but to no effect other than to confuse the scene with smoke, and as the French van ships had been much knocked about La Galissonière was content to disengage by making off to leeward. As it might have been thought that, in the words of the fighting instructions, the main body of the enemy had been 'disabled or run', the admiral might 'think it convenient the whole fleet shall follow them', and Byng mentioned to his flag captain that it was a pity he had not a few more ships so as to enable him to take such action. As things were, however, he did not think he could be justified in pursuing the enemy.

In the subsequent court martial the court had no difficulty in concluding that he had not done his utmost. Of the witnesses who were examined about the *Ramillies* being so much further from the French line than West's division the most succinct answer was given by the captain of the *Intrepid*: 'To be sure the two rears were at the greatest distance from each other because our rear was to windward of our van.'[1] In other words because Byng had gone on sailing close-hauled (even though not quite close) after he had passed the head of the French line, the *Ramillies* was still to windward after he reversed his line, when his division, previously the van, became the rear.

Not unnaturally, both at the time and since, there has been some sincere sympathy for Byng in that ostensibly he suffered the death penalty merely because he was an incompetent tactician. But that he could hardly have handled his fleet worse than he did admits of no doubt.

[1] Quoted in B. Tunstall, *Byng*, p. 224.

Chapter 7

QUIBERON BAY

After the lamentable episode of Minorca there were no further battles between British and French fleets until the Wonderful Year of 1759. But in the meanwhile one of the basic problems of tactics had come into question. This was the action that should be taken when individual enemy ships or small bodies of them had been driven out of their line without the main body having been disabled or run, a problem already mentioned (p. 59) in connection with the battle of Malaga.

That the two highest authorities on tactics of this time should have been in positions to express apparently contrary opinions on the matter was due in the first place to an incident in higher naval circles in May 1758, which took away the breath of the few who knew about it. At that time Hawke was in command of the Channel fleet. In great secrecy Pitt was planning raids on the north coast of Brittany with the aim of attracting thereto considerable French forces and thus to ease the pressure on Frederick the Great. The warships needed for these expeditions on a difficult coast would mostly be small in size and not very numerous, and it was decided to give the naval command to Howe, a young officer who had already shown great enterprise and vigour. (He was only thirty-two years old but had twelve years in as a post captain.) Hawke, knowing nothing of the objectives or the details of the expeditions, was told to give Howe all the assistance he asked for while making his preparations. Upon this Hawke jumped to the conclusion that the affair was to be a repetition of the Rochefort expedition of the previous year in which he had held the naval command and which had petered out so ignominiously, despite the gallant and successful bombardment of the outlying Ile d'Aix by six ships led by Howe in the *Magnanime*. (It so happened that he had just been asked by the Admiralty for the chart of the Basque roads which he had drawn on that occasion.) If this was the case, and if he was to be replaced in command of the active forces by a youngster twenty years his junior, his treatment seemed to him a reproof and a stain on his honour. He thereupon lost his temper and with gross insubordination hauled down his flag, and so reported to the Admiralty. He was then haled before their Lordships and having by this time learnt the true facts and realized how stupid he had been, he did his best to make amends. But it was clear that some change must be made and the decision was that Anson, the First Lord, should once more fly his flag afloat in command of the Channel fleet and that Hawke should re-hoist his flag, but this time as second in command. This post he held only a few weeks because of a breakdown in health.

Anson then spent much time in drilling a fleet which included many more ships than had Hawke's and therefore needed it. In doing this he issued several additional fighting instructions. One was for forming a line of battle on any specified point of the compass irrespective of the course that the fleet was steering, that is on a compass line of bearing. And then there was the one affecting the problem referred to at the beginning of this chapter:

> If upon coming to action with the Enemy, I should think it proper to haul down the Signal for the Line of Battle, every Ship in the Fleet is then to use his utmost endeavours to take or destroy such Ships of the Enemy as they may be opposed to, by engaging them as closely as possible, and pursuing them if they are driven out of their line, without having any regard to the situation which was prescribed to themselves by the Line of Battle, before the signal was hauled down.[1]

In September of that year, on conclusion of the somewhat unsatisfactory raids on the Breton coast, Anson returned to his seat at the head of the Admiralty Board, leaving the squadrons that were to remain at sea during the winter in the hands of junior flag officers. By May 1759, however, Hawke had recovered his health and a self-confidence which seems to

---

[1] *The Barrington Papers* vol. I, Navy Records Society, p. 231.

have been temporarily shattered by his foolish conduct of the previous year. And by this time, too, there was a justifiable assumption that the French were preparing for an invasion, and considerable apprehension that they might achieve their aim. Confidence in Hawke having been restored he was ordered to hoist his flag once more in command of the Channel fleet which was gradually being brought up to the strength needed to frustrate anything the French navy could attempt. It was in these circumstances, with twenty-seven ships of the line in his fleet, that he issued some additional fighting instructions. Most of these were repetitions of those issued by Anson the previous summer, but on one point Hawke's view differed almost, but not quite, fundamentally from that of the First Lord. For the latter's instruction, quoted above, Hawke substituted:

'Whereas many and great inconveniences may arise from every particular Ship in the Squadron strictly preserving her situation in the Line, either immediately at the beginning of, or during an Action, in cases where the whole of the Enemy's Ships shall not be in a direct, or strict line, or their Van, Centre or Rear shall alter the position they were first in; You are to observe, that as soon as I shall have led on the Squadron, so as to be within the distance I think proper to engage at, the moment I hoist the Signal for Engaging, I will haul down the Signal for the Line; When you are hereby required to continue engaging the Ship of the Enemy that shall be immediately opposed to you, in such close manner, according to her position, as will best enable you to take, sink or destroy her; in either of which if you succeed, you are to go to the assistance of the next of the King's Ships engaged ahead or astern of you, as you shall judge most necessary; on the whole having a particular regard to the 21st Article of the General Printed Fighting Instructions.[1]

The difference between this article and Anson's seems at

[1] ibid., p. 259. The copy of these instructions given to Barrington (*Achilles*) is dated 16 July 1759, but it was only at that time that the *Achilles* joined the fleet and it may be that they had been issued to the ships in company with Hawke some weeks earlier.

first sight to be plain enough. Anson says individual ships are to pursue. Hawke says each ship is to have a particular regard to Article XXI (not to pursue till the main body is defeated or run) but his previous sentences might well call for difficult decisions on the part of individual captains. He is legislating for a case in which the enemy is not in 'a direct or strict line' and he enjoins each ship to take up the best position for engaging her opposite number so as to take, sink, or destroy her. Nothing is said about pursuing her if she refuses to be taken, sunk or destroyed and runs to leeward. To continue engaging 'in such a close manner' as is needed to knock her out would, of course, mean pursuit, which would be contradictory to 'having a particular regard' to Article XXI. A puzzling matter, but one which was never in fact put to the test; and it should perhaps be noted in addition that Anson's instructions were qualified by: 'if I should think it proper to haul down the signal for the line of battle', whereas Hawke said that in the circumstances envisaged he would haul down the signal for the line the moment he hoisted the signal for engaging.

In this same year, 1759, Boscawen, commanding in the Mediterranean, issued a short additional instruction, similar in effect to Anson's, enjoining pursuit of an enemy ship forced out of the line 'notwithstanding the general printed Fighting Instructions', his only qualifying clause being: 'when engaged with an equal number of the enemy's ships'.[1] The latter seems to imply that the British fleet should continue in line of battle if the enemy, despite a ship or ships run to leeward, still had as many or more in their line.

That was the last heard on this matter, at least on paper, until the instructions in the Signal Book of 1799, already quoted (p. 59). The problem remained a difficult one, not to be written off merely as a matter of the temperaments of the admirals concerned. Anson, Boscawen, Hawke and Howe were all good men and true, and the two latter (Howe also when he came into authority was an advocate of cohesion) were no less aggressive than the two former. But though there was for the present nothing more on paper, there is a wide gap in our knowledge of the extent to which admirals discussed these

[1] *Fighting Instructions* (Navy Records Society) p. 224.

matters with their junior flag officers and their captains. We know that in ordinary weather when a fleet was blockading or merely cruising there was much ship-visiting, both on service and socially for dinner. Only really dirty weather prevented boat work. But until Nelson emphasized the importance of such consultation, whatever there was seems to have been taken for granted. How much there was and how profitable no doubt depended on the character, and the health, of the commander-in-chief.

Of the fleet actions of 1759 which resulted from the French threat of invasion the first was Boscawen's chase of the Toulon fleet through the Straits of Gibraltar. This fleet of ten of the line commanded by La Clue had been ordered to join the much larger Brest fleet, under Conflans, so as to form a concentration of ships of the line which should have been strong enough, at least in numbers, to protect the transports of the powerful army now being gathered near various ports on the south coast of Brittany. Boscawen had left French waters in July and taken his fourteen ships of the line to refit at Gibraltar, so now was the time for La Clue to make his attempt. He was still at Gibraltar with many of his ships somewhat dismantled when, on the evening of August 17th, a look-out frigate off the African shore reported the French fleet approaching with a fresh easterly wind. In remarkably quick time considering the state of the fleet each ship, as soon as she was ready, slipped her cable and made sail, and by 10 p.m. all were clear of the anchorage and steering for the straits.

When daylight came the bulk of the French, having been shadowed all night by a frigate, were in sight ahead and the British ships were coming up fast, surprisingly so considering that the French were only just out of a dockyard port. What had happened was that before passing Gibraltar La Clue had given Cadiz as the next rendezvous. During the night, however, with the wind favourable and the knowledge that he had been reported, he decided to make for Cape St Vincent without delay. He signalled accordingly but being by that time rather dispersed his three smallest sail of the line (sixty-fours), two fifties and three frigates failed to receive the signal and made for Cadiz. It was therefore only seven ships that Boscawen sighted ahead of him, and at the same time, La Clue, seeing some ships astern, supposed at first that they were his missing rear. He was soon disillusioned, however, and carried on for Cape St Vincent, forming a line of battle ahead with a full spread of canvas. Despite this the British slowly overhauled him, forming for battle in such sequence as they found themselves—presumably by Articles IX and X of the additional fighting instructions quoted above (p. 89).

It was not till 2.30 p.m. that the leading British ship was enabled to engage the nearest Frenchman, and it was 4 o'clock before Boscawen in the *Namur* (ninety) reached La Clue's eighty-gun *Océan*. A hot action ensued in which the *Namur* soon lost her mizzen mast and her fore and main topsail yards. With his flagship thus handicapped in the chase of a flying enemy, Boscawen shifted his flag to the *Newark* (eighty) and continued in pursuit. By nightfall the rear French ship had struck her colours and during the night the British ships kept in touch as well as they were able. The morning, however, showed only four of the French in sight, two having escaped during the night, and these four were now heading for Lagos bay, on the near side of Cape St Vincent. There two of them, including the *Océan*, were run aground under full sail so as at least to deprive their enemy of prizes, and La Clue, badly wounded, was landed on the Portuguese shore. The other two anchored, surrendering to their assailants as soon as they came up with them while at the same time parties from the British ships burnt the now immovable wrecks.

The news of Boscawen's elimination of five good French ships of the line did something to ease the dread of invasion which had been steadily mounting at home. But tension was still high and was not lessened by the fact that a secret agent had conveyed to the government the details of an apparently feasible and probable plan. This was that any army of 20,000 men from Brittany, protected by Conflans' fleet, would be landed in the Firth of Clyde and would then cross southern Scotland and occupy Edinburgh. In the meanwhile the fleet would sail northabout to Flemish waters where it would protect the passage of another army of 20,000 from Ostend to

Maldon in Essex, whence it would march on London. Such a plan could be of no avail if Hawke's fleet could keep Conflans blockaded; but looked on from the other side there could hardly be a doubt of success if Conflans, with a stronger fleet, should put to sea and deliberately and successfully face Hawke in battle. To British eyes this would have been the only sound strategy; but the French navy, though realizing this (Conflans actually voiced it, without contradiction, in a letter to his sovereign), as so often, hoped that good fortune, meaning principally fortunate weather, would save them from putting matters to the ultimate test. For their current plan there was one important item in their favour. The blockade of Brest with its many inshore hazards was too difficult to maintain continuously, even for the main fleet in the offing, in severe westerly gales. The heavy ships had then to make for the shelter of Torbay. In such weather, of course, the French fleet would be unable to leave harbour, but if the westerly weather was followed by good breezes from the eastward, out it could come and perhaps be well away to the westward what time the British fleet, having left Torbay, was still short of its station off Ushant. It might be that frigates, which had been left off Brest despite the weather, would still be able to put Hawke in touch with his enemy but of this there could be no full assurance. Though Scotland was believed to be the French objective a possible descent on Ireland was always much in British minds.

The problem on the French side would have been simplified if the army as well as the navy had been assembled at Brest, but as already noted it was in fact farther south, concentrated round the Morbihan gulf, a complex, island studded sheet of water some ten miles by five, including narrow channels leading to the towns of Auray and Vannes. These channels joined at their seaward ends and debouched through a strongly tidal outlet barely half a mile wide into Quiberon Bay. These well-sheltered waters of the Morbihan were suitable for the transports of those days but too narrow and too shallow for a battle fleet. Lacour-Gayet who wrote (1902) the history of the French navy under Louis XV considered that it would have been more sensible and just as easy to have concentrated the army at

Brest and embarked it there.[1] But the situation and communications of Brest were such that it often proved difficult to keep the crews of a large fleet (say 20,000 men) fully victualled, the coastal traffic, the main source of supplies, being in constant danger from British attack. To have doubled the number of men by bringing the army there instead of spreading it over a wide and more fertile country might well have proved too much. However that may be, the arrangement was that the army should embark at Vannes and Auray, and Conflans must take two bites at his cherry—unless he could steel himself to fight Hawke before considering the army's passage. On the first opportunity he must take his fleet to Quiberon Bay. There, if conditions were still favourable, the transports could join him and he could sail away. If conditions were adverse he must wait there, hoping the Fates, as represented by suitable alternations of westerly gales and east winds, would not keep him waiting too long.

During the summer Hawke's vigilance was able to check any opportunity for a sortie from Brest, even though he sometimes had to leave the watching to a reduced, inshore squadron. But with autumn deteriorating into winter it was another matter. Whenever there were westerly gales Hawke struggled hard to keep his fleet to windward of Ushant, but there were times when he had to admit defeat and on November 9th he anchored in Torbay with fifteen of the line, to be joined in the next few days by reinforcements from Plymouth which brought up the strength of his line of battle to twenty-three ships.

Eager to resume his station he sailed again, only to be confronted by another south-westerly gale; but on November 14th he was at last away and heading for Ushant. On the same day Conflans sailed from Brest with twenty-one of the line, feeling that Hawke was unlikely to confront him with so numerous a fleet after the strain that must have been put on the blockading forces by the recent foul weather. If he could make good time to Quiberon Bay, little more than a hundred miles away, the transports with their 20,000 men could join him from the Morbihan and he could be once more away to sea *en route* for Scotland. But here he was unlucky. He had not

[1] Quoted by Mackay, *Admiral Hawke*, p. 233.

made half the distance before he was confronted by an easterly gale too fierce for his fleet to make headway against it. He therefore gave ground and when on November 18th he could once more shape an easterly course he was further from Quiberon than he had been when he sailed.

Meanwhile Hawke had been making steady progress to regain his position off Ushant and on the afternoon of November 16th he had the good fortune to receive news of his enemy. An empty victualler, returning to Plymouth from the squadron of fifty-gun ships and frigates stationed in Quiberon Bay to watch the Morbihan, was able to tell him that on the previous day she had sighted the French fleet. Conflans was then seventy miles west of Belle-Ile, the island some ten miles by three lying seven miles south of the Quiberon peninsula, and at that time he was still trying to make ground against the easterly winds. Any doubts Hawke may have had were thus set at rest and his endeavours were now centred on steering the best courses the winds would permit for rounding Belle-Ile.

By the night of November 19th–20th both fleets were heading for the south coast of that island, the British somewhat south of west from it and the French farther to the southward. The latter were rather nearer their expected landfall and both fleets had hove to till daylight lest they should find themselves too close to the shore in darkness.

At 7 a.m. when daylight came Hawke believed himself to be about thirty miles from the island and he called the *Magnanime* (Howe) within hail and told her captain to go ahead and make the land. At 8.30 a frigate stationed on Hawke's starboard bow let fly her topgallant sheets, which had been assigned the meaning of a number of ships in sight, and at 9.45 Howe confirmed that it was in fact the French battle fleet. Up till then Conflans had had the satisfaction of chasing the small squadron normally stationed in Quiberon Bay, to which Hawke had previously sent a message ordering it to sea before it could be entrapped and which Conflans had now found in his path. But with the appearance of the British battle fleet all this was changed. He had no intention of engaging a superior fleet, twenty-three to his twenty-one, in the open sea, and he therefore headed for the channel, six miles wide, between the Cardinal

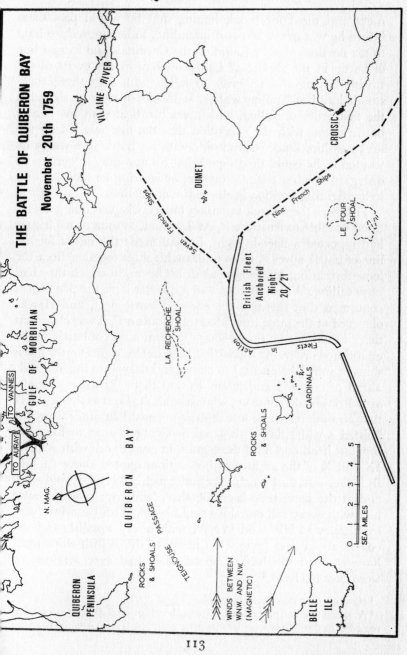

THE BATTLE OF QUIBERON BAY
November 20th 1759

VILAINE RIVER

CROISIC

DUMET

Seven French Ships

Nine French Ships

British Fleet Anchored Night 20/21

LE FOUR SHOAL

Fleets in Action

LA RECHERCHE SHOAL

GULF OF MORBIHAN

TO VANNES
TO AURAY

N. MAG.

QUIBERON BAY

CARDINALS

ROCKS & SHOALS

ROCKS & SHOALS PASSAGE

TEIGNOUSE

QUIBERON PENINSULA

WINDS BETWEEN W.N.W. AND N.W. (MAGNETIC)

BELLE ILE

SEA MILES
0 1 2 3 4 5

rocks and the Four shoal, hoping that he would pass them before he was overtaken and intending, so he averred, to haul to the northward after rounding the Cardinals and form a line of battle in the shelter of Quiberon Bay in the event of the British having the temerity to follow him into these rock-studded and unfamiliar waters. With this in view he signalled the first order of sailing, which was identical with the line of battle ahead with the exception that the line was led by the fleet flagship. Once safely inside with his battle line where he wanted it, he could then signal that his movements were to be disregarded what time by tacking or wearing he took his ship to her fighting position in the centre of the line.

That was the French intention but Hawke was doing everything possible to frustrate it. At 8.30 a.m. as soon as his frigate had reported a fleet in sight, he had made the signal for the line of battle abreast, so as to draw his ships together from the loose formation, somewhere abaft his beam, in which they had been sailing. When an hour and a quarter later the *Magnanime* confirmed that this was the enemy's battle fleet, and Hawke observed at the same time 'that they made off', it was clear that there would not be time enough to form a line of battle in the established order. He therefore 'threw out the signal for the seven ships nearest [the enemy] to chase, and draw into line of battle ahead of me, and endeavour to stop them till the rest of the squadron should come up, who were also to form as they chased, that no time might be lost in their pursuit'.[1] In other words he hoisted a white flag with a red St George's cross at his main topmast head and fired three guns, in accordance with Articles IX and X of the additional instructions quoted above (p. 89). By his account the French were under such sail as they could carry and at the same time keep together, 'while we crowded after him with every sail our ships could bear'. With the wind 'very fresh gales at NW and WNW, with heavy squalls', and the course about east (magnetic) many of the British ships must have reached the highest speeds they had ever attained or were ever likely to.[2]

[1] Hawke's despatch of 24 November 1759.

[2] As noted above (p. 22n) all courses, bearings and directions of wind recorded in those days were by magnetic compass. If one plots the bearings

Of the exact movements of these leading ships and the order in which they engaged the available evidence is anything but precise. It is clear that the seven ships ordered to form a line ahead increased to nine and that Hawke's hundred-gun flagship *Royal George* was not far astern of them. It can also be seen that they were of all sizes (four seventy-fours, two seventies, one sixty-four and two sixties) and came from all three squadrons of the fleet, for they included both of Hawke's seconds, *Torbay* (Keppel) and *Magnanime* (Howe), two other ships of the centre squadron, three of the van and two of the rear. As to their order, it is to be supposed that the leader was Howe for he had been sent ahead at daylight.[1] But it was not the *Magnanime* that was the first to engage as the British drew up on the French rear, perhaps because Howe had ordered his gun crews not to open fire till they were close alongside. Two ships, however, did open fire about 2.30 p.m. at the sternmost of the enemy as they approached the Cardinals, and Hawke without being able to see exactly what was happening ahead now made the signal to engage, a red flag at the fore topmast head.

No more courageous decision in the handling of a navy's main fleet in battle has ever been taken. No doubt the squadron of fifties and frigates that had been stationed in Quiberon Bay knew something of the sheet of water that the fleet was now approaching and from them he may have heard something of its hazards—though he says he was totally ignorant of the details. He had no pilots, and even if he had had an accurate chart in front of him the situation would clearly have been

given in the directions for using the Teignouse Passage, the narrow northern passage into Quiberon Bay (recorded in Marcus, *Quiberon Bay*, appendix 5) it appears that the variation (now 10°W) was at that time about 22° W, i.e. two points. This is confirmed by the only two magnetic variation charts compiled in the eighteenth century other than Halley's original one of 1703. These charts, which probably refer to observations made in about 1750 and 1780 respectively, give the variation as 21° and 25°.

[1] Richard Howe was now a viscount and the head of this distinguished family. Their father had died twenty years earlier and his elder brother, the idol of the army, both British regiments and colonials, had been killed in America the previous year. His younger brother had just been commanding Wolfe's light infantry in the conquest of Quebec.

highly dangerous. There was a gale astern, only two or three hours of daylight remaining, and no certainty that ships rounding-to and close hauled could avoid being driven onto a lee shore. And if he anchored there was no assurance that the anchors would hold—though in fact there was a mud bottom which afforded good holding ground. If he continued on his course after passing the Cardinals there was a tract of clear water ahead of him about six miles square with Dumet island at its north-east corner and the unmarked Recherche shoal to the north-west. But to get into Quiberon Bay itself, that is the waters sheltered by the Quiberon peninsula and the islands and rocks prolonging it, ending in the Cardinals, would have entailed sailing through a two-mile wide unmarked passage between the Recherche and those islands. This was what Conflans intended to do, but the wind having veered a point or two he found it could not be managed. He had to haul round to the eastward and Hawke had to rely, as he was already doing, on the assumption that where his enemy could go he too could go. Many dangers there were but in his eyes, and in ours, to face them was justified by 'the necessity I was under of running all risks to break this strong force of the enemy'—a force which, when considered in conjunction with troops and transports, had so severely shaken English nerves ashore.

The details of the fiercely contested actions which immediately followed the overlap of the British van and the French rear are obscure. Although the British should have been in line ahead by the letter of their instructions, they had been racing for the posts of honour and their line may well have been irregular. Perhaps that did not matter, for the exhilaration of chasing an enemy who was hoping to make his escape if he ran fast enough, however hard he might be prepared to fight when brought to action, gave such a moral superiority as to justify a mêlée—that and the self-confidence nurtured by long months at sea, often in foul weather.

Whether this line, such as it was, was all to windward of the French is not altogether clear. Certainly some ships were to windward and one supposes that all might have been but for the report that it was the starboard side of the French *Formidable*, flagship of their rear squadron, that 'was pierced like a cullender by the number of shot she had received'.[1] While the wind was on the quarter the weather side may well have been the better, but should it have been necessary to haul to the wind, as it would have been if Conflans had been able to steer more to the northward, it might have produced the handicap of making the lower deck guns unusable. As it was, two ships, the *Torbay* and *Dorsetshire*, had to luff right up in a severe squall to clear their lower decks of water and this may have been at the same time as the *Torbay* was engaging the *Thésée* and the latter, apparently with her disengaged (lee) gunports open, heeled over, filled and sank.

It was during this period that the *Formidable*, assailed by several ships and with her admiral dead, at last surrendered. So also did the *Héros;* with all her commissioned officers killed or wounded, she hauled down her colours to the *Magnanime*. But it was too rough for Howe to put a prize crew on board, so she anchored and the *Magnanime* passed on.

When Conflans' efforts to lead his fleet into the security of the Quiberon Bay anchorage were frustrated by the shift of wind he had no alternative but to wear his flagship, the *Soleil Royal*, and head to the eastward towards Dumet island, hoping that the bulk of his fleet would conform but in fact putting most of them in a state of confusion. By this time the *Royal George* had joined up with the advanced line and was soon in contact with this disorganized mass of enemy ships, Hawke hoping to engage the *Soleil Royal*. Some broadsides were in fact exchanged between the two flagships, but he was unable to prolong the engagement, other French ships having interposed themselves and Conflans having again hauled to the wind on the larboard tack and stood to the northward. Hawke then engaged the *Superbe* (seventy) which foundered after receiving two broadsides, perhaps by flooding through open gunports, and as he was now nearing Dumet with the night rapidly closing in he had to haul to the wind on the starboard tack, heading to the south-westward, so as to get his fleet clear. He then signalled for the whole fleet to anchor and came-to in fifteen fathoms four or five miles

[1] Marcus, op cit., p. 152.

west by south from Dumet.[1] All but five anchored close around him; four of those five succeeded in getting clear of the land and making an offing, returning on subsequent days. The fifth, the *Resolution*, which had been out of control for some hours repairing damage sustained in her fight with the *Formidable*, was wrecked on the Four shoal, five miles to seaward of the anchorage, of which she had no knowledge.

At daylight on November 21st Hawke could take stock of the situation. He knew that he had sunk two ships and that two had surrendered, though one of the latter, the *Héros*, had not yet been boarded. She was anchored among his fleet, and so too, strangely, was Conflans in the *Soleil Royal*. The latter immediately cut his cable and made sail in an endeavour to beach his ship in the little harbour of Croisic nearby. So too did the *Héros* but both ships succeeded only in running on the rocks off Croisic point. One ship, the *Essex*, had been sent to try and recapture the *Héros* but she lucklessly ran on the hitherto unknown Four shoal, which thus claimed the only two British losses.

Five Frenchmen were now accounted for and to the northward, three or four miles beyond Dumet island, seven more could be descried in the shoal water off the mouth of the Vilaine river, apparently aground at low water. Hawke's first impulse was to weigh anchor and close nearer to them, but as it continued to blow as hard as ever he decided to remain where he was for that day, sending two frigates to rescue the crews of the *Resolution* and *Essex*. All were saved either then or on the following day except for some men of the *Resolution*, who had misguidedly left their ship on a raft during the first night.

By November 22nd the wind had eased somewhat and some of the fifty-gun ships were sent towards Croisic to burn the *Soleil Royal* and *Héros*. Both were burnt, the French having made this easier by themselves starting to set alight the former. And on November 23rd the weather was good enough for approaching the mouth of the Vilaine. Here it was found that six ships, by jettisoning their guns and stores and taking advantage of the spring tides, had been able to cross the very

[1] Hawke's despatch says between two and three miles, but from cross bearings he took next morning it was evidently more than that.

shallow bar into deeper water beyond—where they remained unarmed and inactive for more than a year. The seventh ship was wrecked outside the river's mouth.

All the remaining nine of Conflans' original twenty-one ships of the line had succeeded in getting clear of the land during the night following the battle and by the next evening eight of them were anchored in the Basque roads, a hundred miles to the southward. The ninth, which had been badly damaged and her captain killed, had made for the mouth of the Loire, closer at hand, but by some accident of navigation she was wrecked near the entrance with the loss of nearly all hands.

Though in the final count the French fleet had not been annihilated it had clearly ceased to exist as a fighting force either physically or morally. But the British navy would continue to blockade the Biscay ports, even if sometimes with less exhilaration than before—for, as the sailors said of their compatriots,

Ere Hawke did bang
Monsieur Conflang
You sent us beef and beer.
Now Monsieur's beat
We've nought to eat
Since you have nought to fear.

Chapter 8

THE BATTLE OF USHANT, 1778

The conduct of the French navy in the Seven Years War had little in it to be proud of and something for shame. In all the seas save in the opening moves off Minorca the British had asserted their superiority, both moral and material. When, therefore, Choiseul became Louis XV's chief minister while the war was in progress he was determined to do what he could to build up the fleet to a strength which, when combined with the hoped-for alliance of the Spanish fleet, would provide an almost overwhelming force for any future war. This he had substantially achieved, at least in numbers, before in 1770 he was cast aside by his king and exiled to his country estate. And soon there was not only the enhanced material strength of the French fleet to encourage renewal of its self-confidence but there was also the evidently worsening relations between Britain and her American colonies. These might well lead to a disregard for seafaring matters which would detract from the British navy's ability to defend the country against invasion and to protect the valuable trade with the West and East Indies.

With the surrender of Burgoyne at Saratoga in the autumn of 1777, therefore, France determined on an attempt to redeem her position at sea (Spain acted more slowly), and in the spring of 1778 a fleet of thirty-two ships of the line was assembled at Brest.

In England the outlook was far from cheerful. Though the Admiralty (the earl of Sandwich at its head) assured Parliament and the public that there were plenty of ships ready, this was based on unjustified assumptions; and when in June, 1778, a Channel fleet at last put to sea it included only twenty-one of the line. Command of this fleet was in the hands of Augustus

Keppel, now an admiral of the blue, who had distinguished himself as second-in-command of the naval forces taking part in the siege and capture of Havana (1762), co-operating with the army commanded by his elder brother, the earl of Albermarle. He neither liked nor trusted Lord Sandwich, either politically or personally, but by seniority and by reputation he was the obvious choice. And as he had agreed previously at a special audience with the king that he would be ready to take up this post if war should be at hand, it was his evident duty to accept the responsibility to which he was now called. He was now fifty-three years of age and in full mental vigour, despite the fact that he was somewhat handicapped physically by an injury to his back which had resulted from a fall down a hatchway in rough weather ten years earlier when on passage to Lisbon in a packet boat. It seems that this was frequently painful and sometimes affected the use of his legs.

Having ascertained in an encounter with some French frigates on June 17th that the Brest fleet had a superiority of three to two over his force he returned to harbour for reinforcements, and on July 9th he put to sea again with thirty of the line. It so happened that on the previous day the Brest fleet also had sailed. In command was the comte d'Orvilliers. The French still retained their partiality for elderly admirals (d'Orvilliers was sixty-eight: Conflans had been sixty-nine at Quiberon Bay) and here there was no inducement to a feeling of rejuvenation such as might have been imparted by a vigorous offensive plan. The ministers of Lousi XVI were not yet ready to consider an invasion of England without the co-operation of Spain, which was still hanging back. But evidently some gesture must be made and d'Orvilliers was ordered to take his fleet to the westward, where if he were lucky it might well do some damage to British trade from the East and West Indies. It was implied that he was not to seek action with any British fleet in his cruising area, but at the same time he was expected to remain at sea for a month. His acknowledgement of these orders included his determination to fulfil his instructions but with the well-justified qualification that if the British really sought to force an action it would be very hard to shun one.

It was on July 23rd that the two fleets first came in sight of one another, being then about eighty miles west of Ushant. At that time the French were steering to the southward on a north-westerly wind and the British were to windward of them, but it was already late in the afternoon with no possibility of Keppel forcing an action on his adversary before dark. Next morning the positions were reversed in that the wind had backed to the south-west and the French were now to windward.

For the next three days the French fleet kept plying to windward in an endeavour to keep clear of their adversaries. During this time two French ships lost touch and were not seen again, so the two lines of battle were now equalized, thirty ships each.

On the fourth day, however, July 27th, there was a change which justified Hoste's surmise in his book of a century earlier that a fleet to windward trying to avoid action was unlikely to succeed in this indefinitely. At daybreak in rather misty weather the situation was much as before: wind south-west and the French fleet dead to windward of the British about eight miles away. Both fleets were on the larboard tack, steering about west-north-west. But they were not in similar formations. The French were in line ahead; but the three British divisions (van, centre and rear) were each severally in loose order of sailing, that is somewhere on the quarters of their flagships, and the three flagships were intended to be on such bearings as would put those of the van and rear ahead and astern of the commander-in-chief if he ordered the fleet to tack together and then stood close-hauled on the starboard tack. This can be deduced from the answer given by Jervis (captain of the *Foudroyant*, Keppel's second astern) in subsequent cross-examination that 'the *Formidable* (flagship of the rear division) was much further to leeward than her station in the order of sailing prescribes'. The exact order of sailing has not been recorded, but from Jervis's evidence and the events of the battle there can be no doubt that the situation was as stated above.[1]

[1] Article VI of the additional sailing instructions of 1778 lays down: 'In case no other order of sailing shall be prescribed every ship is to keep in such station on the quarter of the commander-in-chief as may enable her

It was here that the first sign of animosity between the commander-in-chief and his third-in-command can be perceived. The second-in-command was Vice-Admiral Sir Robert Harland, commanding the van division, who gave Keppel his loyal and faultless support on every occasion, but the rear was commanded by Vice-Admiral Sir Hugh Palliser whose background was notably different from that of his chief. Keppel was a member of the Whig aristocracy and with the influence thereby accruing had been made a post captain just before his twentieth birthday. Palliser, two years older, was of a landowning Yorkshire family and a staunch Tory. He was not without family influence but was not made post captain until he was twenty-five and was thus three years junior to Keppel on the list that established all future relative seniority. His record was beyond reproach; after many active years afloat he had held the office of Comptroller of the Navy for three years during the peace; and then, with a Tory government, he was given a seat on the Board of Admiralty. As was quite usual in those days he remained a member despite his present service with the fleet.

It was soon after daybreak on July 27th that Keppel, seeing that most of Palliser's ships were to leeward (eastward) of their station, particularly some laggardly ones, made a signal addressed individually to seven of these ships to 'chase to windward'. Under these conditions 'chase' was an intransitive verb, as was a familiar usage in those days, and implied standing close-hauled with all the sail that could be carried. As there were but nine ships in Palliser's division, only the *Formidable* and one other were omitted from this order and one might wonder why the signal was not made to the division as a whole. But as yet there were no distinguishing signals for the separate divisions of the fleet, as there were to be later. In this instance, however, Palliser, no doubt roused by signals being direct to his ships, did make more sail so as not to be left behind. But it was evident subsequently that this affair

to join the line of-battle with the greatest despatch, viz. the seconds nearest to him, the leaders on the wings, and the intermediate ships agreeable to the written order'. In this case such an order was presumably intended, substituting 'divisional commander' for 'commander-in-chief'.

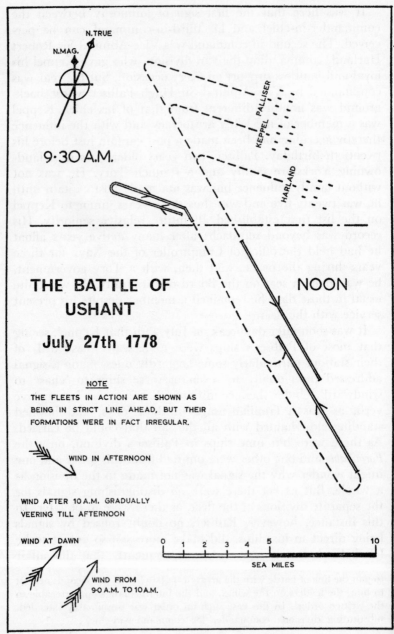

N. TRUE

N. MAG.

9·30 A.M.

KEPPEL

HARLAND

PALLISER

THE BATTLE OF USHANT

NOON

July 27th 1778

NOTE

THE FLEETS IN ACTION ARE SHOWN AS
BEING IN STRICT LINE AHEAD, BUT THEIR
FORMATIONS WERE IN FACT IRREGULAR.

WIND IN AFTERNOON

WIND AFTER 10 A.M. GRADUALLY
VEERING TILL AFTERNOON

WIND AT DAWN

WIND FROM
9·0 A.M. TO 10 A.M.

| 0 | 1 | 2 | 3 | 4 | 5 | | | | | 10 |

SEA MILES

occasioned a strong, and perhaps not unnatural, resentment in his mind, appearing as it did to take the command of his division out of his hands.[1]

At 9 a.m., by which time Palliser's division must have come up to something like its intended position, d'Orvilliers decided to alter his course from the larboard to the starboard tack. For what reason he made this move is not clear. It has been said that he wanted to have a more distinct view of what his enemy was doing—for the weather was hazy. But he had spent three days trying to keep to windward out of harm's way, and although if he had now tacked little ground would have been lost, he decided that it would be best to wear, presumably mistrusting the ability of his ships to tack without risk of missing stays. Even wearing together would not have lost much ground, but he preferred to wear in succession, a manoeuvre which forced the leading ship to sail large until she had reached the rear ship, that is half the length of the line. Not till then could she and subsequently the ships astern of her haul to the wind on the new tack.

By the time, therefore, that d'Orvilliers' whole line was on the starboard tack, steering south-south-east, he had lost ground to leeward, and it so happened that during this manoeuvre the wind backed temporarily one point—to south-west by south. This in the then relative positions of the two fleets allowed the British, still on the larboard tack, to make better ground to windward and to close slightly with the enemy, with the result that they were now almost in the French fleet's wake. Keppel therefore ordered the whole fleet to tack together which brought his ships into a rough line ahead (or rather into a line of three divisions with the individual ships somewhat disordered) close-hauled on the starboard tack, with the leading ship slightly on the larboard quarter of the rear Frenchman. He did not hoist the signal for the line of battle ahead since if every ship were to take up her precise position in the order of battle much time would be lost. He had no doubt that Harland

[1] There was in fact nothing unusual in a commander-in-chief making signals direct to ships in the divisions of other flag officers. During the two hours before fire was opened at Trafalgar Nelson made four signals to ships in Collingwood's division.

and his van division would do what was needed to form a line ahead of the centre, which in fact he did.

The relative positions of the two fleets now seemed to d'Orvilliers to endanger his rear ships. He therefore ordered his fleet to wear together so as to allow these ships, which would now be in the van, to keep out of trouble. This would not lose so much ground as his previous wearing in succession, but wearing necessarily entailed quite a large turning circle to leeward and by the time all his ships were round they were in rather a ragged line and were so nearly pointing towards his enemy that he could not without dishonour attempt a refusal which might sacrifice any of his ships which had fallen too far to leeward. Two or three of his now leading ships did haul to the wind to keep out of shot of the oncoming British van, but the rest maintained their gradually improving line with the result that the two fleets engaged on opposite courses, starboard to starboard. By now, too, the wind was gradually shifting again, veering this time, and this was enabling the British to stand more towards their opponents' line.

The resulting engagement was necessarily irregular but there was brisk fighting while it lasted, apparently for about two hours in all. The fleets passed each other only slowly. They were under easy sail and, as was often remarked of these battles, the heavy cannonade was said to have had the effect of making the breeze die down. Whether there was any meteorological foundation for this view can never now be known, but it was widely expected as a probability and when this expectation was not fulfilled it was sometimes remarked on, for example by Morogues of the battle of Malaga.[1] In this battle Jervis had no doubt about it for he noted in his journal, 'the wind having quite abated by the concussion of the air'.[2]

Another widely held view in those days was that whereas the British always fired at the enemy's hulls, so as to knock out the guns and kill the men and perhaps make the ships unseaworthy, the French always elevated their guns so as to cripple the masts, spars and sails of the British. Whether this was enjoined on the French navy as the universal rule is not

[1] Bigot de Morogues, *Naval Tactics*, translated by a Sea-Officer, p. 93.
[2] Keppel, *Life of Viscount Keppel*, vol. II, p. 41.

clear. It is always risky to accept a theory propounded by someone on one's own side as to what the enemy's practice is and two instances of this are worth noting. A French admiral, de Grenier, writing in 1787, asserted that the English had begun to discard the line of battle at the beginning of the Seven Years War and that in the War of American Independence, knowing the weakness of the single line, had almost always concentrated on part of the French line without regular order.[1] And on the British side Charles Knowles (the younger) who thought a lot about tactics and being bilingual (his mother was Belgian) naturally interested himself in the French aspects, stated that a French fleet, when attacked from to windward, fell off to leeward by alternate ships (by signal) so as to force their enemy's to be constantly heading down to them and so putting themselves in positions liable to raking. Of such a manoeuvre there is no evidence in any of the battles between British and French fleets.

But to return to the matter of French fire control in this battle of Ushant, it seems clear both in the general impression and in the resulting damage that the French were firing to cripple. Among other things it was noted that when at close range they were firing langridge rather than grape shot. When langridge (any old bits of scrap-iron that could be loaded into a gun) hit a sail it tore it to bits, whereas grape only peppered it. Whether this was the French intention is as may be, but the fact was that by the time the two fleets had passed clear of each other five British ships were immobile until they could do extensive repairs aloft, while the French were able to sail on, gradually improving the formation of their line. And besides the five British ships crippled there were others whose sails and rigging needed attention to put them into full manoeuvring trim. These included some of Palliser's rear division which by gradual veering of the wind had been able to stand closer to their opponents, a process which had eventually taken them well to windward of the rest of the British fleet.

On the other hand the British practice of aiming at the hulls of their opponents, though here too transitory to achieve a decision, had resulted in 163 French killed and 573 wounded

[1] *Fighting Instructions* (Navy Records Society), p. 285.

as against British 133 killed and 375 wounded—and the latter would have been lower but for the fact that a considerable proportion of the *Formidable's* 16 killed and 49 wounded were not due to the enemy but to the accidental explosion of some powder.[1]

When Harland and the van division had cleared the French rear at about 1.30 p.m. he lost no time in anticipating his admiral's wishes and tacking in succession to follow the French. When Keppel with the centre had reached the same position he would no doubt have liked to follow, but the *Victory* was in no condition to tack so he had perforce to wear, thus losing some ground to leeward. As there were other ships in the same condition he made the signal for the line of battle ahead, so as to collect such ships as could make sail, at the same time standing on in chase of the enemy. This challenge, however, could not be maintained for long, for the French now wore in succession, thereby threatening the five disabled ships lying on Keppel's lee quarter. And not only that, but on his weather bow were Palliser's ships who, as already noted, had stood well to windward when they had finished fighting and were remaining there, two or three miles away, repairing damage. Keppel therefore again wore his fleet together and subsequently sent Harland, now astern of him, once again into the van, hoping that Palliser would soon join him and form the rear. Both fleets were now on southerly courses sailing large (the wind had veered further to north-west by west), Keppel steering to protect his disabled ships. D'Orvilliers was slightly on his lee (larboard) quarter making no attempt to renew the action though he could easily have done so.

In the British fleet the signal for the line of battle ahead was again flying, summoning Palliser to come into the station indicated to him by the course his commander-in-chief was

---

[1] That the value of crippling the enemy's motive power was not entirely overlooked by British admirals is shown by a note inserted, curiously, in the middle of a list of forty-nine additional signals issued by Arbuthnot on the North American station in 1781: 'N.B. It is directed that in action a portion of every ship's fire be reserved for and directed against the masts and rigging of the enemy.' *Signals and Instructions*, Navy Records Society, p. 251.

now steering. But there was no movement from his division. His ships were still lying-to repairing damage. As each completed she took up her station relative to the *Formidable*, not to the commander-in-chief, a point on which there seems to have been some ambiguity, as already mentioned in the case of Lestock's views in 1742 and his practice in 1744 (p. 69 above). But the *Formidable* remained immobile, making no report of her inability to join the commander-in-chief, either then or when shortly afterwards Keppel sent a frigate to Palliser to tell him what he wanted, a message delivered orally through a speaking-trumpet. Later, exasperated by the delay, Keppel summoned all the rear ships (except the *Formidable*) by their individual pendants to join him, but by the time he had collected a sufficiently powerful line of battle he thought it too late in the evening to assail the enemy who were now lying to leeward of him out of range. Hoping to complete the business in the morning he lay by for the night, deceived in the assumption that the French were still at hand by the three fast-sailing ships which d'Orvilliers had left to windward of his line with full lights burning as if they were flagships, while he made off for Brest with the rest of his fleet. When this became clear to Keppel in the morning and there seemed no hope of overtaking even the three ships in sight, he bore up for Plymouth to make good his battle damage.

Despite his justifiably harsh feelings about lack of support from Palliser, whom he had previously thought his friend, Keppel refrained from any hint of this in his despatch to the Admiralty, and when once more in fighting trim the fleet continued to cruise off Ushant during the autumn. But the feelings of those who thought their commander-in-chief had been badly let down seem to have got about and not unnaturally penetrated to the press, with the result that shortly before the fleet's final return to port at the end of October an indictment of Palliser's proceedings during the afternoon of the battle appeared anonymously in a London paper. Palliser was told of this and was enraged to tthe extent of demanding a personal interview with his commander-in-chief a few days later in London. When this was granted he laid before Keppel a letter not merely exonerating but highly praising his, Palliser's, conduct and demanded that Keppel should not only sign it but himself send it to a newspaper.

This Keppel refused to do. Palliser thereupon published his views on the battle and the stage was now being set for one of those disputes between a commander-in-chief and a subordinate which from time to time have besmirched the fame of the British navy. With the re-assembly of Parliament in November the conduct of the battle was debated in both Houses with little sympathy for Palliser from anyone except the Prime Minister and the First Lord, North and Sandwich. In the Commons, of which both Keppel and Palliser were members, the debates were notably hot and emotional though without any resulting decisions. But thereafter, early in December, Palliser asked the Board of Admiralty of which he was still a member that Keppel should be brought before a court martial to be prosecuted by himself, Palliser, for not doing his utmost to defeat d'Orvilliers. This request Sandwich at once conceded. Keppel was so informed and told that the court would assemble early in January.

The unexpected shock to Keppel at being treated in this way was naturally severe, but although his health was not always as good as it might be, on which account a special act of Parliament was passed allowing the court to be held ashore at Portsmouth, he responded forcefully to the exigences of the trial, no doubt heartened by the backing of many supporters and the evident sympathy which was always extended to him by the court. In intimate support he probably owed most to Jervis, in the way the latter gave his evidence both in his examination and in his subsequent cross-examination by Palliser, and in the advice he gave on the general policy that Keppel should follow in his defence.[1]

---

[1] Jervis was at this time forty-three years old. His father, a lawyer, had strongly opposed his son's determination to join the navy but had eventually allowed him to go to sea at the age of thirteen. He was given just enough money for his outfit as a midshipman but thereafter received neither encouragement nor financial help from his family. His talents, however, were so evident to such of his captains as were themselves outstanding that he became a post captain at the age of twenty-six. He had now been in command of the 84-gun *Foudroyant* for three years and was to remain in her for

The trial lasted five weeks and at the end he was unanimously and honourably acquitted, to the joy of his friends and in fact of all Whigs. In this the London mob joined with a will. North's and Sandwich's windows were broken and Palliser's house was gutted, with a fine bonfire of his furniture in St James's Square.

Two months later a further court martial was assembled with directions to inquire into Palliser's 'conduct and behaviour' during the battle without any specific charge being made. He was acquitted of any misconduct or misbehaviour, but it was the opinion of the court that 'it was incumbent on him to have made known to his commander-in-chief the disabled state of the *Formidable*'. Clearly North and Sandwich could no longer be so barefaced as to retain him on the Board, but he was allowed to have the lucrative office of Governor of Greenwich Hospital when it became vacant shortly afterwards.

another five, attaining for her the reputation of the smartest ship in the British navy.

Chapter 9

BYRON AND D'ESTAING AT GRENADA

Despite the size of the fleets in European waters, sometimes amounting to as many as forty-four British ships of the line, forty-eight French and eighteen of their Spanish allies, it was not here that the main naval battles of the War of American Independence were fought. Apart from Britain's straitened resources it was difficult to find successive commanders-in-chief for the Channel fleet, senior enough and willing to serve under the existing Board, who at the same time were not too senile to pursue a vigorous strategy. In fact the only fleet engagements on this side of the Atlantic were Rodney's destruction of a Spanish squadron south of Cape St Vincent on his way to the West Indies in January 1780 and, after a change of Admiralty had brought Howe once more afloat, his brush with the combined fleets of France and Spain when he relieved Gibraltar in October 1782. But in West Indian and North American waters there was a continuous struggle culminating in Rodney's victory in the battle of The Saints in April 1782.

The opening move was the despatch of a squadron from Toulon under the comte d'Estaing in April 1778 to do what he could to help the Americans. Two months later a similar squadron under Vice-Admiral John Byron was sent across with the specific purpose of keeping d'Estaing in check on whichever of the regular naval stations (North America, Leeward Islands and Jamaica) he might happen to be operating. Both these squadrons suffered from bad weather, not only on passage across the Atlantic but also after arrival in North American waters, with the result that nothing of importance was achieved that summer. Early in November, however, the French were sufficiently refitted, and revictualled to allow them to sail for the West Indies, and on the same day as they left Boston a

British force of five thousand troops under Major-General Grant sailed from New York escorted by a small squadron with instructions to capture St Lucia, the next island south of the French Martinique with its main naval base at Fort Royal. Joining Vice-Admiral Samuel Barrington, commander-in-chief of the Leeward Islands station, at Barbados and not losing a moment, the convoy landed its troops in St Lucia on December 14th and assailed the weak garrison just as d'Estaing came over the horizon with a greatly superior squadron and transports carrying nine thousand troops. French efforts to dislodge Barrington from his anchorage failed and a vigorously pressed attack by the French army which had been landed in the northern part of the island was driven back with heavy casualties. Ten days later d'Estaing re-embarked his army and retired to Martinique, leaving St Lucia in British hands with its valuable anchorage in Gros Islet Bay at the northern end, only thirty miles across the water from the French base.

Byron's squadron, which had left North American waters in December, joined Barrington in January, and as the latter was the junior it was arranged that command of the Leeward Islands station should be transferred to Byron, Barrington remaining in his flagship the *Prince of Wales* (seventy-four) as second-in-command. The situation was then quiescent for a few months with the two fleets facing each other, so to speak, across the channel between St Lucia and Martinique. Each from time to time received reinforcements from home and by June this had resulted in Byron having twenty-one of the line under his command and d'Estaing twenty-five.

The next move arose from the need to despatch a large British convoy which had been collecting at St Kitts, two hundred miles to the northward, and to see it well clear into the Atlantic on its homeward-bound voyage. Byron had accordingly to sail with his whole fleet and inevitably to leave the coast clear for d'Estaing to put in train any enterprise against the southern islands that he might think fit. The latter's first move was to send a small expedition to capture the ungarrisoned St Vincent, thirty miles south of St Lucia. That achieved, he sailed from Fort Royal on June 30th with his whole fleet and army to attack the more valuable and almost equally defenceless island of Grenada, sixty miles further on. There he arrived on July 2nd and on July 4th the island capitulated.

The British fleet arrived back at St Lucia on July 1st and there Byron heard of the capture of St Vincent, and heard also a little later that d'Estaing had sailed with a considerable force to the southward, probably bound for Grenada. He therefore embarked General Grant's five battalions in their transports, to defend, or if necessary retake, Grenada, and by July 3rd he was on his way south. It appeared from an imperfect reconnaissance of Fort Royal that there were still some ships of the line there, and from this and some reports he received from ships which had sighted the French fleet on its passage south it seemed that d'Estaing had only sixteen or so ships of the line with him with which to oppose Byron's twenty-one.

It was at 4 a.m. on July 6th while still dark that the British fleet, standing to the southward, sighted the northern end of Grenada on its larboard, weather, bow about eight miles away. General Grant's convoy, with three of the line guarding it, was some way astern and the remaining eighteen were in loose cruising formation, sailing free with the wind somewhere in the north-east quarter.[1]

Half an hour later, as day was breaking, Byron hoisted a blue flag at the peak (Article VI of the printed fighting instructions) for ships to form in line ahead or astern of him, and about this time two French frigates were seen inshore making all sail towards St George's Bay on the south-west coast of the island. There, not long afterwards, the French fleet was sighted at anchor and Byron then, at 5 a.m., made the signal for a general chase in the south-east quarter, evidently meaning towards the enemy in sight. At this time Barrington in the

[1] The Caribbean islands are, of course, in what is generally known as the north-east trade wind belt, but in these longitudes the winds are usually deflected clockwise to the extent of being more easterly than north-easterly though with variations depending on the disposition of the islands. This can be seen from the naming of the island groups, for Grenada, the southernmost of the Windward Islands, bears due south from Antigua, the headquarters of the Leeward Islands station. Contributing to a similar effect on strategy was the fact that the Equatorial current which percolated between all these islands at a rate of one knot or more had a general direction of west-north-west.

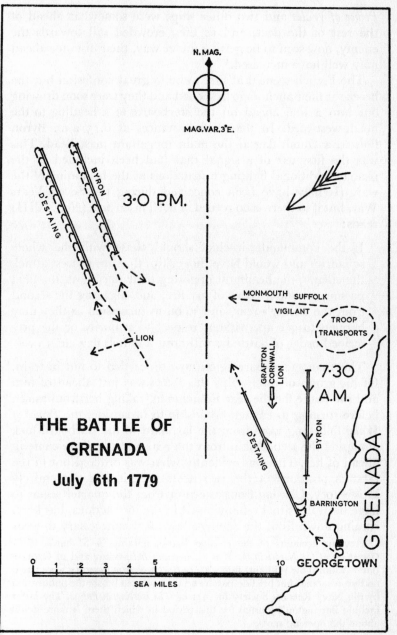

N. MAG.

MAG.VAR.3°E.

D'ESTAING

BYRON

3·0 P.M.

LION

MONMOUTH SUFFOLK

VIGILANT

TROOP
TRANSPORTS

GRAFTON
CORNWALL
LION

7·30
A.M.

BYRON

THE BATTLE OF
GRENADA
July 6th 1779

D'ESTAING

BARRINGTON

GRENADA

GEORGETOWN

0 1 2 3 4 5   10
SEA MILES

Prince of Wales and two other ships were somewhat ahead of the rest of the fleet, and as they crowded sail towards the enemy, now seen to be getting under way, their distance ahead may well have increased.[1]

The French seemed at first to be in great confusion but the breeze at their anchorage freshened and they were soon drawing out into a line ahead on the starboard tack heading to the north-westward. In these circumstances at 6.15 a.m. Byron hoisted a Dutch flag at the main topgallant mast head. This was the first use of a signal that had been included in the issue of additional fighting instructions at the beginning of the war. (It may have been conceived during the Seven Years War, but if so there is no record of it.) This article (No. XVIII) reads:

> If the commander-in-chief should chase with the whole squadron and would have those ships that are nearest attack the enemy, the headmost opposing their sternmost, the next passing on under cover of her fire, and engaging the second from the enemy's rear, and so on in succession as they may happen to get up, without respect to seniority or the pre-scribed order of battle he will hoist a Dutch flag etc. . . .

This manoeuvre Barrington now proceeded to put in train. Of his group of three ships the *Sultan* was just ahead of him and she made for the rear Frenchman, raking her from astern before turning to engage broadside to broadside, the *Prince of Wales* following wore from the larboard to the starboard tack alongside the second ship from the rear and the *Boyne* came in ahead of her. This was evidently what was ordered but in the relative positions of the two fleets here it was not entirely satisfactory. Chasing from astern or from the quarter seems to have been the situation envisaged in the instructions, but here, coming down from the enemy's bow, it was necessary to wear

[1] Previous accounts of the coming battle, notably in Mahan's *Major Operations of the Navies in the War of American Independence* and in Captain (later Admiral Sir William) James's *The British Navy in Adversity*, were based on Byron's somewhat brief despatch and were written before the publication by the Navy Records Society in 1941 of *The Barrington Papers*. The latter include Barrington's journal for this period in which there is more detail about the opening moves.

ship under fire before coming into action, thus increasing the well-known though normally accepted danger of attacking from a weather position.

It was at 7.35 a.m. that the French line opened fire on Barrington's approaching detachment but once he had engaged his opposite number with his larboard broadside it was not long before 'she bore up from us', and he then noticed that Byron had hauled down the Dutch flag and hoisted a red flag with a white cross. This was Article XIX of the new edition of the additional instructions, which was identical with Articles IX and X of the old instructions (see p. 89 above) except that the above flag had been substituted for the original Genoese ensign (a white flag with a red cross), presumably to avoid confusion with the flag of an admiral of the white. Why Byron had changed his mind has not been recorded. Perhaps it was because he now saw that there were twenty-four ships of the line opposed to his twenty-one, instead of the sixteen he had expected, or perhaps he now realized that the relative positions of the fleet made Article XVIII unsuitable for his purpose. However that may be, Barrington 'got the main-tack on board, and made all sail I could in order to gain the enemy's van, engaging the ships in the Rear and Centre as I passed and attempting several times to close with them, but which they as industriously avoided by always bearing up to prevent it, and three of their ships absolutely quitted their line and ran to leeward (one of them with studding sails set) and did not rejoin the Line till after the action'.[1]

It was at about this time that there was a set-back to a group of British ships, the details of which have never been made clear. It is said that three ships, the *Grafton*, *Cornwall* and *Lion*, who were to leeward of Byron's main body and much closer to the enemy because the British were approaching from the latter's starboard, weather, bow 'sustained the fire of the enemy's whole line as it passed on the starboard tack'. What is not clear is whether they were trying to get to the rear of their own fleet or whether they were still influenced by Byron's original signal (Article XVIII) which would have brought them into the line ahead of Barrington. However that may be they certainly

[1] *The Barrington Papers* (Navy Records Society), vol. II, p. 309.

suffered much damage and were left crippled as the battle passed to the westward.

Barrington gradually forged ahead and about 10 a.m., that is two hours after he had come into action, he noticed that Byron had hoisted the signal for line ahead at two cables. He had previously had the signal for close action flying and was now presumably trying to dress his line and press on ahead so as to forestall any attempt of d'Estaing to make to windward towards the convoy. By 11 a.m. Barrington had progressed as far forward as the fifth ship from the enemy's van and so had virtually reached his objective, for the three ships with the convoy, the *Monmouth*, *Suffolk* and *Vigilant*, had left their charges and were racing down towards the head of the battle line. The *Monmouth* was already fiercely in action with the French leaders and the other two were following her. By noon most of the British ships were in action but many of them, besides the three that had been left behind crippled, were much damaged, Barrington's *Prince of Wales* and the gallant *Monmouth* in particular. By 1.20 p.m. all firing had ceased. Though there were now only eighteen in the British line opposed to the French twenty-four d'Estaing made no attempt to press the action, and at 3 p.m., being then out of range, he tacked his fleet together to head back towards Grenada. Byron conformed.

This move, it was clear, put the *Grafton*, *Cornwall* and *Lion* in grave danger, for they could easily have been in d'Estaing's path had he cared to steer such a course. But for this he showed no inclination. The *Grafton* and *Cornwall* could make just sufficient sail to draw slowly to windward and the French were contented with some desultory firing at them as they went by. The *Lion* could only run to leeward, hoping to be left alone, which to general British astonishment she was. No French ships were detached to engage her and the gallant Cornwallis, the steadfast blockader of Brest in the Napoleonic war, arrived at Jamaica a fortnight later.

D'Estaing now resumed his anchorage in St George's Bay and the British forces, with no hope recapturing Grenada, made the best of their way to St Kitts to make good their damage. This they were unable to complete for some time because of the shortage of stores on the station. Casualties in the battle had been fairly equally divided—the British 183 killed and 346 wounded; the French 190 killed and 759 wounded. But the material damage (masts, spars, rigging and sails) had been greater on the British side; so much so that a fortnight later d'Estaing, now with twenty-six of the line in good repair, was able to appear off St Kitts without fear of battle with Byron's twenty who had at present to remain at anchor in the defensive formation in which he had arranged them.

By this time Byron had decided to send Barrington home with his despatches so that he might explain verbally the very poor situation in the Leeward and Windward Islands, both in the numbers and fitness (or unfitness) of the ships and in the defenceless state of the islands. A month later Byron himself came home, somewhat worn out by his anxieties but with no doubts as to his having done everything possible to defeat d'Estaing in battle. But as a British fleet had met a French one and could not claim to have won a resounding victory there were, of course, people ready to blame the commander-in-chief. and Barrington noted that Byron's initial reception was not over cordial, but 'after a great deal of bustle about nothing', he was graciously received by the king and was sent a letter of appreciation from the Admiralty.

The letter from the Secretary, having summarized Byron's despatch, continued:

In return I have it in command from their Lordships to acquaint you that they very well approve of your proceedings and animated conduct, and that the relation you give of the spirited example and gallant behaviour of Vice-Admiral Barrington, and the Commanders of the ships who were principally engaged, the endeavour and strong desire of coming to a close engagement, which prevailed universally through the Squadron, and the bravery of the Officers and Men in general does great honour to them individually, as well as generally, and has afforded the highest satisfaction to their Lordships which I am to desire you will please signify to them.[1]

[1] *The Barrington Papers* (N.R.S.), vol. II, p. 319.

There is, of course, some of the polite hyperbole of the eighteenth century in the above wording. But, allowing for that, the facts of the battle make one wonder why Mahan castigates Byron with particular severity: 'Byron's disaster was due to attacking with needless precipitation, and in needless disorder. He had the weather gage, it was early morning, and the north-east trade wind must freshen [?] as the day advanced. . . . There was time for fighting, an opportunity for forcing action which could not be evaded, and time also for the British to form in reasonably good order.'[1] This comes somewhat strangely from a critic whose usual target is the hidebound nature of British tactics and who, though a biographer of Nelson, seems to have forgotten the latter's dictum that 'time is everything: five minutes may make the difference between a victory and a defeat', as also his comment on unnecessary manoeuvring that 'a day is soon lost in that business'.

Surely any admiral sighting an enemy fleet at anchor, believed to be inferior in numbers to his own, would be guilty of serious negligence if he refrained from pressing on with all sail set in the hope of reaching it before it was fully under way. To follow this by holding back and forming a regular line of battle, because the enemy was subsequently found to be more numerous and further advanced than expected, would have lost much time in bringing to action an antagonist who, in the event, showed himself disinclined for close action and might well have denied his opponent 'an opportunity for forcing action'.

[1] Mahan, op. cit., pp. 111, 112. He overlooked the fact that on the western side of these islands the trade wind was frequently cancelled or reversed by the sea breeze which sprang up in the afternoon when the land had been heated by the sun.

Chapter 10

RODNEY AND DE GUICHEN,
17 APRIL 1780

That in popular esteem George Brydges Rodney has been given
one of the leading places among Britain's naval heroes is readily
explainable on two major counts. On 12 April 1782 the many
disappointments of the naval war between Britain and France
were at last assuaged by a victory which, though it fell well
short of annihilation, had no untoward later conflict to set
against it and could be rated satisfactory enough to entitle the
commander-in-chief to a peerage. And during the course of this
battle it so happened that some of the French ships in the centre
of their line were thrown aback by a shift of wind, thus enabling
(in fact almost compelling) the British flagship to pass through
a gap in the French line. This manoeuvre in conjunction with
similar movements through a gap some way astern contributed
to the disarray of part of the French fleet and so, it was presumed, to the victory. There was nothing new in the idea of
passing through an enemy's line from the lee side if there was a
suitable gap. The matter had been discussed during the Dutch
wars and it had been well summed up by Hoste (see above,
p. 47). But it had been thought of simply as passing through
a gap. 'Breaking the line' was the term usually applied to a
ship falling out of her place in her own line and thus breaking
its continuity. But when, as now happened, the expression came
to mean breaking the enemy's line the word had an altogether
different ring. To break his line conveyed the idea of breaking
his fleet to pieces and chewing it up. From this it came to be
assumed that Rodney had initiated a new and startlingly
successful battle manoeuvre. St Vincent, a man of no illusions,
commented twenty years later: 'Lord Rodney passed through
the enemy's line by accident, not design, although historians

have given him credit for the latter'. But that was not the general view. He had broken the line and won the last battle of the war and that for most people was enough to establish his place in our naval annals.

Of this battle of The Saints, so called from a small group of islands (Les Saintes) between Guadeloupe and Dominica, more must be said later, but in the meanwhile there is his unsatisfactory action two years earlier, on 17 April 1780, soon after his first arrival in the West Indies.

As a young captain in Hawke's battle of 14 October 1747, Rodney had shown a fine fighting spirit together with initiative and enterprise; and in the Seven Years War he had distinguished himself in bombardments of the French coast and in co-operating with General Monckton in the capture of Martinique in 1762. In the peace which followed he had been for three years commander-in-chief on the Jamaica station and while there he had strongly convinced himself that he should succeed to the governorship of Jamaica when it fell vacant, which it soon did. In this, however, he was disappointed and he had no other resource than to return to the fashionable life of London, to which he was suited in all respects except financially. It was on the latter count that he moved to Paris and it was there that he found himself when, in 1778, it was evident that war was imminent. Appeals by letter to the Admiralty for employment, which might have raised enough credit to release him from the debts which now tied him to Paris, proved of no avail. Despite some qualms, however, he eventually accepted the repeated offer of a loan, sufficient to satisfy his creditors, from a chivalrous old Marshal of France. He then returned to London and by some means or other immediately repaid his debt to the generous Marshal Biron.

He could now make personal application both to the King and to the First Lord for employment; but to find a suitable post for him was not easy and he had to wait in idleness for a year until, in October 1779, he was appointed commander-in-chief of the Leeward Islands station to which he was to take a squadron of reinforcements, escorting some supplies to besieged Gibraltar *en route*. He was now sixty-one years of age and still masterful and enterprising, to the extent, that is, that his health would allow. But in the latter respect he was undoubtedly ageing. It has been said that he was suffering from both gout and gravel (afflictions that had troubled Lestock and Mathews severally), and though his brain remained vigorous he had often to take to his bed. During the successful elimination of a smaller Spanish squadron which he now encountered off Cape St Vincent he was in his cot throughout this afternoon and moonlight night action and his decisions had to be taken on the information and advice given him by Walter Young, his flag captain in the *Sandwich* (ninety). Young had an unusual background in that he had entered the navy with a master's warrant, probably aged between twenty-five and thirty, had been commissioned as a lieutenant two years later, and after fourteen years in that rank had just recently been promoted to commander and then to post captain, apparently because Lord Sandwich thought he would do well as Rodney's flag captain. This was a very successful choice, for after the battle of 17 April 1780, shortly to be related, Rodney wrote to Sandwich: 'Many many, thanks for your Lordship's recommendation of Captain Young. There is nothing he does not deserve. Had every captain been actuated with his spirit, more than half of the French fleet had belonged to his Majesty'.[1]

Young undoubtedly served his master well, particularly in smoothing the admiral's relations with his other captains as far as this could be achieved. Not an easy matter, for Rodney's personal conceit was such that his manner was not endearing to his subordinates. But Young evidently had a hard task. As he confided to his correspondent Middleton, Comptroller of the Navy: 'My situation requires great patience with so unsteady and irresolute a man'.[2] This irresolution, it seems, was not such as resulted in any hesitation in giving orders, but in fact that they were so often followed by counter-orders. This partnership of admiral and flag captain continued as satisfactorily as could be expected until the latter's death in May 1781.

It was in March 1780 that Rodney arrived at St Lucia with

[1] *The Sandwich Papers* (Navy Records Society), vol. III, p. 212.
[2] *Barham Papers* (Navy Records Society), vol. I, p. 62.

reinforcements that brought the fleet on the Leeward Islands station up to twenty sail of the line. His prospective opponent was no longer d'Estaing, who had gone home the previous autumn, but the comte de Guichen who had just arrived at Martinique with a squadron that brought the French strength to twenty-two. De Guichen, now sixty-seven, had served at sea from his youth up, unlike d'Estaing with his mainly military background, and he had a reputation as a handler of ships and squadrons—though this does not seem fully justified by what was to come. In conjunction with the governor of Martinique he now planned the conquest of Barbados and on April 13th he sailed from Fort Royal with three thousand troops on board his warships. His intention was to steer away from St Lucia and round the northern end of Martinique, thence making for Barbados. But the winds had been light and unfavourable and three days later he was still to leeward of his base. It was there, about twenty miles from the land, that Rodney, hastening from St Lucia, first sighted him, and chasing to the north-westward after him he was able to gain a full view of his enemy's fleet before dark. He then formed a line of battle ahead on a northwesterly course and with two frigates scouting ahead he kept touch during the night. At 1 a.m. on April 17th de Guichen also formed a line of battle ahead on the same course until 5.30 a.m. when he tacked his fleet together and steered to southward. The two fleets were then apparently steering to pass each other on opposite courses but at a distance of some twelve miles apart, the British on the starboard tack, with the enemy on their larboard bow and the French on the larboard tack, to leeward.

What followed was the subject of much discussion, discontent and vilification at the time and of differences of opinion that have continued even into the present century.

The basis of the trouble was Rodney's laudable wish to launch his whole force against part of the enemy's; laudable, that is, if his opponent so misconducted his line as to make this practicable. Some six years later he made some marginal notes in a book on tactics and these included: 'During all the commands Lord Rodney has been intrusted with, he made it a rule to bring his whole force against part of the enemy's, and never was so absurd as to bring ship against ship, *when the enemy gave him an opportunity of acting otherwise*'.[1] (The words in italics have too often been omitted in quotations.) It was no doubt for this reason that he added three new signals to the additional fighting instructions then in use. These were:

When the commander-in-chief means to make an attack, upon the enemy's centre he will hoist a flag half blue half yellow at the main top gallant mast head.
Ditto his van ditto flag with a red pennant over it.
Ditto his rear ditto with a white pennant under it.[2]

There is no direct evidence, however, as to how he intended to achieve those concentrations. All there is is a statement in the *Naval Chronicle* twenty-nine years later by Dr (by that time Sir) Gilbert Blane, the distinguished physician of the fleet and a friend and supporter of Rodney, who was with him in this battle and the battle of The Saints:

Lord Rodney himself at various times informed me that two days before the action [of 17 April 1780] he did either by oral or written communication, acquaint each captain in his fleet that it was his intention to attack that of the enemy; not their entire fleet of 23 sail [in fact 22] with his inferior one of 20, but a part of theirs—as for example 15 or 16—with his whole fleet.

To this one may add the comment of Laughton when he edited the *Barham Papers*:

If Blane's memory was not playing him false, if Rodney really did this, we can only say that power of exposition was altogether wanting to him; for it is quite certain that not one man to whom he thus explained his intention had the faintest notion of what Rodney wanted to do or how he wanted to do it.[3]

So much for the setting: now for what happened. At 5.45 a.m. the British fleet was ordered once more to form line of battle

[1] J. Clerk, *Naval Tactics*, 3rd edition (1827), p. 18.
[2] *Signals and Instructions* (N.R.S.), p. 230.
[3] *Barham Papers*, vol. I, p. 1.

ahead at two cables, still on its north-westerly course, and at white pennant nnder it signifying his intention to attack the 6.45 a.m. Rodney hoisted the flag half blue half yellow with a enemy's rear. A quarter of an hour later he ordered the line to close up, the ships to be one cable apart, and after a further hour and a half, thinking himself then in an appropriate position for attacking the rear of the southbound French fleet, now twelve miles to leeward of him, he ordered a line abreast at two cables apart on a line of bearing north by west and south by east, that is steering west by south. De Guichen, it seems, reluctant to accept battle, had already decided to wear his fleet together to the northward and this he now did. Rodney, seeing that his attempt had been foiled for the present, hauled together onto the opposite, larboard, tack so as to put his fleet into a relative position from which to make a second approach.

At 10.10 a.m., being then on the weather, eastward quarter of the French, the British fleet wore together and began to overhaul the enemy keeping well to windward of them. And at 11.50 a.m., being about five or six miles from the enemy as far as can be judged, Rodney hoisted the Union flag at the main topgallant mast head, the signal for the twenty-first article of the additional fighting instructions then in force in his fleet. This ordered that 'every ship in the squadron is to steer for the ship of the enemy, which, from the disposition of the two squadrons, it must be her lot to engage notwithstanding the signal for the line ahead (a Union flag at the mizzen peak) will be kept flying; making or shortening sail in such proportion as to preserve the distance assigned by the signal for the line, in order that the whole squadron may, as near as possible, come into action at the same time'. This, it will be remembered, was almost identical with Hawke's memorandum of 1756 (see above, p. 32). It did not specify exactly what was to be done if the enemy had more ships than you had, nor if his line was not in as good order as yours. Such matters could only be dealt with adequately by an admiral who made his tactical ideas known to his captains. But it was the generally accepted doctrine that in almost all circumstances both the leading ship and the rear ship of the enemy should be engaged, so as to

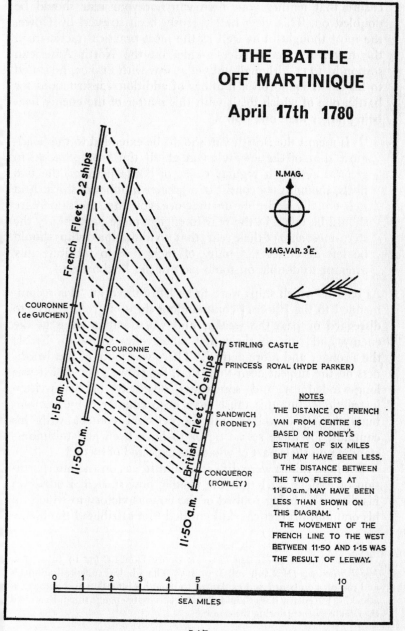

THE BATTLE
OF MARTINIQUE

April 17th 1780

N.MAG.

MAG.VAR. 3°E.

French Fleet 22 ships

COURONNE
(de GUICHEN)

COURONNE

STIRLING CASTLE

PRINCESS ROYAL (HYDE PARKER)

British Fleet 20 ships

SANDWICH
(RODNEY)

CONQUEROR
(ROWLEY)

1·15 p.m.

11·50 a.m.

11·50 a.m.

NOTES

THE DISTANCE OF FRENCH
VAN FROM CENTRE IS
BASED ON RODNEY'S
ESTIMATE OF SIX MILES
BUT MAY HAVE BEEN LESS.
THE DISTANCE BETWEEN
THE TWO FLEETS AT
11·50 a.m. MAY HAVE BEEN
LESS THAN SHOWN ON
THIS DIAGRAM.
THE MOVEMENT OF THE
FRENCH LINE TO THE WEST
BETWEEN 11·50 AND 1·15 WAS
THE RESULT OF LEEWAY.

0 1 2 3 4 5   10

SEA MILES

ensure that neither your own van nor your rear should be doubled on. This view had recently been stressed by Howe, the most thoughtful as well as the most practical tactician in the navy. As commander-in-chief on the North American station in 1777, although not yet at war with France, he issued to his small squadron a number of additional instructions for battle, one of which dealt with this matter of the enemy fleet being larger than one's own.

'It is meant the British van should be extended to the head-most ship of the enemy's van at all times preparative to general action in regular order of battle between the two fleets, though they consist of a greater number of ships. And it is equally desirable on that occasion that the same care should be taken in the rear to engage more particularly the stern-most ship of their rear, that no unoccupied ships should be left at either extremity of their line to facilitate any attempt to double on some part of the British fleet.'

As regards which ships were to be left unfired at, 'it is recom-mended to the [those?] commanding ships of greater force to disregard or pass the weaker and worst sailing ships of the enemy and confine their first endeavours solely to disable the stronger and more active'.[1] There was more of this wordi-ness on the subject even than that, for Howe's one defect was long-windedness and sometimes obscurity of his written instructions. But this must have been countered by frequent manoeuvring exercises and by personal contact with his captains, for there seems never to have been any misunder-standing on their part of what was expected of them.[2]

But here things were different, and it was on the interpreta-tion of Article XXI that the trouble now started. Rodney in his disgust at being robbed of the famous victory to which, in his opinion, his tactical skill entitled him attributed the blame

[1] *Signals and Instructions*, pp. 108–9.
[2] *See* the journal of his flag captain, Henry Duncan, for 13 July 1782, *Naval Miscellany* (N.R.S.), vol. I, p. 215: 'The admiral called all admirals and captains on board and explained to them his intention and manner of attacking the enemy if we should find it necessary to engage them. Exercised the fleet frequently during the cruise.'

in the first place to the disobedience of his rear-admirals and captains in that they failed to adhere to the signal he had made five hours earlier to the effect that he would attack the enemy's rear; and this despite the fact that since then the French fleet had reversed its course and his own fleet had reversed its course twice. But his main grievance was that his van and particularly the leading ship, the *Stirling Castle* (Captain Carkett), had cracked on ahead to engage the enemy's van despite the fact that the latter, according to Rodney's subsequent letter of reprimand to Carkett, was six miles ahead of the centre. This was probably an exaggeration when one considers the fact that in his official despatch he notes that some of his van ships, which had followed Carkett, had opened fire before his flagship, the *Sandwich*, which presumably had much less distance to go and would be sailing well off the wind. If the enemy's line was really so far extended it was, of course, a good opportunity for concentrating on his rear; but if that was so why did Rodney invoke Article XXI? Why did he not come down in line abreast as he attempted to do earlier in the morning? Or slant down together on any other course maintaining the same line of bearing, parallel to the enemy, for which signals were provided in the additional instructions?[1] And why, one wonders, did he not repeat the signal for attacking the enemy's rear? Possibly because of the former occasion he says in his despatch, 'this signal was penetrated by (the enemy), who, discovering my intention, wore, and formed a line of battle on the other tack'—though in fact de Guichen had already decided to wear before this signal was made, and there is no evidence that the signal had been 'penetrated' by the French.

Another reason Rodney adduced for blaming the behaviour of his van was that Article XXI enjoined that ships should keep at the distance apart already ordered, in this case two cables. By any ordinary interpretation that meant that they were to keep in a regularly spaced formation, with the presumption that the enemy would do likewise, but to his self-esteem it was plain to him that he was justified in putting forward any possible item that would put the blame on others.

[1] *Signals and Instructions*, p. 217.

How did Rodney himself interpret his intention to attack the rear of the enemy? In normal circumstances where each commander-in-chief was in or near the centre of the line it had long been the custom, however theoretically lacking in justification, for the flagships of the rivals to come to grips as soon as they could. But here this would not suit Rodney's plan. He had nine ships astern of him and he steered to engage the French ship that had eight or nine astern of her—the number is uncertain. As she was only a sixty-four, the ninety-gun, three-decker *Sandwich* had no difficulty in knocking her out of the line, and then the ship next to her, either a sixty-four or a seventy-four, identification from existing accounts is conflicting.[1] The situation ahead of the admiral, however, was not so satisfactory. De Guichen with his seconds ahead and astern had little to face. His flagship, the *Couronne*, though only an eighty-gun two-decker, was of a type hardly inferior to the small British three-deckers and his seconds were both seventy-fours. Opposed to him were only the *Cornwall* (seventy-four), Rodney's second ahead, and the sixty-four-gun *Yarmouth*. The other ships ahead were engaging the French van and the *Yarmouth* (Captain Bateman) did not close the *Couronne* as, according to Rodney's ideas, he should have done. When Bateman was court martialled some months later he was specifically acquitted of cowardice (he had been commissioned from the lower deck for his gallantry in the *Marlborough* at the battle of Toulon in 1744), but it seems that he was puzzled about the interpretation put on Article XXI by the ships ahead of him, including the commodore (his next ahead) who was leading the British centre division. So he just hung about doing nothing until he was signalled later to come into the admiral's wake. In consequence he was convicted of not supporting his admiral and was dismissed from the navy.

De Guichen now had no ship opposed to him, so, in company with his two seconds, he wore out of the line and then came in again to engage the *Sandwich*. A fierce action followed for an

---

[1] The difference between these two classes was not merely in number of guns. In the British navy the seventy-fours mounted 32-pounders on the lower deck, while the sixty-fours mounted only 24-pounders and were of somewhat lighter scantling.

hour and a half in which, according to Rodney's account, he was entirely unsupported, though it seems clear from the evidence given in Bateman's court martial that the *Cornwall* and eventually the *Yarmouth* took some part. But there is no doubt that the *Sandwich* had to fight hard until eventually de Guichen fell off to leeward and disengaged. She had been heavily battered and had to keep her pumps going for several hours until all her shot holes had been plugged.

Although there is no evidence of it in Rodney's despatch, there were also some sharp actions both in his van and his rear divisions under their rear admirals, Hyde Parker and Rowley respectively, both of whom he castigated severely in a letter to the First Lord. Fortunately, orders were already on the way for Hyde Parker to return to England with the next convoy. He arrived in explosive mood but was dissuaded from making any official complaint. (In the following year he commanded the small British squadron against the Dutch in the fiercely fought battle of the Dogger Bank. In 1782 when on passage to take up the East Indies command his flagship was lost with all hands.) Rowley, who had also strongly resented the unmerited verbal rebukes he had received from Rodney, was transferred to the Jamaica station a few months later.

Despite the extent of bad feeling which resulted from this battle and the impression Rodney strove to give that no ship but the *Sandwich* had done anything worth while, the facts remained that the French casualties were notably heavier than the British and that the French endeavour to invade Barbados had been frustrated. De Guichen, prevented by the British squadron from return to Fort Royal, was forced to go to the northward, to Guadaloupe and beyond, to make good his damages, and a few days later Rodney returned to St Lucia. In the following month there was some manoeuvring to windward of the islands while de Guichen was on passage back to Martinique. With the French reluctance to engage, however, Rodney was unable to achieve anything more than some partial and brief encounters at long range.

Chapter 11

THE BATTLE OF CHESAPEAKE,
5 SEPTEMBER 1781

Despite the evident friction between Rodney and his subordinates in 1780 there was no doubt about his remaining in
command in the West Indies. (His backer was believed to be
Lord George Germain, Secretary of State for the American
Colonies, rather than Sandwich.) It was clear, though, that it
would not be easy to find a second-in-command of adequate
ability who would loyally support his chief. Tactful approaches
by Sandwich to at least two vice-admirals produced no willing
response, even though to one of them (Darby) his letter
included the inducement that there was 'a great probability,
from Sir George's infirmities, that the chief command will
devolve soon on the next in rank to him'.[1] All that remained,
therefore, was to make a promotion that would delve down in
the list of captains far enough to include someone suitable.

The man whom Sandwich had in mind was Samuel Hood,
six years younger than Rodney, who had only recently been
given the civil post of Commissioner of Portsmouth Dockyard.
This was a position that was usually thought of as ending any
expectation of a subsequent seagoing career, and Hood's
immediate reply to Sandwich's suggestion was a polite refusal,
because 'those bodily infirmities, with which I have been
afflicted for nearly twenty years, are of late become so very
heavy and severe that I have no spirits left and can scarcely
keep myself upon my legs'. That was on a Saturday. But on
Monday, perhaps exhilarated by the thought of going to sea
again, he felt 'so much better' and flattered himself 'that a
warm climate will tend more towards removing my complaints

[1] *The Sandwich Papers*, (Navy Records Society), vol. III, p. 222.

than any assistance I can get at home'. So he wrote again, hoping it was not too late to cancel his refusal.[2] (Later correspondence and the acidity of some of his comments on his seniors suggest that his 'infirmities' may have been digestive. But despite them, whatever they were, he lived to the age of ninety-two.)

The suggested promotion, which gave Hood his flag as rearadmiral of the blue, quickly followed his acceptance, as did also his appointment to the West Indies; and at the end of November 1780 he sailed with a squadron of reinforcements flying his flag in the ninety-gun *Barfleur*. Early in January he joined Rodney at St Lucia.

The early months of 1781 were concerned mainly with the affairs of St Eustatius, the richly stocked Dutch island, which had fallen into British hands. This was followed by some manoeuvring among the more southern islands between the two fleets, the French being now commanded by the comte de Grasse who had arrived in April with strong reinforcements. No encounter resulted, however. Later, with the approach of the hurricane season, the ships needing extensive repairs and the St Eustatius convoy left for home. They sailed on August 1st and Rodney left on the same day in the *Gibraltar* (eighty) heading for more temperate latitudes, still undecided whether he must go home for the relaxation and medical attention which he felt he needed but soon making up his mind that this was essential if he was to be fit for the next West Indian campaigning season. He therefore shaped his course accordingly.

As had become the custom for the hurricane season, Hood sailed with what remained of the Leeward Islands squadron, now fourteen of the line, a few days later, heading for the North American station. Here the interest ashore had been centred for some time on Lord Cornwallis's campaign in the south. Starting from South Carolina in January he had advanced into Virginia but had now come to a halt at the York river where it debouches into Chesapeake Bay and had dug himself in at Yorktown to await reinforcements by sea or co-ordinated operations from the north.

This was known to Hood, as was also the fact that de Grasse

[2] *The Sandwich Papers*, (Navy Records Society), vol. III, pp. 228–9.

too was coming north and might get there before him. He therefore made all sail possible for New York, passing close to the entrances to Chesapeake Bay and the Delaware on his way without sighting anything. On arrival on August 28th he refrained from taking his ships in across the bar at Sandy Hook but immediately consulted with the commander-in-chief of the North American station as to the quickest means of getting the largest available squadron to sea. This was Rear-Admiral Thomas Graves, a year younger than Hood though a year senior to him as a rear-admiral. He had previously been second-in-command to Vice-Admiral Arbuthnot but had succeeded him temporarily on the latter returning to England.

How much these facts affected the subsequent unsatisfactory battle it is impossible to judge. Though there was no doubt that Hood and his second-in-command, Rear-Admiral Drake, must take their orders from Graves, the fact was that the West Indian squadron had fourteen ships of the line and the North American squadron could contribute only five, for two of its ships were refitting. Beyond that there was a technical point which may have contributed to some misunderstandings, or at least to some hesitation on Graves's part.

This was the fact that ships in the West Indies and those in North American waters had been using different signal books. The former had worked with a set of additional fighting instructions probably printed by the Admiralty but modified here and there in manuscript as ordered by Rodney; but on the North American station Arbuthnot had issued his own additional fighting instructions in 1779–80, and in 1781 had supplemented these by a list of forty-nine signals: 'In addition to the General and Additional Signals and Instructions which you have already received from me'.[1] This must have been confusing for ships which had to change from one book to the other only a few days before going into battle, as now happened to Hood's squadron, and the confusion must have been enhanced, one can well suppose, by the fact that nearly all the manoeuvres needed were described in the same, or almost the same, wording in both books though the signal for each manoeuvre was different.

[1] *Signals and Instructions* (N.R.S.), p. 249.

For three days after Hood's arrival off Sandy Hook, Graves had to wait for a wind that would allow him to bring his five ships out across the bar; but then, on August 31st, the combined squadron sailed and headed for Chesapeake Bay, hoping that de Grasse would be found in those waters and expecting also that he would not have been able to bring more than eighteen of the line with him, for it was estimated that he had had to send about ten home to refit, as in fact he had been ordered to do. But so urgent had been the appeals from Washington and his French colleague, Rochambeau, that de Grasse had decided to bring all his ships, twenty-eight of the line, and had embarked in them three thousand troops from Cap François (now Cap Haitien), the main French base on the north coast of Hispaniola.[1] With these he had arrived in Chesapeake Bay the day before Graves and Hood sailed from Sandy Hook. The troops had been disembarked and four of the line had been left in the bay to assist in the operations against Cornwallis. The other twenty-four had anchored in Lynnhaven roads, just inside Cape Henry, the southern cape of the Chesapeake entrance.

It was there they were sighted by one of Grave's frigates at 9.30 a.m. on September 5th, the British fleet being then about twenty miles east of Cape Henry. At 11 a.m. the log of Graves's flagship, the *London* (ninety-eight), stated, 'discovered a fleet of large ships at anchor near Cape Henry, supposed to be the enemy'. Graves himself in his official despatch states that this fleet 'seemed to be extended across the entrance of the Chesapeake from Cape Henry to the Middle Ground'. The latter shoal lay five miles north of the cape and with further shoals beyond it virtually blocked the remaining five miles to the northern shore of the entrance. If, as Graves seemed to think, the French were anchored clear to the north of Cape Henry,

[1] The island of Hispaniola was so named by Columbus and Santo Domingo was established as its capital on the south coast towards the eastern end. Two centuries later in the treaty of Ryswick (1697) the western half of the island was made over to the French who called their colony Saint Domingue. British sources in the late eighteenth century, however, usually refer to the whole island, whether French or Spanish territory, as San Domingo. Saint Domingue later became Haiti.

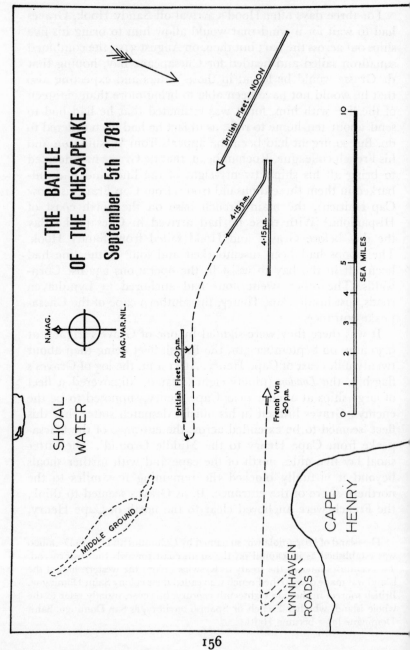

THE BATTLE
OF THE CHESAPEAKE
September 5th 1781

British Fleet—NOON

4·15 p.m.

4·15 p.m.

British Fleet 2·0 p.m.

French Van
2·0 p.m.

N.MAG.

MAG.VAR.NIL.

SHOAL
WATER

MIDDLE GROUND

CAPE
HENRY

LYNNHAVEN
ROADS

SEA MILES

0 1 2 3 4 5 6 7 8 9 10

there was nothing to stop them making sail immediately and coming out to meet him; but in fact they were three miles beyond and somewhat embayed by the Cape, and with the wind at north-north-east as it then was many of them had to make one or two boards to windward before they could get clear, and they could not well do that until the tide turned to the ebb which it did about noon. They should have been able to steer east but would have had to make allowance for a point or two of leeway before being far enough to the northward to clear Cape Henry, even with the help of the ebb tide of about $1\frac{1}{2}$ knots as it is thereabouts and trending somewhat south of east. But that was a matter which could hardly be apparent to Graves when he first sighted his enemy, so he made the signal for the line of battle ahead at two cables apart and stood towards him.

By noon he was some fourteen miles from Cape Henry and seems to have been steering west-north-west with the Cape bearing west 1/2 south, and at 12.30 p.m. he saw that the French were getting under sail. As he expected them to come out close-hauled on the larboard tack, that is steering east on the north-north-east wind, he hauled down the signal for the line ahead (he had recently closed it to one cable) and hoisted that for forming an east-west line. The injuction accompanying this signal specified only 'yet steering the same course as I do', which was presumably still about west-north-west. By 2 p.m. the van of the enemy was bearing south from him (that is from the *London* in the centre of the line) three miles distant; and a quarter of an hour later, finding he was getting close to the Middle Ground he wore his fleet together and brought-to on the larboard tack 'in order to let the enemy's ships come abreast of us'.

Just when he again filled and stood on he does not say, nor does he say when he made the signal for a line ahead to supersede his last formation signal which had been for a line of bearing. But presumably he must have made those signals quite soon, at least that to stand on, perhaps leaving the line ahead to the imagination of his captains, for they would have found themselves so formed after wearing. At all events they must have been in some such line, for a quarter of an hour later, at 2.30 p.m., he made the signal for the leading ship to lead more to starboard.

It was here that Graves started allowing circumstances to get the better of him. He had manoeuvred, or so he supposed, to place his line parallel to the enemy's but was yet too far from it to make the signal to attack. Why, then, did he not close the distance by ordering his ships to alter course together so many points to starboard, retaining their existing compass line of bearing? This manoeuvre was prescribed in the same terms (though with different signals) both in Arbuthnot's book and in the one in use in the West Indies. Was it because he did not trust his mixed fleet to keep station in a line of bearing which was, and still is, more difficult than keeping station in line ahead? Or was it just that he did not see what trouble an alteration of course in succession would get him into? There was no doubt that when ships were in line ahead and the leader was ordered to alter so many points to port or starboard each ship was to follow the ship ahead of her, a simple matter. One may well suppose that it was that which was in Graves's mind. What we are not told in his transcript of the *London's* log is the amount that he ordered the leading ship to alter. This depended on the number of guns fired after the signal was hoisted—one gun for each point of the compass. As the signal already mentioned (2.30 p.m.) was succeeded by two others, at 3.17 and 3.34, the total alteration before fire was opened cannot have been less than three points. Graves was, in fact, going into action at much the same angle to his enemy's line as had Byng off Minorca twenty-five years earlier, and with much the same results.

This result could have been less inept had it not been for the fact that Arbuthnot's book did not include in the signal to engage the stipulation originated by Hawke and included in the additional fighting instructions Article XXI which Hood's ships had been previously using. This, as already noted above (p. 146–150), ordered every ship to steer for her opposite number 'notwithstanding the signal for the line ahead will be kept flying'. What happened here was that at 3.46 p.m. Graves again ordered a line ahead at one cable and a few minutes later made the signal worded in the *London's* log as 'to bear down and engage the enemy'. This in the Arbuthnot book was: 'When I would have each ship to steer for and engage his opponent in the enemy's line, I will hoist the signal for close action [that is a red flag at the fore topmast head, as it had been since Blake's days] and a white pennant over it'. According to her log the *London* then 'filled the main topsail and bore down to the enemy'.

But not for very long, or not at least in the account given by Hood, viewing the situation from the centre of his division which was now in the rear, According to him the *London* was engaging at much too long a range and not pressing on or closing with the enemy, 'having her main topsail to the mast the whole time she was firing'. By Graves's account he now hauled down the signal for the line ahead (4.11 p.m.), expecting the rear to go down and engage, hoisted it again at 4.22 as a reminder that ships should be properly spaced and finally hauled it down at 4.27. But that was not Hood's impression nor the recollection of one of his midshipmen in the *Barfleur* who wrote very heatedly on the subject fifty years later.[1] According to them the signal for the line was flying throughout the action until it was hauled down about 5.30 p.m., and then, and not till then, Hood bore down with the rear division. By the time he neared the enemy it was already too late and the action was broken off soon after sunset.

In the meanwhile, since about 4 p.m., the ships in the van and part of the centre had gone into action, not together as they should have done, but successively because of the three points or more angle with the French line. The leading ship, the *Shrewsbury*, suffered severely and had her captain wounded and first lieutenant killed. The second in the line, the *Intrepid*, was 'much disabled in every respect', and the *Ajax*, *Terrible* and *Montagu* (fifth, sixth and eighth in the order of battle) were 'full of complaints' afterwards, that is much damaged. In the case of the *Terrible* this was partly because of her previously unseaworthy condition due to two groundings and a collision in recent months, with the result that a few days later she had to be abandoned and burnt. Drake's flagship, the *Princessa*, fourth in the line, had her main topmast much damaged and

[1] Thomas White in *Naval Researches*.

feared she would lose it over the side though in fact it survived. But beyond the eighth ship (the *London* was tenth) there was no serious damage and few casualties.

Both Graves and Hood wrote accounts of the battle to the First Lord, the former's letter being in addition to his official despatch to the Admiralty. The ineptitude of the way in which this battle was handled and the subsequent extinction of any hopes of a British recovery of the initiative in the southern colonies (Cornwallis was forced to capitulate on October 19th) were of course entirely the responsibility of Graves, and on his part there was no attempt to make excuses. But he knew that Hood had held off on the plea that the signal for the line ahead had been kept flying until 5.30 p.m. (though in the *London* it was asserted that this was not so), and on the day following the battle he issued a memorandum which conveyed the same effect as Article XXI of the additional fighting instructions, that once the signal to engage was hoisted the signal for the line of battle ahead should be interpreted merely as referring to the spacing ('the line of extension') and that the line must be kept parallel to the enemy. That was all very sound, of course, but unfortunately it had not been included in the signal book he was using.

Sandwich's letter from Hood was in quite a different vein and it enclosed a memorandum of 'my sentiments upon the truly unfortunate day, as committed to writing the next morning, which I mentioned to Mr Graves when I attended his first summons'. These sentiments were in effect a thorough castigation of Graves's tactics on several points. On the most important of these, however, he overreaches himself, for he says: 'Now had the centre of the British line gone on to support the van, and the signal for the line hauled down, or had Rear Admiral Graves set the example of close action *even with the signal for the line out* [my italics], the van ships of the enemy must have been cut up; and the rear division of the British fleet would have been opposed to those ships the centre fired at, and at the most *proper* [Hood's italics] distance for engaging, or the Rear Admiral commanding it [himself] would have had a great deal to answer for'.[1] In other words if Graves had

---

[1] *The Sandwich Papers*, vol. IV, p. 190.

behaved as Hood thought he should, he would have been prepared to disregard the signal for the line ahead; but as he considered that Graves was engaging 'at a most improper distance' he thought himself justified in adhering to what he held to be the letter of the law.

The basic motives of Hood's behaviour on this occasion must for ever remain conjectural. That he was, and had no doubt that he was, an admiral of the highest competence can well be accepted, and his skill and leadership were to be displayed conspicuously a few months later in West Indian waters where he was opposed to de Grasse's more numerous fleet (twenty-nine against his twenty-two), and yet by the speed and adroitness with which he took up a defensive anchorage off St Kitts in his enemy's presence he was able to maintain his squadron intact. But that he was thoroughly impatient and highly critical of his superiors when they did not do what he thought they should have done were also marked characteristics—as was to be shown conspicuously after the battle of The Saints. And here, off the Chesapeake, he had been put under an admiral who was only temporarily commanding the station, awaiting the arrival of Arbuthnot's successor before moving on to be second-in-command on the Jamaica station, an officer moreover of whom it is clear that he had a poor opinion. It is difficult not to conclude that on this occasion he allowed his annoyance to get the better of his judgment and his loyalty.

Whether there could have been any difference in the eventual outcome, however inspired the British tactics had been, is a matter of doubt. For one thing de Grasse evidently had no intention of pressing the action: his fleet was all the time inclining to ease off to leeward and on subsequent days when the two fleets were still in sight of one another and the French were to windward he made no attempt to close. And for another thing he was joined within a few days by the French squadron of eight of the line which had been based on Rhode Island and he then had thirty-six ships to oppose only eighteen British—now that the *Terrible* had been scuttled. It was sometimes suggested that if Graves had entered Chesapeake Bay a day or two after the battle, while it was still open, and had anchored his fleet in some such skilful way as Hood did the following January at St Kitts, he could have stood up to any attack. But what Cornwallis needed at Yorktown was reinforcements, not seaward protection. The latter would not have been able to save him any more than Hood was able to prevent the surrender of Brimstone Hill, the citadel of St Kitts, in the following February.

Of course, if on the morning of September 5th de Grasse's twenty-four of the line had presented the British nineteen with 'the rich and most delightful harvest of glory' that Hood said they offered and the harvest had been well and truly gathered, quite a different face would have been put on Cornwallis's troubles provided reinforcements from New York had been hurried to him by sea. In Hood's view such a victory was not achieved because in the first place Graves failed to attack the French van closely as it came out of Lynnhaven Bay and secondly because when the van had in fact cleared Cape Henry and was, according to Hood, much extended beyond the centre and rear, 'it was not attacked by the whole force of the British line' at a time, or so he said, when there was a full hour and a half in which to have demolished the van before the rear could have come up.

The idea of assaulting an anchored enemy before he could form a line of battle was, of course, what had occurred to Byron when he sighted the French fleet anchored off Grenada. But not having the luck to achieve this aim he was given no credit and some blame for his subsequent manoeuvres. And it would certainly have occurred to Nelson if he had been commanding a band of brothers—which was not Graves's fortune—and in that case it might have resulted in a resounding victory. But both this and Hood's second suggestion quoted above depended on appreciating the French fleet's difficulties in clearing the bay—the need to make some tacks to windward and to wait for some assistance from the ebb tidal stream, matters which must have been difficult to realize from a distance of ten miles in the offing, as Graves was when the French fleet began to get under sail. To such genius as would be needed to deal with these problems successfully Graves was evidently unable to aspire.

Chapter 12

THE BATTLE OF THE SAINTS,
APRIL 1782

More has been printed about the battle of the Saints on 12 April 1782 than on any other victory under sail except Trafalgar. A scholarly and judicious account was included a few years after the event by the historian Robert Beatson in his *Naval and Military Memoirs of Great Britain from 1727 to 1783*. Much was written in private letters at the time, some of which were incorporated fifty years later in the biography of Rodney by his son-in-law, Major-General G. B. Mundy, and many more in the volumes of the Navy Records Society, starting with the *Letters of Sir Samuel Hood* in 1895. But the most intensive flood of print began to flow just before Mundy's book appeared. This had its source in the action of descendants and friends of John Clerk of Eldin (who had died eighteen years earlier and of whom more must be said in a later chapter), who now put forward the extraordinary and groundless claim that Clerk deserved a large share of credit for the victory because, so they said, he had previously conveyed to Rodney the idea of breaking through the enemy's line—a manoeuvre to which this victory was generally supposed to have been due. This was a claim which Clerk himself had never made specifically in his published work, though he had hinted that it might well have been the case. This not unnaturally aroused the fury of Major-General Sir Howard Douglas, son of Rodney's first captain, Sir Charles, who was sure, probably with justification, that this manoeuvre was suggested by his father to Rodney on the spur of the moment.[1]

---

[1] An admiral commanding twenty or more ships of the line was entitled to two captains in his flagship, the first captain being equivalent to a modern

Many pages of the *Edinburgh Review* and the *Quarterly Review* were covered by both parties to this dispute, and finally Howard Douglas published a book of 120 pages, closely printed and with scarcely a break, in which the claims of Clerk's supporters were thoroughly castigated. A year or two before this final word appeared another vigorous contestant, and a more convincing one, had joined in the battle—Captain Thomas White, who has already been mentioned (p. 159) as one of Hood's midshipmen in the *Barfleur*. He thought nothing of Clerk, either of his fantastic claims or of his subsequent descriptions of the battle, and he did not interest himself in the question whether Rodney or Douglas was primarily responsible for the decision to pass through a gap in the French line. He gave, however, a more coherent account of what happened at that juncture than any other that had appeared, even though the *Barfleur* was too far off to observe Rodney's exact movements in the prevailing smoke of battle.

With all this information available it might be supposed that a guaranteed narrative of, and commentary on, the battle would now be forthcoming. This cannot be claimed, but such doubts as remain are few.

It was on 19 February 1782 that Rodney arrived at Barbados after his five months' leave in England, bringing with him twelve sail of the line including his new flagship, the *Formidable* (ninety-eight). Here he heard that Hood had been facing de Grasse off St Kitts and after rapidly completing with water he sailed to the northward to join his second-in-command. The latter had in fact quitted his defensive anchorage a week earlier, cutting his cables by night at a prearranged time and making sail to windward. He had then visited Antigua to complete with stores before shaping course for Barbados in expectation of his chief's arrival. Rodney missed Hood at Antigua, arriving two days after the latter had sailed, but

chief of staff (though he had no staff except his secretary), while the second was the flag captain. The first captain later became known as the captain of the fleet and during the long peace of the nineteenth century had specific responsibilities assigned to him by Admiralty regulations. It was usual for a commander-in-chief's first captain to be senior to all, or nearly all, captains of private ships, and in several instances he was in fact a rear-admiral.

shortly afterwards the two parts of the fleet made contact to windward of that island. Unsuccessful in his hopes of intercepting de Grasse on the French fleet's route back to Martinique, Rodney then took his whole fleet to St Lucia. There he remained, watching de Grasse, save for an abortive attempt in mid-March to intercept a convoy from France. For once the British had a superiority in number of ships of the line, thirty-six opposed to the French thirty-three.

There was little or no doubt that the French aim was now the conquest of Jamaica, by far the most valuable of all the British islands, and in fact de Grasse was preparing to sail with five thousand troops to Cap François, there to join forces with a Spanish squadron and further troops from Havana which would give him a marked superiority in numbers both in sea and land forces. The troops he was taking from Martinique would be embarked in his warships and the bulk of their ammunition, baggage and supplies in a convoy of transports.

The convoy sailed from Fort Royal during the night of April 6th–7th hoping to get an unobserved start, but as they were in fact sighted they put back on April 7th. On the next day de Grasse, hearing that Rodney had already sailed from St Lucia, decided not to wait any longer for one of his ships which was not ready and put to sea with fleet and convoy, clearing the harbour by 10 p.m. and steering under the lee of Dominica for Guadeloupe. By next morning (April 9th) the heads of both fleets were clearing the northern end of Dominica in a steady easterly breeze, the French inshore having benefited by the land breeze of the hours before dawn to give them a lead. Not only that, but it also allowed de Grasse to send the convoy on to the anchorage at Basse Terre in Guadeloupe, twenty-five miles to the northward, where it would be out of harm's way. The main body of the British fleet, however, the centre and rear, which were further from the land and not so far advanced, were becalmed for most of the morning, and Hood's van division was now exposed to a much stronger body of the enemy and had to sustain their attacks as they sailed by him from his sternmost to his headmost ships. This was around 10 a.m. and they then came round to the larboard tack, sailed to the rear of Hood's division and soon after noon repeated their attack on the same lines. Hood could do nothing but return their fire, mostly with his main topsails to the mast so as not to widen his distance from the becalmed centre and rear, but though these two actions were sharp while they lasted it does not seem that either side received much serious damage, and by the time the second encounter was in train the leading ships of the British centre were at last making sufficient headway to enable them to join in.

Considering that there seems no doubt that de Grasse's plan was to get to Cap François without a battle, it is not clear why he had decided to attack on this occasion when he could easily have taken his whole fleet clear to windward without suffering any damage. It was evidently a splendid opportunity for any admiral who was prepared to press his attack home, but this he did not do. But maybe it was too obvious an opportunity to be refused, even if it were not pressed home, for it has been suggested that despite the general preference given by the French to long distance strategical aims there was an undercurrent of feeling among de Grasse's officers that he was a shade too battle-shy.

During the next two days the French fleet plied to windward in the waters between Dominica and Guadeloupe and Rodney followed. On the whole the French seemed to gain ground. One of their sixty-fours had been sent to Guadeloupe because of damage received in the action, and another was sent after her on the morning of April 10th because of damage incurred in a collision with the *Zélé* (seventy-four) during the previous night. Then during the night of April 11th–12th, the *Zélé* once more collided, this time with the flagship, the *Ville de Paris* (106), pride of the French fleet. On this occasion the *Zélé* was so much damaged that she had to be sent in tow of a frigate to join the other two cripples at Basse Terre and at dawn on April 12th she was sighted from the British fleet.

During most of the previous night Rodney had been standing on the larboard tack, to the southward, with Drake's division, the nominal rear, ahead of him and Hood's astern, the order of battle having been inverted since the action of April 9th so that the leading ships should be undamaged ones and could therefore be sure of standing close to the wind. In this formation

Hood's ships were the most northerly at dawn and therefore closest to the *Zélé* and Hood was ordered to send four ships to intercept her. Seeing her danger de Grasse then brought his fleet to leeward to protect her and Hood's ships had to be called off; but by that time the French had sacrificed the position clear to windward which they had been intent on keeping for the last three days. Meanwhile at about 6 a.m. Rodney had ordered his fleet to tack in succession, to the northward, led by the *Marlborough*, with Drake in the *Princessa* sixth in the line, and it soon became apparent that the French line of battle, the thirty ships still in company, though once more standing close to the wind could not hope to avoid an encounter with Rodney's thirty-six because they were now perforce on the larboard tack so as to keep clear of the Saints. Had they had more sea-room they might have avoided battle by hauling to the wind on the starboard tack, for if they sailed better on a wind than the British, as they probably did, they could have gained ground ahead and to windward, perhaps sufficient ground to be clear of their opponents before they had to tack. But these were narrow waters, only thirteen miles from Dominica to the Saints, and their line would have been about eight miles long. With the wind at south-east as it was then, the French fleet on the starboard tack might have been able to point to the eastward of the Saints, but with their leeway when close-hauled and the lee current through the passage between Dominica and Guadeloupe they could not have cleared this cluster of islets.

In the British fleet two cables was the distance apart ordered by the simplest signal for the line of battle ahead, the Union flag at the mizzen peak, and this was the normal formation. But a closer line with ships one cable apart could be signalled by hoisting another flag under the Union and this was in fact hoisted by Rodney at 7.10 a.m., thus in theory reducing his nearly ten mile-long line to about five miles. This was just five minutes before Hood's *Barfleur*, eighth ship from the rear, came round on to the starboard tack to follow Drake's and Rodney's divisions. How long it took to close up this very long line it is impossible to say. Perhaps some of the rear ships cut the corner when it came to their turn to tack. All one can tell now is that

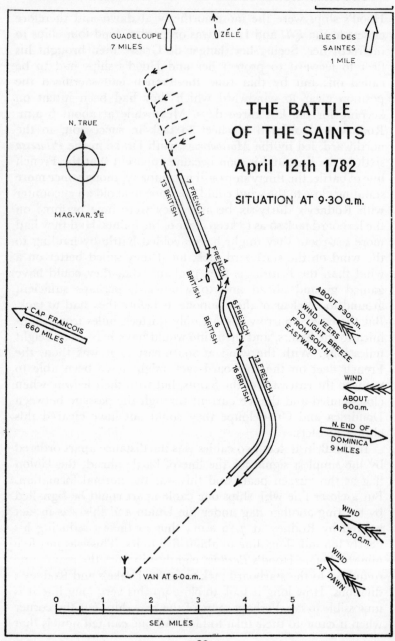

GUADELOUPE
7 MILES

ZÉLÉ

ÎLES DES
SAINTES
1 MILE

THE BATTLE
OF THE SAINTS
April 12th 1782

SITUATION AT 9·30 a.m.

N. TRUE

MAG. VAR. 3° E

13 BRITISH

7 FRENCH

FRENCH

1
BRITISH
0

6
BRITISH

6 FRENCH

CAP FRANCOIS
660 MILES

16 FRENCH

13 BRITISH

ABOUT 9·30 a.m.

WIND VEERS
TO LIGHT BREEZE
FROM SOUTH-
EASTWARD

WIND
ABOUT
8·0 a.m.

N. END OF
DOMINICA
9 MILES

WIND
AT 7·0 a.m.

WIND
AT DAWN

VAN AT 6·0 a.m.

0   1   2   3   4   5

SEA MILES

when the van came round onto the starboard tack (6 a.m.) there seemed a possibility that the British fleet might cross ahead of the French if the wind remained at south-east. But soon afterwards it backed two points, to east-south-east, with the result that the *Marlborough*, sailing as close as she could, was now closing with the ninth ship in the French line. As she neared her about 7.40 a.m. she hauled to port, parallel to the French line on an opposite course, and with the rest of the fleet following her the French centre and rear were engaged progressively under easy sail. At the same time the eight leading French ships, hitherto with no opponents, now put up their helms so that they could engage the British ships that were still approaching.

An action on opposite courses had usually proved ineffectual, as in Keppel's battle in 1778, but on this occasion much damage was inflicted at least by the British fleet on the French. This may have been partly to the credit of the improvements in gunnery on which Douglas had concentrated when comanding the *Duke*, before he joined Rodney (see above, p. 91). If, as he claimed, though perhaps with exaggeration, the *Duke* and some other ships could fire all their guns from three points before to three points abaft their beams and other ships could employ at least part of their armaments on those bearings, then three broadsides could be fired at each enemy ship as she was passed if the opposing lines were as close together as a distance of one cable, and it seems that each French ship was unlikely to get off more than two broadsides, perhaps only one, as she passed each opponent. That was on the assumption that the fleets were under such easy sail that it took three and a half minutes from being abreast one ship to being abreast the next, as was calculated to be the case in this battle.[1] It is perhaps apposite to note here that a broadside in this and other battles of those days was not an accurately simultaneous discharge of

[1] '*Rodney's Battle of 12th April*' in the *Quarterly Review* of January 1830, p. 69. The article is signed 'Art'. but it is understood to be by Sir John Barrow who had been Second Secretary of the Admiralty since 1804. The combined speeds of the two lines to effect this would, of course, depend on the spacing of the ships. If they were all at exactly one cable it would be $2\frac{3}{4}$ knots, but if not as well drilled as that it might be 3 or 4 knots, i.e. $1\frac{1}{2}$ or 2 knots for each line.

all guns, as it has been with the director firing of the twentieth century, for it was the general opinion that the shock of such a discharge, particularly in a three-decker, would put an unnecessary strain on the ship's timbers. As to whether there was any drill for avoiding this, for example platoon firing by sections of guns, or ripple firing, no information has survived but it seems probable that the exact moment of firing was left to the captain of the gun and that this resulted in a sufficient spread.

It was about 9 a.m. after more than an hour of heavy firing, and hence in dense smoke, that the *Formidable* and *Ville de Paris* engaged each other and passed on and it was soon after this that a crisis in the battle was reached. This derived from an unexpected shift of wind in this part of the field of battle from the steady east-south-east breeze which had been blowing for the last hour or more to light and variable winds from the southward. In the northern part where Drake's division was now engaged with the French rear there was little or no change, but in the French centre, headed by these southerly airs, there was necessarily some confusion. Ships naturally put their helms to port so as to fill again on the larboard tack and re-form their line, but at least three failed even to do that and found themselves heading to the eastward.

The main features of what probably happened at this point are most convincingly related in White's narrative, presumably founded on what he had been told soon afterwards.

At about ten o'clock, the southerly wind having reached the centre division and the *Duke* [Rodney's second ahead] having hauled up more in consequence thereof, it was observed from on board her, through the dense smoke that covered all that part of the fleet, that a ship was right ahead of, and apparently standing towards her: as they approached each other nearer, she proved to be an enemy's ship which had been compelled to break off, from the change of wind, as stated above. Each ship put her helm a-weather to endeavour to get to leeward of the other, in which effort the *Duke* at length succeeded, This of course caused a great opening in the French line (if the straggling and irregular position of the French ships at that moment can be called a line) between the ship attempting to clear the *Duke* [the *Diadème*], and the *Glorieux*, her second ahead, which for the same cause found herself on the starboard bow of the *Formidable*. Sir George Rodney being thus situated it was generally understood that he had no choice left him but to go through the opening in the French fleet, or to become entangled, as the *Duke* was at that moment with the French ship above alluded to.[1]

Exactly what happened on the quarter deck of the *Formidable* at this juncture, the question which caused so much ink to be spilt fifty years later, can never be fully determined. It seems clear, though, that Douglas wanted the flagship and the ships following her to go through the gap and that Rodney thought it would be better to follow the *Duke*. The flippant version which had some currency at the time was that Douglas, thinking it was the obvious thing to do, said port the helm, Rodney objecting to this said starboard the helm, and the master, thinking the helmsman must be getting rather confused, said midships. And through the gap they went, Rodney having in the meanwhile told Douglas to do as he liked.

This was the movement which was afterwards generally supposed to be a master stroke and the battle winner. It was not, however, admitted to be such by Beatson the historian, who says it must be doubted whether it was a fortunate evolution, nor by Cornwallis whose ship, the *Canada*, was three places astern of the *Formidable*.[2] This was for the very cogent reason that by going through to windward Rodney's flagship and the ships following him allowed the already battered French ships in his neighbourhood to get a start in retreating to leeward. And further astern there was a similar effect when the *Bedford* (Commodore Affleck), the last ship of the centre division, went through a gap two or three places ahead of the *Ville de Paris* and was followed by the whole of Hood's division, though it is doubtful whether Affleck knew he had gone through until he came clear of the smoke, the French formation being now in such a state of confusion.

[1] White, *Naval Researches*, p. 106.
[2] Cornwallis-West, *The Life and Letters of Admiral Cornwallis*, p. 122.

Rodney naturally did not disclaim responsibility for the movements of his flagship even though his first impulse had been to keep to leeward—especially so since in the event the whole world concluded, erroneously, that it was by the movement to windward that he had gained his victory. But at the back of his mind he must have known that this conflicted with his firmly stated principles and that it would in fact have been better to have kept to leeward following the *Duke*—supposing that had been possible. This is shown by his comments seven years later when he was given a copy of the original edition of Clerk's *Naval Tactics*, which had been distributed privately in January 1782, and asked if he would remark on it. This was Part I of Clerk's complete work, published later, and dealt only with attack from the weather gage, but Rodney's marginal comments included some which touched on this matter and all his comments were printed in the third edition of Clerk's book published by his heirs in 1827. The most relevant of these was 'as he [Rodney] told the King before any of his actions took place, he would always take the lee gage: because it prevented the enemy's retreat; secondly, because if any of his ships were disabled, by putting their helms a-weather the next ship closed the line, and secured the disabled ship'.[1] This was a sound principle, or would have been were it not for the fact that to bring the usually unwilling French to close action from the lee gage was unlikely to be possible except on opposite courses, a situation which was usually considered ineffectual. But having in fact become closely engaged from the leeward, despite being on opposite courses, it would evidently have been best to have remained to leeward if practicable. Another marginal comment of Rodney's to much the same effect was: 'A lee gage has certainly a very great advantage, and should always be taken when a proper opportunity offers of being close'.[2]

In this battle the *Formidable*'s passage to windward through the enemy's fleet followed by the five ships astern of her did in fact result in a heavy local concentration which might have been supposed to counterbalance the disadvantage of throwing open to the enemy their line of retreat. While she was still firing at the *Glorieux* in a very close action on her starboard hand

[1] Clerk, *Naval Tactics*, p. 18.   [2] ibid., p. 40.

there was a bunch of four ships within range to larboard, one at least of which had payed off on the wrong tack after the wind had headed her. And beyond these was the *Duke* who was now making her way round them to rejoin her admiral. The *Glorieux* was so battered by the *Formidable* and her followers that she was completely dismasted and inevitably fell into British hands later, and in this situation all attention could be concentrated on these four French ships by the seven British which were virtually surrounding them. It therefore comes as a surprise to find that none of them was numbered among the four ships (in addition to the *Glorieux*) that subsequently surrendered. These latter were presumably those which were most battered and therefore unable to make good their retreat, and they were in fact the *Ville de Paris*, two of her division who were ahead of her, and one of the van division.

This was a situation which one could not expect Rodney to allude to once he had decided to take credit for going through the French line whatever the facts may have been, and in a narrative of the battle which he wrote for Clerk in 1789, at the same time as he commented on Part I of Clerk's book, his description of this episode is as follows:

The British Admiral's ship, the *Formidable*, reached the enemy's fourth ship from their van, and began a very close action within half musket-shot, and continued such action close along the enemy's line, under easy sail, till an opening appeared at the third ship astern of the enemy's Admiral, which gave an opportunity of breaking their line, and putting their rear in the utmost confusion; when six of their ships falling onboard each other, in that condition the Admiral and division attacked them, tore them to pieces, and the moment they had disengaged themselves, they bore right away before the wind.[1]

This was a very vivid description. The only omission apt to mislead was the fact that none of these ships was so torn to pieces as to prevent her reaching Cap François.

Of what happened in the afternoon the clearest and probably most reliable picture is that derived from three sketches (2 p.m.,

[1] Clerk, *Naval Tactics*, p. 286 n.

4 p.m. and sunset) made by John Knight, Hood's flag captain, which were reproduced by Boswall in an appendix to his translation by Hoste (1834). From these and other information it is clear that the French were making off to the westward as best they could and that the three British divisions were rallying to their flag officers as well as their damage and the light breezes allowed and engaging such enemy ships as they came up with, the first of these being the dismasted *Glorieux* which had to be abandoned by the frigate that had been towing her. But according to Hood the commander-in-chief was unduly concerned with keeping his fleet together and on that account 'he pursued only under his topsails, the greatest part of the afternoon, though the flying enemy had all the sail set their very shattered state would allow.[1] This example, however, did not restrain Hood and by sunset the *Barfleur* had come up with the *Ville de Paris* and 'opened such a tremendous fire as he could not stand for more than ten minutes when he struck.'[2] By that time the bulk of the French had got clear enough to the westward to be able to come round more to the northward *en route* for Cap François, and soon after sunset Rodney made the signal to bring to and continue to lie-to the whole night, satisfied by his fleet having taken five prizes and particularly by the fact that these included de Grasse and his magnificent flagship. He justified himself for not pressing on in chase by the assumption that the remaining twenty-five French ships of the line were in an organized body which should not be approached until his own fleet was once more re-formed and sufficiently refitted. To Hood the majority of the French were thought of as being in a shattered state, morally as well as physically, as no doubt they were, and to his mind the haul of prizes should have been not a mere five ships but twenty.

In fact, far from the retreating French ships being the close-connected body of Rodney's imagination, de Vaudreuil, who was now in command, had only ten ships in sight the following morning. Five more joined him two days later and on April 25th he arrived at Cap François where he found some others.

[1] Hood to Middleton, *Barham Papers* (N.R.S.), vol. I p. 161.
[2] ibid.

But there were still four absent. These had been so badly damaged that they had been enable to shape a course that would have taken them to windward of San Domingo and they had run down to Curaçao to refit, finally arriving at Cap François on May 12th. All these ships, together with fourteen Spanish sail of the line and ten thousand Spanish troops from Havana which were there to meet them for the conquest of Jamaica, could be supposed a formidable enemy. On paper, Jamaica was still threatened by large and menacing forces. But the spirit had gone out of them and nothing further was attempted.

From what has been written above it is clear that the British fleet on April 12th had won a victory that was in the end decisive, even though it had not come up to Hood's view of the possibilities. It also seems clear that this victory was not attained by the *Formidable*'s passage through the French fleet. And it seems impossible to arrive at any more detailed narrative for, in the heartfelt words of the Second Secretary of Admiralty fifty years later, 'it is not easy, from such jarring and contradictory materials as the ships' logs are, in time of battle, at least those that we have seen, to ascertain [a number of things]'. What, then, were the principal causes of the victory?

It would be not unnatural to suggest that thirty-six ships could well expect to win a battle against thirty opponents. Rodney reasonably pointed out that the preponderance was not quite as marked as that, for whereas ten of his thirty-six were only sixty-fours the French had only three of this smaller type in their line. Douglas, who was mathematically minded, went much further than that, in fact too far. He made out detailed lists of the weights of the broadsides of each fleet and came to the surprising conclusion that the French fleet was not weaker than the British but had a perponderance equivalent to two normal ships of the line; in fact that the thirty-six British were opposed to what would have been thirty-eight French if the latter had carried on the average the same type of armament as their enemies.[2] Copies of these lists he distributed widely.

[1] Sir John Barrow in the *Quarterly Review*, vol. 42, p. 69.
[2] Gilbert Blane's *Select Dissertations*, quoted in Mundy's *Rodney*, vol. II, p. 231, and *Barham Papers*, vol. I, p. 283.

Of course if the average French ship embodied a much greater concentration of fighting power than the average British ship it would have been to the French credit. Concentration should always be aimed at if it can be brought to bear effectively: for example a three-decker in those days was thought to have an advantage over a two-decker (in battle, if not in coping with heavy weather) greater than would be adjudged on a strict comparison of their weights of broadside— and here, incidentally, the British had five three-deckers and the French only one. But Douglas's comparison was mainly illusionary. He based his figures on the fact that the lower deck guns of the British ships were 32-pounders whereas those of the French were 36-pounders, and beyond that the difference between the French pound and the English brought the French ball up to forty-two pounds English. (According to careful calculation by James, the historian of the next war, the weight of the ball of a French 36-pounder was thirty-nine English pounds.) What Douglas overlooked, however, was that in the previous war the British hundred-gun first-rates had mounted 42-pounders on their lower decks but that recently, at the instance of Keppel, it had been decided to replace them with 32-pounders as being easier to handle and capable of a better rate of fire as well as for several other reasons. To assume, therefore, as Douglas did in effect, that the difference in size between the French 36-pounders and the British 32s gave the French lower decks a marked superiority of fire was to contradict a view recently accepted by the British.

Disregarding Douglas's calculations and accepting that the British had a preponderance of force, the question still remains of the major causes of the French rout. A higher rate of fire, which was particularly telling when the fleets were on opposite courses, was probably one reason though there is no direct evidence of this. On the contrary, some British prisoners (taken the year before and exchanged in May 1782) who were on board the *Hercule*, the leader of the French line, stated that at the end of the battle she had only two rounds a gun remaining for her upper deck guns. So the *Hercule* at all events must have fired vigorously, at least from her upper deck guns; but she had apparently been more heavily engaged than the majority for she was one of those who was so badly crippled that she had to run down to Curaçao to refit before rejoining de Vaudreuil at Cap François. Another prisoner who was in the *Bourgogne* said that at cease fire she had only three rounds of shot left. And yet another, formerly the gunner of a sloop, who was on board the *Diadème* stated that 'on her ceasing fire she had not more than six rounds of powder left: and was informed that throughout the whole fleet no ship had more; some indeed had none at all'.[1]

But these reports were only hearsay and whether true or not it is difficult to believe that the French guns, however often they were fired, were fired as effectively as the British. A basis for the victory which seems more probable is one derived from the fact that the French officers, though not lacking in personal courage, were deficient in leadership. Gilbert Blane averred that 'in breaking the line the, *Formidable* passed so near the *Glorieux* that I could see the cannoneers throwing away their sponges and handspikes in order to save themselves by running below, while our guns were served with the utmost animation'.[1] This is supported by the prisoner in the *Diadème* quoted above who stated that in 'the latter part of the action in the forenoon the men did not stand to their quarters, but run down into the hold'.

[1] *Barham Papers*, vol. I, p. 186.
[2] Blane, op. cit., p. 232. He could see this because Rodney, having no midshipmen messengers at hand, had sent his physician of the fleet down to the lower deck with an order to the lieutenant in charge there.

Chapter 13

REFORM OF THE SIGNAL BOOKS

From very early in the American war there were several flag officers and captains who gave much thought to tactical affairs. There was no doubt in their minds that the basic aim was to take the ships of one's line of battle into action well ordered, well knit and simultaneously, but it seemed that more attention should be paid to the variety of manoeuvres which might contribute to that result. For such a purpose it was thought that the old signal books, the General and Additional Sailing and Fighting Instructions, hardly afforded the scope needed, based as they were on a comparatively small number of flags whose significance depended on the position in which they were hoisted. In the first, limited reform, instituted by Howe on the North American station in 1777, though the number of flags was increased, their positions still affected their meanings. But that arrangement was soon altered to a simple numerical system in which ten flags, numbered 1 to 0, were hoisted either singly or in pairs or threes wherever was thought best. To these were added fifteen or so special flags which were used either singly, for the more urgent or more frequently needed orders, or as qualifying some other signal hoisted at the same time, such as the Preparative flag.

This gave a virtually unlimited scope for conveying all sailing, manoeuvring and fighting orders that an admiral could wish to give, but there were no written instructions on how a battle was to be joined or fought, other than those which were evident from the wording, printed or in manuscript, in the signal book. As noted earlier, the old books contained very few instructions that were not in fact signals, and when Howe decided to introduce a new system of signalling he compiled at the same time a book of *Instructions respecting the Order of*

Battle and Conduct of the Fleet preparative to, and in Action with, the Enemy. When he issued these instructions to his small squadron in North America at the same time as his new signal book of 1777 they were covered by a statement that they were 'explanatory of and relative to the signals', and because of this it has sometimes been thought that all subsequent issues of similar instructions were merely 'explanatory'. These subsequent instructions were those drafted by Kempenfelt during the American war, followed by those of Howe at the end of that war and during the Nootka Sound Armament of 1790, and also in the early years of war of the French Revolution. They were followed by those included in the *Signal Book for the Ships of War*, 1799, the first of such instructions to be issued on the authority of the Admiralty instead of on that of the commander-in-chief as had been the previous practice. As already mentioned it had become usual for the Admiralty to undertake the printing of the general instructions and to make copies available to commanders-in-chief on hoisting their flags, and it was therefore natural that they should be accepted as common doctrine and issued by admirals as they were until such an enterprising tactician as Howe thought it better to write a completely new set for use in his own squadron. Even then, however, there was nothing in his instructions that contradicted the spirit of the old ones and in one article he pointed out that his manoeuvre conformed to the doctrine of bringing his leading ship 'to attack their leading ship in the van, as is generally understood to be required in such relative positions of the two fleets by the 19th article of the General Printed Fighting Instructions, the most necessary purposes of which the particular Signals and Instructions delivered for the government of ships on the present occasion are meant to supply'.[1]

The word 'explanatory' in connection with these instructions had again been used in prefacing those drafted by Kempenfelt when serving as first captain to successive commanders-in-chief of the Channel fleet (Hardy, Geary and Darby), and also later when he hoisted his flag as commander of a squadron. But these instructions were virtually copies of Howe's earlier ones. The word was not used thereafter, but when, in 1905, Corbett

[1] *Signals and Instructions* (Navy Records Society), p. 112.

edited a volume of *Fighting Instructions* for the Navy Records Society, his attitude to the introduction of the various new signalling systems and the instructions that went with them was that 'it was no mere substitution of a new set of Instructions but a complete revolution of method. The basis of the new tactical code was no longer included in the Instructions, and the Instructions sank to the second place of being "explanatory" to the signals.'[1] To modern minds, with the experience of two great wars to call on, it must seem a strange idea that the tactical aim to be achieved should be considered secondary in importance to the tools for achieving it. But perhaps not so strange to writers on the subject in 1905. In those days the Fighting Instructions had been labelled with a bad name and as with a dog given a bad name it was assumed that they should be hanged.

That, however, was not the view at the end of the eighteenth century. The authorization on the first page of the 1799 book, 'By the Commissioners for executing the Office of Lord High Admiral etc.', was followed by: 'You are hereby required and directed to pay strict obedience to the following instructions and signals, etc. etc.' And though, as will be shown later, Nelson felt himself justified in disregarding the 'strict obedience' if circumstances and his personal views conflicted with them, these instructions remained as the basis of tactical doctrine to the end of the sailing ship era.

In the tactical ideas that Howe set out in his instructions of 1777 there were only two that were new, or rather one that was original and one which was very old but had never before been indicated officially in writing. The former enjoined that 'if the Admiral should think it proper' to preface a general action by attacking the enemy's rear ships when coming up with an enemy 'waiting under easy sail by the wind in line of battle ahead', he would make a signal which ordered his leading ship to engage the enemy on their weather or lee quarter and then tack or wear and take station at the rear of his line—and so on in succession. Sometimes the order would be to a division of the fleet only, and the instructions seem to indicate that several of the sternmost ships of the enemy should be attacked in this

---

[1] op. cit'., p. 233.

way. The object of these preliminary tactics was obviously to ensure a fight to the finish unless the enemy was prepared to sacrifice his sorely battered rear ships by leaving them in the lurch. But it is difficult to understand why, if the latter was a possibility, he should have allowed the British fleet to overtake him in the first instance. However that may be, this manoeuvre was not mentioned in the instructions included in the Admiralty book of 1799 though the signal for it was still given therein.

The other new feature in these instructions lay in specifying the drill to be followed if the admiral wanted to change his position in the line so that, when his fleet went into action, the enemy's commander-in-chief would be his opposite number. The idea that a commander-in-chief was not merely in command of his fleet but also its champion, though perhaps unscientific from the geometrical point of view, had usually been assumed by admirals of spirit. And not without reason. The geometrical aspects of naval tactics were essentially limited in scope, unlike those ashore where the general's place should evidently be well in the rear of the fighting—even though Marlborough had sometimes found himself in the forefront of the battle. Because of this the moral encouragement derived from the admiral being seen to be engaging his adversary boldly and giving him a thorough trouncing must have enhanced the fighting power of the whole fleet. Curiously, though, it was at this same time that the contrary view, that an admiral should control his fleet in a similar way to a general conducting his army, was being advocated. In fact Howe himself when confronted by d'Estaing's much stronger squadron off Rhode Island in August 1778 (though he was none the less determined to give battle) shifted his flag to a frigate so that he could get closer to his enemy, who was to windward, and from there decide how he would take his squadron into action. It seems probable that he intended to return to his flagship before battle was joined, but in the event a violent storm intervened to scatter and damage both fleets, so that there was no battle, and it was not till next day that he could leave his frigate for a ship of the line.

Rodney, also, when manoeuvring off Martinique in May 1780, endeavouring to bring de Guichen to action, several times transferred to a frigate, though apparently leaving his flag flying in the *Sandwich* and telling his flag captain, Young, to make signals to the fleet when needed. Against this way of doing things Young protested, and in one of his series of letters to Middleton (the Comptroller) he commented: 'His being in a frigate was of no service, as he always kept to leeward of our line. The enemy being to windward he could never be a judge of it; but, at last, I got him persuaded to keep between us, which he attended to the last encounter'.[1]

The French, too, at one time leant towards this seemingly logical idea, and after the battle of the Saints, perhaps partly because of the capture of de Grasse, the authorities gave orders that commanders-in-chief were in future to conduct their battles from frigates.[2] But no doubt such an arrangement did not appeal to the ardour of the revolutionaries and there is no further instance of it being entertained either by the French or the British.

Because he did not see eye to eye on the American policy of Lord North's government, Howe asked to be relieved of the North American command, and on return to England in October 1778 he hauled down his flag. There was then no prospect of further employment for him while the existing government remained in power, but his interest in tactics was not abated and he was evidently in touch with Kempenfelt when the latter advocated the use of the North American instructions in home waters.

On the change of government early in 1782, however, Howe was once more employed afloat, this time as commander-in-chief of the Channel fleet. Promoted to admiral of the blue, he hoisted his flag in the *Victory* in April with several flag officers under his orders, including Kempenfelt until the latter lost his life in August, when the bottom of the *Royal George* caved in while she was at anchor and nearly all were drowned. During Howe's summer cruises he devoted much time to manoeuvring his fleet for exercise, at first not at all to his satisfaction despite the fact that he was now using Kempenfelt's version of his

[1] The *Barham Papers*, vol. I, p. 62.
[2] A. T. Mahan, *The Influence of Sea Power upon History*, p. 353.

own previous battle instructions and signals. But by September, when he was ordered to prepare for the relief of Gibraltar, taking with him thirty-four sail of the line to protect some thirty victuallers and store ships from the powerful Franco-Spanish fleet in those waters, practice had improved the situation, and he then issued a slightly revised set of instructions and, apparently, a new signal book.

The evidence for the latter is derived from Jervis's remarks at a meeting of captains and admirals on board the *Victory* while the fleet was southward bound, a meeting which also illustrated the current view on the perennial question whether a fleet should seek battle at night. This meeting is vividly described by St Vincent's biographer, the son of his secretary.

A battle with the combined fleets of France and Spain was fully expected; and the enemy being in very superior force [forty-eight to the British thirty-four] Lord Howe was desirous of ascertaining the sentiments of the senior officers under his command, whether, if an option presented itself, the day or the night would be more eligible for the action. It was understood, that, as against such an outnumbering force, his lordship's own prepossession was in favour of the night, in confidence that the discipline and practice of the British fleet would compensate for their inferiority in numbers, while in the darkness the disparity would be less perceptible.

On the first opportunity during the passage, his lordship assembled all his flag officers and captains on board the *Victory*, and having fully stated the probable chances, commencing with the junior officer, according to the practice of courts-martial, he requested their voices separately.

Every officer accorded with what was supposed to be also the commander-in-chief's views until it came to the turn of Sir John Jervis: but he dissented. Expressing regret that his duty compelled him to offer an opinion contrary, not only to that of his brother officers, but also, as he feared, to that of his commander-in-chief; he was satisfied, that if the choice of a day or night battle were afforded, the former would be greatly preferable. In the first place, it would give the fleet the able direction and tactics of his lordship, who might take the more prompt advantage of any mistake on the part of the enemy, or of any fluctuation of the wind, to make a successful impression on the most vulnerable point. Then the execution of any evolution they attempted, would be materially aided by the admirable code of day-signals, which his lordship had lately introduced. While in the mêlée of a battle at night, there must always be greater risk of separation, and of ships receiving the fire of their friends as well as foes. Sir John concluded by strongly urging the advantages of a daylight fight.

After him the senior captains, and then Rear-Admiral Sir Richard Hughes, and Vice-Admiral Milbanke, gave their opinion in conformity with the junior captains, Vice-Admiral Barrington alone concurring with Sir John Jervis, only further observing, 'that he could not comtemplate that any ship should be found wanting in the day of battle: and yet, should there unfortunately be a shy cock amongst them, daylight would expose him'.[1]

As things turned out, the need for Howe to decide whether he should fight by night did not arise. The enemy made no attempt to do more than exchange a few shots at long range, and as the merchant ships were successfully shepherded into Gibraltar, despite having overshot their mark in the first place, there was no call to force an action against so much more numerous a foe. So one cannot tell what Howe's view on this point was after he had listened to all his captains and admirals. But evidently he had the matter still in mind eight years later when the navy was again mobilized because of a threat of war with Spain over the Nootka Sound quarrel, and he was again in command of a Channel fleet, of thirty-five sail of the line. At that time, in addition to other sailing and fighting instructions, he issued six articles, headed 'Separate Instruction', of which the first was: 'The general purpose of this signal [a white flag with a blue cross] is to give timely notice of the Admiral's intentions meant to take effect at, or after the close of the day; that the divisions of ships to which they may relate may be

[1] J. S. Tucker, *Memoirs of the Earl of St Vincent*, vol. I, p. 77.

suitably prepared when it is thought expedient, later in the evening or course of the night, to make the different signals expressive of those intention'[1]—by night signals which were composed of lanterns, sometimes as many as five, hoisted in various patterns and in various places. These are the only known instructions envisaging the deliberate choice of action by night in preference to a day battle. In the 1799 book of night signals and instructions there are eleven instructions regarding battle by night but their background is 'the sudden discovery of a strange fleet' mentioned in Article I, and in fact there is no trace of any subsequent enthusiasm for a night action between fleets of heavy ships until the matter was revived in the British fleet in the nineteen-thirties.

During this 'armament', as it was called, of 1790, Howe spent much time in exercising fleet manoeuvres and was not at first at all satisfied with their performance. So, in the following year, did Hood, when there was a further armament because of a disagreement with Russia and he had been given the Channel fleet command and was using Howe's books. How much these exercises had led to modifications of the instructions and signals that Howe issued when war with France was declared in 1793 and he was again afloat as commander-in-chief is not clear, but it was on this occasion that a new battle manoeuvre first made its appearance: a move designed not merely to bring the enemy to action but to hold him there.

No doubt it had often been realized that the difficulty of achieving a decisive victory stemmed from the tendency of a French fleet to break off action by falling off to leeward soon after a British fleet had attacked from the weather gage, particularly if they had succeeded in their usual aim of crippling the British ships aloft. Knowles, as already mentioned, had stated that the French had a signal for a deliberate manoeuvre to do this, falling off by alternate ships, though in fact this was not so. He had also brought to Howe's notice his own observations as a lieutenant in Barrington's flagship at the battle of Grenada: how nearly impossible it seemed to keep the enemy in close action however close to windward one engaged them in the first place, a point which Barrington himself had

[1] *Signals and Instructions*, p. 327.

noted in his journal at the time. (Sir Charles H. Knowles was a keen student of tactics as his father, also Sir Charles, had been before him. A captain of 1780, though by St Vincent's standards a very unsatisfactory one in the 1790s, he eventually went through all the grades of admiral but never hoisted his flag.) There is no reason to suppose, however, that Howe had not already thought all this out for himself.

The crux of the matter was that unless you had the weather gage you were unlikely to be able to bring a reluctant French fleet to action. In every other respect it would have been better to engage from to leeward, as Rodney so clearly pointed out in his comments on Clerk's *Naval Tactics*. In practice, however, he had never succeeded in conforming to his theory. The fact was that there was no possibility of *forcing* a battle from the lee position. An opportunity might come when the two fleets were on contrary tacks but in that case the opportunity was usually too fleeting for reaching a decisive result. At the Saints the damage inflicted on the French had certainly been severe, despite the fleets being on opposite courses, but the shift of the wind had made it impossible for Rodney to maintain his position to leeward whether or not he had wanted to.

Howe's solution to this problem, though he knew it was a hazardous one, was that his fleet should bear down on the enemy's line, with his own line well formed and parallel to it as had always been the aim; but that each ship as she neared her opposite number, instead of rounding up to windward of her, should pass under her stern, raking her, and should then round up close under her lee. This would evidently need consummate ship-handling if the enemy was in a close knit line, but to Howe's mind it was worth trying.

In fact some such idea seems already to have occurred to him as early as 1777, for in his additional instructions of that year, as part of an article dealing with the procedure for an attack from the weather gage, he inserted: 'They are permitted to bring up against the enemy to take their stations on either part, to windward or to leeward of their opponents, as they may see most suitable for boarding or closing with them at advantage to disable them more speedily'.[1] At the same time

[1] This sentence had been omitted from the subsequent instructions of

he had cautioned ships engaging on the lee side of their opposite numbers not to allow themselves to get too far to leeward, out of touch with the rest of the fleet.

Now, however, in 1793 he determined to go the whole hog, ordering each ship to break through the line, if she could manage it, and engage from the lee side. The wording of this signal (No. 34) was: 'If when having the Weather Gage of the Enemy the Admiral means to pass between the ships in their line for engaging them to leeward'. In Howe's signal book there were references against many of the signals to the 'Instructions' or to the 'Additional Instructions', which were evidently in separate books which have not survived, but there was in fact no such reference against this signal.[1] Perhaps what had to be done seemed clear enough, given some previous discussion on the subject with junior flag officers and captains. In the Admiralty book of 1799, which was laid out in much the same form as Howe's, though with all the instructions in the same book as the signals, the meaning of the signal (now No. 27) was: 'Break through the enemy's line in all parts where it is practicable, and engage on the other side', and the instruction was: 'If signal 27, to break through the enemy's line, be made without a Blue Pendant being hoisted it is evident that the line of battle [the British line] must be entirely broken. . . . If any of the ships should find it impracticable . . . to pass through the enemy's line, they are to act in the best manner that circumstances will admit of for the destruction of the enemy'.

But this was not the whole scope of either of these signals.

Kempenfelt and Howe in 1781–2 but was reinserted at the time of the 1790 armament. Corbett, as editor, assumed in a footnote that the latter was the first hint of individual ships going through the enemy's line and engaging on the lee side (*Signals and Instructions* p. 324), curiously overlooking the fact that he had not only included the 1777 version earlier in his book but had commented on it (p. 85): 'It was this line of thought that brought Howe to the eighth article [the one already quoted], where he foreshadows his immortal form of attack which was finally to solve the problem of decisive action at sea.'

[1] A comparison of the instruction numbers quoted against various signals in the 1793 book makes it clear that most of these instructions and additional instructions must have been the same as, or similar to, those he had issued n 1777.

To the meaning in Howe's book quoted above was added, 'or being to Leeward to pass between them for obtaining the Weather Gage'. And in the later book, in which there is no mention of windward or leeward, the main meaning is followed by: 'If a Blue Pendant is hoisted at the fore topmast head, break through the van; if at the main topmast head, break through the centre; if at the mizzen topmast head, break through the rear'. And the corresponding instruction lays down: 'If a Blue Pendant be hoisted at either masthead, the fleet is to preserve the line of battle as it passes through the enemy's line, and to preserve it in very close order, that such of the enemy's ships as are cut off may not find an opportunity of passing through it to rejoin their fleet'. It is perhaps curious that this time there was no mention of windward or leeward, but maybe it was considered obvious that the blue pendant would only be hoisted if the British fleet was to leeward of the enemy.

This anomalous mixture in one basic signal of two tactical ideas which had nothing in common except that both entailed passing through an enemy's line, though in entirely different fashions, with different aims and for different reasons, is not easy to explain. Because it was the popular view that the victory at the Saints should be credited to Rodney's breaking the French line and thus concentrating on part of the enemy fleet, it was natural that a signal for this manoeuvre should be added to most of the books in use at the end of the American war. But this does not seem to have interested Howe at the time. What he was aiming at was a swift attack down wind followed by a station close to leeward that would prevent the enemy breaking off action by putting their helms up. For this his signal was drafted, but having so written it seems probable that he felt that some mention should be made of passing through from the lee side as Rodney had done. So he added, 'to pass between them for obtaining the Weather Gage'. There was nothing in the signification about why one should want to obtain the weather gage—nothing about concentrating on part of the enemy and nothing about keeping in a strict line ahead, if you could, while passing through. This only came later, with the publication of the Admiralty book, as the justification of a manoeuvre which was in fact never thereafter put into practice. As already related (p. 47), Howe did try to do something of the sort on 29 May, 1794, so as to leave no stone unturned in an endeavour to bring his enemy to close action, but his attempt had little success in passing through the French line and no effect at all on the outcome of that day's battle.

John Clerk, laird of Eldin, a small estate four miles from Edinburgh, was born in 1728 and born an enthusiast. From quite early days he had been interested in naval affairs though his only first-hand experience of the sea was in sailing small boats in the Firth of Forth and in watching merchant ships put to sea from the port of Leith. But he had read everything he could lay his hands on about British naval history, and by the time he had reached the age of fifty he had come to the conclusion that, although British fleets had always fought valiantly and had therefore not been worsted, their tactical ideas were all wrong. He therefore conceived the view that his mission for the remainder of his life was to teach them tactical principles which were based not on experience but on theories evolved from his own intellect, which was considerable, slightly tempered by somewhat unreliable history and any conversation with naval officers that came his way.

With this background it may seem strange that any admirals or captains should have taken him seriously. But it seems that he did in fact interest people. When he got down to writing for publication he illustrated his book with many and beautifully drawn diagrams in which you did what he advised and the enemy ships did just what you wanted them to. And he always carried in his pocket handfuls of small model ships with which he was to eager to demonstrate his theories, on dining-room tables, to anyone who would listen—and it seems that many did. Perhaps the basis of the interest that he induced in others was the fact that there were no similar, well-illustrated books available. There were translations of Hoste and Morogues published in the 1760s, of which Clerk does not seem to have been aware, but neither of those authors had had the temerity to draw diagrams showing admirals exactly what manoeuvres they should adopt in various circumstances in order to be sure of winning their battles. Now that Clerk provided such a book, interest naturally quickened and an anonymous friend of Rear-Admiral Ekins, historian of eighteenth century battles, told him that 'of Clerk's Treatise on Naval Tactics Lord Nelson was very fond, and frequently, at his leisure, would desire his Chaplain, Mr Scott, to read a little to him about the *wild geese*; to flocks of which the figures of ships are thought to have a resemblance'.[1]

Clerk's resolve that his interest in tactics should result in a treatise arose, he tells us, from studying the battle of Ushant of 1778 and the subsequent courts-martial of Keppel and Palliser. The 'many things in this engagement which seemed to me palpable blunders . . . roused a desire which could not be resisted, and hurried me on to putting in writing a number of strictures, accompanied by drawings and plans, containing sketches of what might have been attempted in this new kind of recounter of fleets upon contrary tacks'[2]—with the British to leeward. His first essay in this direction he communicated to a friend to whom he 'particularly explained my doctrine of cutting the enemy's line'. How this was to be done in a continuous formation if the enemy was in a strict line ahead with ships one cable apart, without the enemy ships astern of the supposed cut riposting with a similar cut through the British rear, is not mentioned. Nor is this explained when, twenty years later, his published work described his views on an attack from to leeward. There he simply repeats his comment of 1779: 'Perhaps it may be said, that the risk or danger of an attack of this kind might be greater than the advantage proposed. To which it is answered: As soon as ever we shall have the spirit and steadiness to make the experiment, conviction will follow, that the risk and damage to shipping making the attempt will be found less than any other mode of attack.'[3] And it was not difficult for such a skilled draftsman as he was to sketch out superficially convincing plans of such a manoeuvre.

[1] Ekins, *Naval Battles of Great Britain*, 2nd edition, p. 311.
[2] *Naval Tactics*, p. xxxv.   [3] ibid., p. 203.

But that was not to come till later. Though it was the unsatisfactory result of the battle of Ushant that had roused him, he realized that in all previous battles of the eighteenth century the British fleet had been to windward and that he had better deal with that situation first. This he did, and in January 1782 about fifty copies of this part of his work were printed as Part I of an *Essay on Naval Tactics* and distributed privately. Eight years later this part was published with an announcement that the rest of the work (which became: II, The Attack from the Leeward; III, History of Naval Tactics; IV, The Battles of 1782) would follow—which it did in 1792.

The main theme of Part I was that the long-established and approved practice that a fleet to windward should bear down on the enemy's close-hauled line if he was prepared to fight was evidently wrong because the attackers had to go through a period during which the enemy could fire their broadsides at them and they could not reply. This was, of course, a risk, but it was one which had always been accepted, particularly in a battle with the French who were unlikely to be brought to close action if the British fleet acted in any other way. But to this way of attacking Clerk objected and he therefore concocted many ingenious plans and diagrams in which his 'wild geese' were given full scope, the British fleet performing complicated manoeuvres and the French, if not standing to be attacked, as was hoped, did what might perhaps have been expected of them. It must have been on this part of the treatise that Howe commented: 'After studying the whole work, I think it very ingenious: but for my part, when I meet with an enemy, I am still resolved to fight in the old way'[1]—which he did, in the 'old way' with an improvement, on 1 June 1794.

The basis of Clerk's plans for attacking from the weather gage was that the British fleet, instead of being in the traditional single line of battle, should be formed in three columns disposed abeam of each other which should start their attack from a position on the enemy's weather quarter, and from there steer an overtaking course, presuming that the enemy was willing to be overtaken, such as would bring them into action without being raked. They would then overwhelm the enemy's

[1] White. *Naval Researches*, p. 124.

rear if he continued ahead with his van and centre. On the other hand he might take such counter-action as wearing the head of his line. To meet this case and others Clerk drew diagrams of the various movements he thought the enemy might make and his suggestions for meeting them.

When it came to Part II, The Attack from the Leeward, there was little in it beyond the principle that when the occasion for this was a meeting between fleets on opposite courses, as it was almost bound to be, the lee fleet (either the whole or a part) should break through the enemy's line, maintaining its own formation. This was what he had already advocated privately after Keppel's battle and no doubt his views on the subject were now stiffened by the general belief that this was done deliberately at the Saints and had been the main cause of victory.

Though Clerk's driving force was his enthusiasm he evidently believed that his contribution, as he supposed, to subsequent victories deserved some reward. When he first suggested this is not known, but it is clear from St Vincent's correspondence, and from the copy of a letter from Hardy, Nelson's flag captain, to an unspecified addressee, that in the spring of 1806 some of his friends were seeing what could be done about it. On June 2nd of that year St Vincent, then off Ushant with the Channel fleet, replied to an enquiry from the First Lord, Viscount Howick:

My dear Lord
Not having Mr Clark's [*sic*] treatise on naval tactics with me, I am unable to give you a detailed opinion upon the influence it has had on the several victories our fleets have obtained over those of France, Spain, and Holland, since its publication. I would not for the world subtract from the merits of Mr Clark, which I have always admitted; yet, on referring to the encyclopedia, wherein are copious extracts from the pamphlet, I perceive evident signs of compilation from Père le Hoste, down to Viscount de Grenier. In truth, it would be difficult for the ablest seaman and tactician to write upon the subject without running into one or all the French authors.

Inclosed your Lordship will receive the best judgment I can form of the claim Mr Clark has of any merit in the battles of the 1st June, and the attempts on the preceding days by Lord Howe, the battles of Camperdown and Trafalgar: that fought off *Cape St Vincent is totally out of the question.*

I do not see, however, that Ministers can withhold some reward to Mr Clark, after what has been lavished by former Administrations.

Yours ever,

ST VINCENT.

St Vincent's enclosure reads as follows:

Observations of the Earl of St Vincent on 'Clark's Naval Tactics'

Lord Rodney passed through the enemy's line by accident, not design, although historians have given him credit for the latter; this action is, however, not in question, the book having been first published in 1790.

Lord Howe's attacks upon the fleet of the enemy were at variance with the tactics of Mr Clark: on the 28th of May signals were made for a general chase to windward, and to harass the enemy's rear as the ships came up, which was not effected till the close of day, when the French suffered a three-decker to be cut off, at the risk of being taken possession of, in order to avoid a general action.

On the 29th May a manoeuvre, by which Lord Howe proposed to cut off the rear of the enemy, by passing through his line, failed in its effect, owing to the mistake or disobedience of signals; the only advantage gained was the weather gage, which he preserved to the first of June, when he run down in a line abreast, nearly at right angles with the enemy's line, until he brought every ship of his fleet on a diagonal point of bearing to its opponent, then steering on an angle to preserve that bearing until he arrived on the weather quarter, and close to the centre ship of the enemy, when the *Queen Charlotte* altered her course, and steered at right angles through the enemy's line, raking their ships on both sides as she crossed, and then luffing up and engaging to Leeward.

Lord Duncan's action was fought pell-mell (without plan or system); he was a gallant Officer (but had no idea of tactics, and being soon puzzled with them); and attacked, without attention to form or order, trusting that the brave example he set would achieve his object, which it did completely.

The attack at Aboukir furnishes no observation for or against the tactics of Mr Clark, but his position 'that a fleet to windward bearing down at right angles upon the fleet of the enemy must be crippled, if not totally disabled, before it can reach the enemy', has been disproved by the more recent action under Lord Nelson, bearing down in two columns at Trafalgar.

Mr Clark is most correct in his statement of the advantages to be derived from being to leeward of the fleet of the enemy. His mode of attack in columns when to windward has its merit, as have also his statements of the advantages and disadvantages of shifts of wind.

Upon the whole, his tactics are certainly ingenious, and worthy the study of all young and inexperienced Officers. But the great talent is to take prompt advantage of disorder in the fleet of the enemy, by shifts of wind, accidents, and their deficiency in practical seamanship, to the superior knowledge of which much of our success is to be attributed, and I trust it will never be sacrificed to frippery and gimcrack.

ST VINCENT.[1]

Some comment is called for on what St Vincent said about his old friend and contemporary Duncan, because Clerk had made a particular claim with regard to the battle of Camperdown. It seems that he had given a copy of his original treatise of 1782 to his fellow countryman Duncan while the latter was still a captain, in other words, before 1797, and he claimed later that on meeting Duncan again after the battle the latter had 'acknowledged in person to Mr Clerk how much he was indebted for the victory to his Tactics'.[2] This is certainly to the

---

[1] Tucker, *Memoirs of the Earl of St Vincent*, vol. II, pp. 281–3.
[2] quoted by C. Lloyd, *Battles of St Vincent and Camperdown*, p. 141.

credit of Duncan's courtesy, but Clerk's implication has no connection with the facts. Duncan had made Howe's new signal for passing between the ships in the enemy's line for engaging them to leeward—which had never been suggested in anything Clerk had written. And further, Duncan had written to the First Lord, Spencer: 'For the particulars of our victory shall leave your Lordship to my public letter [that is to the Secretary of the Admiralty], and shall just say I was obliged to lay all regularity and tactics aside, we was so near the land, or we should have done nothing'.[1]

There is no doubt that it was the brave example which Duncan set in getting to leeward of the enemy as quickly as he could, without waiting to form a regular line, and so putting his fleet between his adversaries and a lee shore just in time, that gave him his overwhelming victory. Whether he was 'soon puzzled by' tactics, as St Vincent asserted, can only be left to the imagination. If it was so, it was his only shortcoming, for his conduct was never less than admirable in this battle or on any other occasion.

[1] *The Spencer Papers* (Navy Records Society), vol. II, p. 197.

Chapter 15

THE GLORIOUS FIRST OF JUNE

In January 1793, the French beheaded their king and declared war on Britain and the Netherlands. Howe, who had served for several years during the peace as First Lord of the Admiralty and was now an earl and an admiral of the white, was at once appointed to command the Channel fleet which was being mobilized as fast as men could be made available. Given the acting rank of admiral of the fleet, he then hoisted the Union flag at the main on board the hundred-gun *Queen Charlotte*. A French fleet was also fitting out with, as usual, some excellent ships, but in other respect at a disadvantage. Many of the aristocratic officers of the royal fleet had emigrated or at least left the service: some had already been executed and in the Reign of Terror, now approaching, many more were to go to the guillotine. Besides that, the task given to this fleet was not an exhilarating one. The main fear of the Committee of Public Safety, now the virtual government, was that their enemies would land forces on the south coast of Brittany to back up the counter-revolutionaries in that part of the country who were being held in check only with difficulty. Howe occasionally sighted the French ships of the line, but as they always retreated inshore he could not get at them, and in the autumn after some mutinous outbreaks they went back to Brest, where some heads rolled, both of men and officers.

In the spring of the following year the general situation in France was deteriorating. There had been a bad harvest the previous summer and food supplies were short. But the navy was being pulled together under the impulsion of Jean Bon Saint-André, a 44-year-old and somewhat villainous looking member of the Committee of Public Safety to whom this task had been entrusted. And it could be pulled together with a more inspiriting object in view than in the previous year. Because of the shortage of food more than a hundred ships were being loaded with supplies from the United States and assembled in Chesapeake Bay, and it was clear that if these ships were to reach Brest in safety there must be a force, in addition to the normal convoy escort, which was prepared at need to give battle to the British Channel fleet. The emphasis of the French orders was on 'at need'. Action with the British fleet was not to be invited unless it was necessary for ensuring the convoy getting through, but with the Reign of Terror still dominant it must have been clear that if the convoy failed to reach France the admiral's head would have been at risk.

By calling on captains of merchant ships as well as officers of the old navy who were willing to serve under the new government all requirements were now met, and lest there should be any commanding officers who were not quite whole-hearted it was made clear that if any ship hauled down her colours her captain could expect no mercy. As commander-in-chief of this fleet Saint-André selected Villaret de Joyeuse, aged forty-six, who in his previous service in the royal navy had never risen beyond the rank of lieutenant but was to show himself not unworthy of the post he had now been given. So that the behaviour of admirals and captains in battle, if battle there was to be, should be reliably reported to the Committee of Public Safety, Saint-André himself embarked in the flagship, the 120-gun *Montagne*.

It was early in May 1794 that Howe's fleet put to sea to escort the East and West Indies convoys clear of the Channel, at the same time hoping to intercept the convoy from America, some news of whose intentions had become known. That the East Indiamen might have strong protection somewhat further on their southerly voyage than those bound for the West Indies, six ships of the line were detached from the main fleet to augment the regular escort as far as Cape Finisterre with orders that they should then cruise to the westward of the southern part of the Bay of Biscay in case the French convoy should take that route.

Meanwhile Howe with the remainder of his fleet, now numbering twenty-six of the line, had arrived off Ushant on

May 5th, and reconnaissance of Brest had shown that twenty-five sail of the line were at anchor there. As he was in hopes of intercepting the convoy, which might be expected at any time now, before it was so close to the coast as to give individual ships chances of escaping, he at once made sail to the westward on its most probable approach route, cruising there for a fortnight but sighting nothing. He therefore returned to Ushant and, on May 19th, found that Brest was empty, Villaret de Joyeuse having in fact sailed three days earlier. It seems that the two fleets had passed so close to each other in a dense fog on May 17th that the French had heard the guns of some of the British fog signals. Howe returned once more to the westward and on May 28th the two fleets were at last in sight of one another, being then about 350 miles west of Ushant.

It was at 9 a.m. that the French fleet was seen from the *Queen Charlotte*. The wind was then south-south-west and very squally and the enemy were dead to windward, distant about fifteen miles. They were at first sailing large and therefore closing on the British, but at 9.45 a.m. they were seen to be forming line on the larboard tack, that is heading to the westward. Howe, who had been previously standing to the eastward on the starboard tack, now tacked his fleet in succession and carried as full a press of sail as the strong winds and heavy sea permitted, the *Queen Charlotte* sailing with two reefs in her topsails. Three hours later he made the signal for harassing the enemy's rear, the manoeuvring which he had introduced in his first revision of the battle instructions sixteen years earlier. This, it will be remembered, assumed that the enemy was standing under easy sail, waiting to be overtaken. They were in fact at this time nearly stationary, dressing their line, but shortly afterwards it was seen that they were again standing on. Howe therefore made the signal for a general chase, followed by that for engaging the enemy on arriving up with them.

The French then tacked in succession, heading east-south-east and an hour later Howe did the same, with the result that the fire of his leading ship, the *Russell*, could just reach the rear enemy ship which replied. At that time the range was too great for effective gunfire but later three further ships of the British van succeeded in getting within range of the rear

199

French ship, the *Révolutionnaire*, a three-decker which had just taken up this post of evident danger, and they harassed her to some extent as well as the ship next ahead of her. At 7.30 p.m. the British ships were called off but just at this time a further ship, the *Audacious*, came into action with the *Révolutionnaire*, now somewhat crippled, and disregarding Howe's signal to re-form the British line continued to engage her for the next two hours—a British seventy-four against a hundred-gun first-rate.[1]

The French ship having lost all her masts then steered for Brest. The *Audacious* hoped to make sufficient repairs to join her fleet in the morning, but when morning came there was nothing in sight except some French ships to windward. As she was still by no means in fighting trim, she had to put her helm up and steer for Plymouth.

At dawn on May 29th both fleets were still standing to the south-eastward with the French about five miles to southward of the British. Howe had repeated his signal of the night before: 'to form line of battle ahead and astern of the Admiral as most convenient without regard to the established order'. This resulted in the new eighty-gun two-decker *Caesar* leading the line followed by the *Queen*, 98-gun three-decker, flagship of Rear-Admiral Gardner, and the fleet was again carrying all sail possible consistent with keeping an ordered line, endeavouring to make ground to windward. The *Queen Charlotte* was tenth in the line and had set her mainsail.[2]

At 7 a.m. the fleet was ordered to tack in succession with the

[1] By this period the majority of line of battle ships, both British and French, were 74-gun two-deckers, but there were a number of three-deckers in each fleet—the British having 100-gun first-rates and 98- and 90-gun second rates, the French 120-gun and 110-gun ships. There were also a few 80-gun two deckers in both fleets which in the British organization were classed as third-rates, like the 74s. The French 80s were particularly well thought of.

[2] References in ships' logs as to the sail they were carrying were only occasional. It was usual to go into action under the three topsails, either reefed (often with two reefs: the maximum was four) or whole, and perhaps with the foresail as well, the mainsail being clewed up. The *Queen Charlotte's* log for June 1st notes that as she was nearing the French line to pass through it (as will be related below) and was presumably under her whole topsails she 'set the foresail and topgallants'.

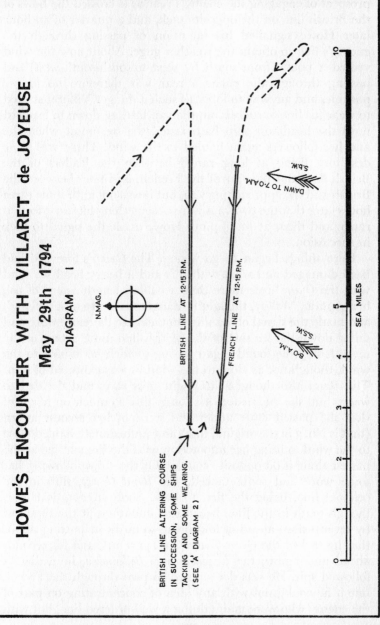

HOWE'S ENCOUNTER WITH VILLARET de JOYEUSE
May 29th 1794
DIAGRAM I

N.MAG.

BRITISH LINE AT 12·15 P.M.

FRENCH LINE AT 12·15 P.M.

BRITISH LINE ALTERING COURSE
IN SUCCESSION, SOME SHIPS
TACKING AND SOME WEARING.
(SEE 'A' DIAGRAM 2)

DAWN TO 7·0 A.M.
S.b.W.

8·0 A.M.
S.S.W.

SEA MILES

prospect of engaging the enemy's rear as it crossed the bows of the British line on the opposite tack, and a quarter of an hour later Howe signalled his intention of passing through the enemy's line to obtain the weather gage. About now the wind veered a point (from south by west to south-south-west) and passing through the enemy's rear was therefore no longer possible, and anyway to forestall such a danger Villaret started to wear his line in succession, the van leading down to leeward until the headmost ship had passed the sternmost when she and her followers again hauled to the wind. There was some desultory firing at long range between the leaders of the British fleet and the rear of the French, and later between the British and the approaching van, but it was not until some three hours later that the two vans were at something like an effectual range and then, at 12.15 p.m., Howe made the signal to tack in succession.

Here things began to go wrong. The *Caesar*'s foreyard had been damaged and what with this and a heavy head sea, and with the *Queen* 'little more than a cable's length astern of us', her captain, Molloy, thought it 'dangerous to attempt tacking', and made the signal of inability to tack. He therefore wore and sailed down the lee side of the British line until, astern of the seventh ship, he found a gap through which he hauled to the wind, though not as close to the wind as was expected of him. The *Queen* also thought she might miss stays and decided to wear, but she succeeded in doing this so much on her heel that she passed close under the stern of her second astern (that is No. 3 in the original line) and immediately hauled close to the wind to bring her into action with the French line as she passed along it on opposite courses. Of the ships following her some wore and some tacked, the *Royal George*, fifth in the original line, being the first to tack. Soon afterwards Howe, though tenth in the line, became so impatient at the time lost by several ships ahead of him being so tardy in putting about that he tacked the *Queen Charlotte* (1.30 p.m.), and his seconds ahead and astern, the *Leviathan* and *Bellerophon*, immediately followed suit. He was determined to pass through the French line if he could, not with any idea of concentrating on part of the enemy who were maintaining a well-ordered line, but with

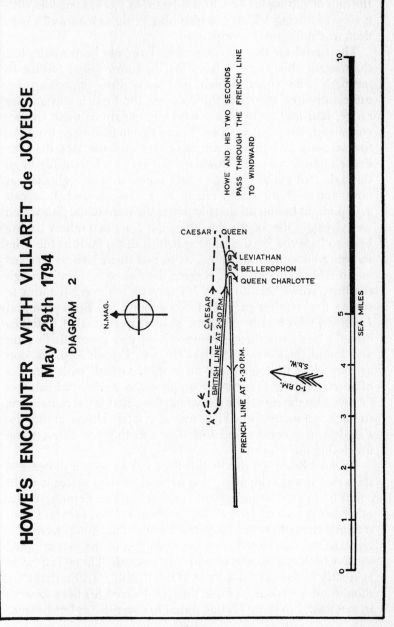

HOWE'S ENCOUNTER WITH VILLARET de JOYEUSE
May 29th 1794

DIAGRAM 2

N.MAG.

CAESAR   QUEEN

LEVIATHAN
BELLEROPHON
QUEEN CHARLOTTE

HOWE AND HIS TWO SECONDS
PASS THROUGH THE FRENCH LINE
TO WINDWARD

CAESAR

BRITISH LINE AT 2·30 P.M.

FRENCH LINE AT 2·30 P.M.

'A'

S.b.W.

1·0 P.M.

SEA MILES

the aim of getting his fleet to windward as soon as possible with a view to forcing Villaret to give him battle as soon as his own fleet was sufficiently reorganized.

The signal for this manoeuvre had already been made, but the *Caesar*, which should have led, had now fallen too far to leeward. The *Queen*, which had succeeded in luffing up sufficiently to engage the third ship of the French van at long range, had gradually closed with the enemy as their courses converged, but what with sustaining so much damage from the fire of each French ship in succession and the fact that the French line was so well closed up she found it impossible to go through. Not so the *Queen Charlotte*, however. Although she was now approaching the French rear she succeeded, about 2.30 p.m., in luffing up sharply under the stern of the *Éole* which was virtually the fourth ship from the rear, two others having been so battered by the leading British ships, both in the brief morning encounter and now, as to put them well to leeward and unable to manoeuvre. Raking the *Éole* as he went through the line, Howe was now on his way to achieving his aim of seizing the weather gage. His two seconds, the *Bellerophon* and *Leviathan*, who had been astern of him, were unable to follow directly but went through respectively two spaces further on and round the stern of the last effective French ship. As soon as they were through these three ships tacked, with the aim of overtaking the French line on its weather side, and this was followed by the signal for the whole fleet, that is the remainder, to tack in succession. Five minutes later Howe made the signal for a general chase and after a further ten minutes one for closing the admiral.

By now, however, the British fleet was in such a disordered state that it was evidently going to be some time before it could again be in any sort of a battle formation. The French, on the other hand, now on Howe's lee (starboard) bow, who had been steering virtually a steady course since the morning, were in a well formed line ahead with the exception of the two crippled ships which were astern and to leeward. These last were evidently in danger from some of the British rear. So that they should not be taken or sunk Villaret ordered his fleet to wear in succession, to bring his line round to cover them; but because his signal was not seen or not understood by his leading ship, who showed no sign of coming round, he shortly afterwards wore his flagship out of the line and took the lead. (This leading ship, the *Montagnard*, carried on the westward and though a frigate was sent to order her back she lost touch and never rejoined the fleet. It is believed that she had been damaged during the first encounter between the two vans in the forenoon, but though damage aloft often prevented a ship from tacking it would hardly prevent her from wearing unless she had lost her formast, which does not seem to have been the case.)

Villaret's manoeuvre succeeded in reaching his two cripples and protecting them under his lee though one, the eighty-gun *Indomptable*, was so badly damaged that he sent her back to harbour with a seventy-four to escort her. Fortunately for the British he did not continue to the eastward where the *Queen*, much shot-about aloft, was lying well to leeward. Instead he wore and steered large to the north-westward, and Howe conformed to the extent of forming his line on the same (larboard) tack but keeping closer to the wind so as to make no doubt of retaining the weather gage while both fleets repaired their damage aloft.

Next day, May 30th, came in foggy. Some clearance during the forenoon revealed the French fleet to the northward and Howe prepared for action, but before long it closed down again thicker than ever and at times he had only one of his ships in sight from the *Queen Charlotte*. From subsequent estimates it seems probable that it was on this day that the highly valued French convoy from America passed on its route to Brest not far to the southward of the British fleet.

It continued foggy all night, but about 10 a.m. on May 31st it began to clear, and by the afternoon the French fleet was in sight six miles to the northward. From the signals he made Howe evidently had in mind the possibility of engaging the enemy that evening, but it seems that he then decided it would be better to wait for the next morning, when, if it remained clear, he would have the whole of a summer's day before him. It will be remembered that twelve years earlier he was believed to be in favour of a night action. But that was in different circumstances, for he would have been engaging a Franco-Spanish fleet much superior in numbers but probably not in cohesion and in handling their ships in a night battle, whereas the British fleet had put in much sea time by day and by night in the previous four years. On the present occasion, however, there seemed to be no reason to doubt the handiness in man-oeuvre of Villaret's fleet despite the junior and humble origins of many of his captains; and on the other hand it is by no means sure that Howe had complete confidence in all his, having noted particularly the inadequate display of the *Caesar* two days previously.

The weather remained clear all night with a fresh breeze from the south and both fleets stood to the westward five or six miles apart, close-hauled on the larboard tack.[1]

At daylight on June 1st the French were seen to be still to the northward in a much extended line with their van on the lee beam of the British centre. Their line of battle comprised twenty-six ships, the same number as had sailed from Brest a fortnight earlier, despite the fact that four of the original fleet had parted company: the much battered *Révolutionnaire* on May 28th and the crippled *Indomptable* on May 29th with the ship that was escorting her back to harbour, as well as the ineptly missing *Montagnard*. But in the meanwhile four fresh ships had joined Villaret's flag. Howe had lost the *Audacious*, now on her way to Plymouth after her hard battle on the evening of May 28th, thus leaving him with one ship less than his adversary.

At 5 a.m. the British fleet bore up together so as to lessen their distance while keeping their line of battle parallel to the enemy, and now that the French were closing up into a well-formed line and their order could be clearly distinguished some minor re-arrangement of the British line was ordered so that

[1] Up to this time it had been the accepted customs of the British and French fleets that a line of battle should be formed six points from the wind, but in the British fleet greater flexibility was introduced about now (certainly by 1796) by changing this to seven points 'unless they be directed to haul close to the wind'. Whether this arrangement was in force in 1794 is not known, but it is clear from the *Queen Charlotte's* log that during this night she was steering west-south-west with the wind at south, i.e. six points, and it seems that the French were doing the same.

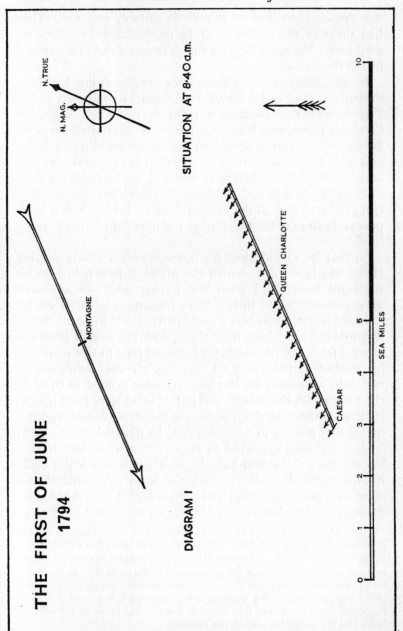

THE FIRST OF JUNE
1794

DIAGRAM I

SITUATION AT 8·40 a.m.

N. TRUE

N. MAG.

MONTAGNE

QUEEN CHARLOTTE

CAESAR

0   1   2   3   4   5   6   7   8   9   10

SEA MILES

the French three-deckers should be suitably opposed. (They had three to the British five.) In particular Howe made no doubt that Villaret's flagship the *Montagne* should be engaged by the *Queen Charlotte*.

By something over two hours later the British line had been dressed in good order about four miles to windward of the French with the *Montagne* a point or two abaft the *Queen Charlotte*'s beam, and Howe then hove-to and passed the word for the crews to go to breakfast, the enemy standing on under easy sail. At the same time he signalled his intention 'to pass between the ships in their [the enemy's] line for engaging them to leeward'. At 8.12 a.m. he made the signal 'to make sail after lying by' and at 8.38 the executive signal for 'each ship independently to steer for and engage her opponent in the enemy's line'.[1]

So that he should close his opponent on a steady bearing Howe was now steering with the *Montagne* four points on his starboard bow, the French line having relatively advanced somewhat while the British were hove-to. The wind on his larboard quarter gave him a speed of five knots while his enemy was making something over three, and the British fleet was aligned from five points on his larboard bow to five points on his starboard quarter. This was not an easy formation to maintain accurately for the hour or more needed to come to close grips with the enemy, and in fact there were some irregularities in the line despite signals made by Howe and his junior flag officers to various ships. In particular the *Caesar*, leading the line, appeared to many observers to be carrying less sail than she should have been. These irregularities made it even more difficult to effect the inevitably difficult and dangerous manoeuvre that had been ordered: each ship to pass through the line close astern of her opposite number and engage

[1] Until a 'preparative' flag had been introduced by several admirals in the previous war signals had been obeyed as soon as seen, but where it was important that ships should put their helms over simultaneously it had now become the practice to hoist the preparative at the same time as the signal for the manoeuvre required. The executive order was then given by hauling down the preparative, the main signal being kept flying until it was no longer of importance. On this occasion the interval between the original hoist and the executive was eleven minutes.

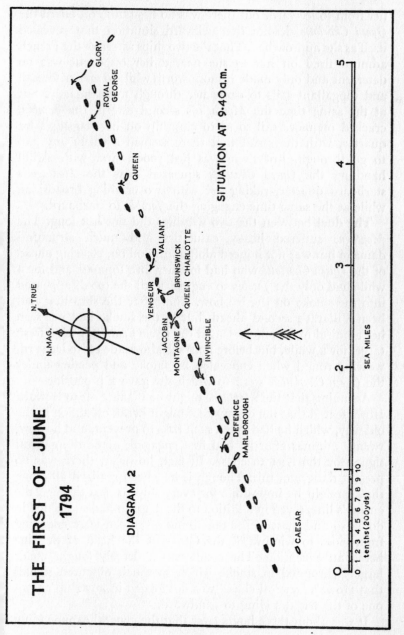

THE FIRST OF JUNE
1794

DIAGRAM 2

N. TRUE

N. MAG.

GLORY

ROYAL
GEORGE

QUEEN

VENGEUR

VALIANT

JACOBIN

BRUNSWICK

MONTAGNE

QUEEN CHARLOTTE

INVINCIBLE

DEFENCE

MARLBOROUGH

CAESAR

SITUATION AT 9·40 a.m.

SEA MILES

0 1 2 3 4 5 6 7 8 9 10
tenths (200 yds)

O

her from to leeward. But there was no hesitation on board the *Queen Charlotte* despite the awkward situation that revealed itself as she approached. That the two ships astern of the French admiral fired on her as she neared her opponent was no deterrent and only made it more worth while to set her foresail and topgallant sails to carry her through more smartly. But at the same time the *Montagne*'s second astern, the *Jacobin*, cracked on more sail so as to close up on her flagship's lee quarter, with the result that there seemed scarcely any gap to go through. But there was just room, and with skilful handling the *Queen Charlotte* squeezed past the *Montagne*'s starboard quarter, raking her with two crashing broadsides, while at the same time engaging the *Jacobin* to starboard.

The duel between the two flagships did not last long. The *Montagne* suffered heavy casualties and much structural damage but was not injured aloft and stood on, clearing ahead of the *Queen Charlotte* who had lost her fore topmast and for a while had only the *Jacobin* to engage, until she too disappeared into the smoke on the lee bow. Thereafter the ship that had been Villaret's second ahead, but in the smoke had not seen her admiral move on, presented the *Queen Charlotte* with a fresh target for a while, but before long she also made off to leeward, wearing round when concealed by smoke and passing under the *Queen Charlotte*'s stern to which she gave a broadside.

Assuming that the *Montagne* might be making off to leeward Howe feared that the enemy fleet might break off action in the old way, which he had taken such risks to prevent, and he now, twenty minutes after he had first engaged, made the general signal for the fleet to chase. In fact, however, there was no present danger of this. Though it had been realized all along that it might be impossible for every ship to pass through the enemy's line, seven in addition to the flagship had succeeded in doing so and most of the remaining seventeen were engaging from close to windward, the *Caesar* at the head of the line being an exception. The result was a fiercely fought mêlée largely shrouded in smoke which so much obscured signals that Howe's 'general chase' was not logged in any ship except one of the frigates lying to windward.

It was about three hours later that the general cannonading

eased up and Howe endeavoured to gather his fleet round him and form a line of battle on the starboard tack—heading to the eastward. Villaret was doing much the same same though more to leeward and not standing so close to the wind. Nine of the enemy had been completely dismasted, as had two of the British, and the fiercest individual battle, that between the *Brunswick* and the *Vengeur*, had now ceased though its eventual conclusion, the foundering of the *Vengeur*, was still some hours ahead. This epic contest had originated in the *Brunswick*, Howe's second astern, while endeavouring to pass through the line astern of the *Jacobin*, having been frustrated by the next French ship making more sail, followed by the *Vengeur* with the same intention. This was more than Captain Harvey of the *Brunswick* would put up with. Though he knew he could not pass clear ahead of the *Vengeur* he continued to stand on across the French line, until his starboard anchors caught in the *Vengeur*'s fore chains and shrouds. And there, locked together, these two ships remained for three hours pounding each other to pieces, during which time Harvey was mortally wounded. They then drifted apart and some hours later the *Vengeur* went down, about half her crew being rescued by such British ships as were near at hand.

Prior to this final event of the battle, six of the nine completely dismasted French ships had been secured as prizes. The other three had succeeded in rejoining their admiral to leeward, two of them in tow and one under a jury rig, and there was some subsequent talk to the effect that they too should have been taken. There was at least one undamaged British ship standing towards them, but it seems that Howe's first captain, Sir Roger Curtis, was becoming anxious lest there should be any dispersal of the British fleet with so many badly damaged ships. Howe, who at the age of sixty-eight was not unnaturally somewhat exhausted after five days in contact with the enemy, including two in close action, now relied on Curtis's advice and allowed him to recall such ships as were still in chase to the eastward. This was regretted by some of those who were aware of what was happening, but Curtis had not only been long trusted by Howe but had also greatly distinguished himself as naval commander under the Governor of Gibraltar at the climax of the great seige in 1872. Laughton, the naval historian, wrote of his 'personal courage tempered by prudence'.[1]

The whole fleet therefore lay to during the night and much of the next day, repairing damage and taking the prizes in tow. The French were no longer in sight and were making the best of their way home with their dismasted ships in tow.

On June 11th Villaret anchored in Bertheaume roads just outside Brest, but Saint-André was disinclined to face immediately the reception to be expected by a depleted and battered fleet with its sad tale of killed and wounded and he therefore postponed going up harbour. The following day, however, saw the arrival of the long-awaited convoy of 116 sail from America, which, on its two months passage from Chesapeake Bay, had been sighted by no ship other than the errant *Montagnard* which had joined it soon after she had parted company with her admiral on May 29th. With this drastic change for the better in the general outlook previous forebodings could be forgotten and the fleet entered Brest harbour.

On this same day, June 12th, nine ships which Howe had detached to Plymouth anchored in Cawsand Bay, and on June 13th the main body with their six prizes anchored at Spithead.

Though there was subsequently some talk of the victory having been less complete than it might have been, Howe was averse to allowing the fleet's undoubted triumph to be sullied by recriminations, and for this there was good reason in the obscurity of the main action, covered as it was by the smoke of battle. So widespread, however, were the strictures on the *Caesar*'s unenterprising conduct that Molloy asked for a court martial so that he might have an opportunity to clear his character. This request was based on Howe's adverse comment on the handling of the *Caesar* on May 29th in his report to the Admiralty, but when it was granted it was decided that the charge should also include June 1st. When, eleven months later, the court martial was held, Molloy was exonerated of any taint of cowardice but convicted of not having done his best to pass through the French line on May 29th, and also of not having taken a proper station for coming into action on June

[1] *Dictionary of National Biography.*

1st. He was, therefore, dismissed his ship and never employed again.

It is of interest that Molloy was one of the only four captains (out of fifteen) of ships not carrying an admiral or commodore whose behaviour in the battle of 17 April 1780 was commended by Rodney, and there was general applause for his gallant bearing as second ship in the line in the battle of the Chesapeake. Perhaps he had deteriorated in the subsequent thirteen years, for it is certainly clear that he now found reasons for not pressing forward, which, however plausible, did not convince the generality of his brother captains.

Chapter 16

THE BATTLE OF CAPE ST VINCENT

In the winter of 1796-7 the fortunes of Britain's armed forces were at a low ebb. Corsica, which had been occupied for two years, originally at the wish of the native Corsicans, had been evacuated in November and the garrison withdrawn to nearby Elba. In the previous month Spain had declared war on Britain in fulfilment of a treaty of alliance with France. What with this and the increasing French grip on Italy, leaving no source of victualling available nearer than Gibraltar, a British fleet at its then strength of fifteen sail of the line could no longer be maintained in the Mediterranean. Sir John Jervis was therefore ordered to withdraw. His command was extended to Cape Finisterre and though it retained its old title its extent was in fact limited for many months to come to Atlantic waters, with Lisbon as its main base. He reached Gibraltar on December 1st *en route* to the Tagus and while there his strength was reduced by a severe easterly gale in which three ships parted their cables or dragged their anchors, one being wrecked and two damaged by grounding. And when entering Lisbon a further ship, in the hands of a local pilot, was wrecked on a shoal at the mouth of the Tagus. What with these mishaps, the calls for repairs and a further grounding when he sailed from the Tagus on January 18th, necessitating the ship concerned returning to Lisbon, he had only ten sail of the line with him as he made his way towards his rendezvous off Cape St Vincent. But there, three weeks later, he was fortunately joined by a reinforcement of five of the line sent to him from England.

Meanwhile in mid-December Commodore Nelson with two frigates had been sent from Gibraltar to Elba to bring back such British troops and naval stores as were still there. The general in command, however, had heard nothing from home about evacuating the island and was not prepared to do so without Government orders. Nelson remained there for a month, hoping that such orders would arrive, but since nothing came he than sailed for Gibraltar with the remaining naval supply ships, taking with him Sir Gilbert Elliott who had been viceroy of Corsica, and rejoining his commander-in-chief off Cape St Vincent on February 13th. (The three thousand troops left in Elba sailed three months later with a weak escort and were so fortunate as to reach Gibraltar without encountering an enemy.)

Such, in brief, were the British movements during this period. As for the Spaniards, their main fleet had joined the French in Toulon soon after their declaration of war and on December 1st they sailed thence in company with five French ships of the line. The latter were urgently required at Brest and the French government were also hoping, somewhat optimistically, to welcome a Spanish fleet there to further their project of an invasion of England. Arriving off Cartagena on December 6th the French stood on, but the Spaniards entered harbour and remained there till February 1st.

On that day the Spanish fleet, comprising twenty-seven ships of the line, sailed under the command of Don Josef de Cordova and shaped course for the Straits of Gibraltar. His flagship was a four-decker, there were six three-deckers and the rest eighties and seventy-fours. Under his protection was a convoy of seventy transports carrying reinforcements for the army camped outside Gibraltar, and once they had been delivered his immediate destination would be Cadiz where the question of a further move to join the French at Brest would no doubt be considered. He also had with him four *urcas*, large merchant ships which in the distance could well be mistaken for warships. These were also bound for Cadiz with very valuable cargoes of mercury, though their eventual destination was across the Atlantic where their cargoes would go to the silver mines of central America.[1]

[1] A Spanish-English dictionary of the last century translates *urca* simply as 'storeship', but it seems that these must have been unusually large ones. The senior officer at Gibraltar, when sending a cutter to Jervis reporting

Cordova passed Gibraltar on February 5th with a strong easterly wind astern and sent the troops into Gibraltar Bay to disembark at Algeciras. Three seventy-fours went with them. One of these rejoined the fleet very soon afterwards, but the others remained with the transports for a further four days and thereafter did not succeed in regaining contact with their admiral until late in the afternoon of February 14th. It seems, therefore, that Cordova had now in company twenty-five of the line and possibly four *urcas*. In his despatch Jervis gave a list of names and number of guns of twenty-seven Spaniards, but it may well be that this was derived from an order of battle found in one of the ships now to be captured. Collingwood wrote in a private letter '27 or 28 sail (for we scarce had time to count them)'.

The news sent from Gibraltar of the Spanish fleet having passed through the straits reached Jervis off Cape St Vincent on February 9th. There was, of course, no indication of their destination but what was most to be apprehended was that they would go north to join the French. This, as already noted, was not Cordova's immediate aim, but it seems that once clear of the straits the wind was of a strength and direction that prevented him fetching Cadiz. (It is generally stated that it was blowing a gale from east-south-east, but that would have been east (true) and though Cadiz bore north-west by north (true) from Cape Trafalgar it would have borne more to the northward by the time he had cleared the Trafalgar shoals, and his ships, particularly the three-deckers, would not have been able to make any ground to windward.) For three days,

Cordova's passage of the Straits, said that there were two or three large ships 'resembling two-deckers'. The mercury came from mines at Almaden in the centre of southern Spain which was one of the few sources of this valuable mineral, used in the process of extracting silver from its ore. The presence of *urcas* and the possible confusion they caused in British estimates of the strength of the Spanish fleet when sighted had never been mentioned by any British historian until Rear-Admiral A. H. Taylor contributed a note on the subject to the *Mariner's Mirror* in 1954. This was based on a study of Cordova's report which, as he says, is by no means clear even when read in conjunction with the comments of Duro, the Spanish historian. But it is evident that there may have been as many as four of these vessels in the vicinity of the fleet on February 14th.

therefore, he was driven farther and farther to the westward, without being sighted. Nelson, who had arrived at Gibraltar on February 9th with his two frigates and heard that the Spanish fleet had passed four days previously, wasted no time in pressing on to rejoin his commander-in-chief, and incidentally when he sailed on February 11th he was chased by the two seventy-fours which were now leaving Algeciras to rejoin their fleet. It is related that that night he found himself in the middle of a collection of ships which he believed to be the Spanish main fleet making for Cadiz, a supposition which it is difficult to reconcile with Cordova's known position two days later. And in the morning he had nothing in sight. When he joined the fleet in the evening of February 13th, therefore, he had no reliable news to give his admiral, but his mission in the Mediterranean having been completed he could now transfer his broad pendant to his former ship, the *Captain* (seventy-four).

By this time the easterly winds had dropped. Soon after midnight, February 13th–14th, there was a steady breeze from south-west for some hours and at 2.30 a.m. a Portuguese frigate (with a Scots captain) hailed Jervis's flagship, the hundred-gun *Victory*, to tell him that the Spanish fleet was about fifteen miles to windward of him. The *Victory* and her fourteen consorts (including the flagship there were six three-deckers) were then about thirty miles west of Cape St Vincent, steering south-east, and they were sailing in two columns well concentrated.

St Valentine's day came in with hazy weather but by 6.30 a.m. some ships could be seen to the south-westward and half an hour later more were sighted on various bearings between south-south-west and south-east. Those on the latter bearing were probably frigates though one or two of them may have been *urcas*, but evidently some of those more to windward were ships of the line. At 7.40 a.m. Jervis sent his best sailing sloop to windward to reconnoitre. At 9.20 a.m. three of the line were ordered to chase and half an hour later two more were sent to follow them. A few minutes before 11 o' clock the reconnoitring sloop reported that there were twenty-five of the line and it could now be seen from the British fleet that the

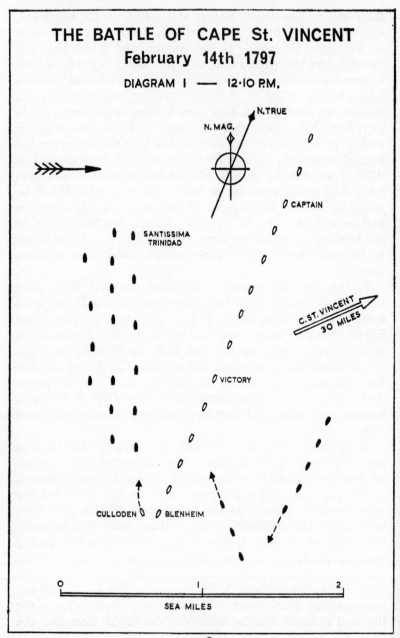

THE BATTLE OF CAPE St. VINCENT
February 14th 1797

DIAGRAM I —— 12·10 P.M.

N.TRUE

N. MAG.

CAPTAIN

SANTISSIMA
TRINIDAD

C. ST. VINCENT
30 MILES

VICTORY

CULLODEN BLENHEIM

0   1   2

SEA MILES

bulk of this force was on the larboard tack. The wind had by this time veered to west by north so they were steering to the northward, and Jervis, observing what then seemed to be a gap towards the rear of their ragged line, ordered his fleet to form 'line of battle ahead and astern as most convenient' and steered south-south-west towards the gap, to make sure it could not be closed.

In fact it was more than a mere gap in the Spanish line and here one arrives at one of the marked dissimilarities between this battle and any of those previously fought by a British fleet in this century. On all previous occasions except the convoy battles of 1747 the enemy had been a French fleet of about the same size as the British, formed in a well-ordered line of battle. Here, however, the enemy was greatly superior in numbers but so badly handled that they were little more than a mob. (It is said that their poor performance derived not only from the lack of seagoing experience of their officers but also from the fact that the seven hundred or more of each ship's complement included only seventy or eighty seamen, the rest being soldiers or inexperienced landsmen.) Thus it soon became evident to Jervis that there was little in the accepted tactical procedures that was applicable here, though the common-sense move of keeping a divided enemy divided was obviously the first step to be taken.

Why Cordova allowed the division of his fleet that was now being emphasized has never been fully apparent. His destination was Cadiz for which the compass course was about east-south-east (the magnetic variation was 21° west) and with the wind now westerly he would have been sailing large and might well have passed to the southward of the British. But a few days previously he had encountered an American ship whose captain told him that the British fleet in the vicinity comprised only nine ships of the line; this being before the reinforcement of five ships had reached Jervis and while one of his previous ten was temporarily out of sight. So it may be that with some twenty ships fairly close round him he thought it his duty to give battle to a mere nine. Apart from the evident call of honour this should enable the four valuable *urcas*, or such of them as were still in the vicinity, to reach Cadiz in safety with the escort of two of his ships which had been detailed to look after them. Whether for this reason or some other he had turned to the northward as already noted and attempted to form a line of battle on the larboard tack.

As the British approached, headed by the *Culloden*, Captain Troubridge, who had been leading the chasers sent forward at 9.50 a.m., it soon became evident that this was no mere gap in the line that they were heading for, but a wide space between two bunches of ships. To windward, on the starboard bow, were nineteen or twenty ships heading to the northward but in a ragged formation that was almost a square with only six in the front (leeward) rank, so to speak, headed by Cordova in the four-decker *Santissima Trinidad*, and with the rest sometimes three deep to windward. And on the *Culloden's* larboard bow and to leeward was a group of six ships, including a three-decker, five of which hauled to the wind on the starboard tack and the sixth, probably an *urca*, made off to the south-east. This group was joined soon afterwards by a vice-admiral with two further three-deckers and a two-decker from the main body, who stood across the *Culloden's* bows at about the time (11.30 a.m.) that she was beginning to engage the ships on her starboard side. At what range the *Culloden* engaged and whether she engaged all the front rank of the Spaniards which she was passing on opposite courses is not clear, but it is stated that all the guns of her first two broadsides were double-shotted so she must have been moderately close, and it seems that her course was converging with the tail of the Spanish line and that she was near to colliding with their last ship.

At this same time Jervis made Howe's signal denoting the admiral's intention to pass through the enemy's line, in the same wording (see p. 188 above) though differently numbered in his signal book. Just what he meant by this, which he repeated three quarters of an hour later when on the other tack, cannot be derived from any literal interpretation of the signal—as is evident from the various and confusing forms in which it is noted in the logs of his ships. But it was perhaps clear to all that his aim was to ensure that the two parts into which the enemy had separated were kept apart. And his other signals and movements did ensure this. These latter showed that he had no intention when 'being to leeward to pass between them [the enemy's ships] for obtaining the weather gage', nor of dealing with the smaller body of the enemy, of which he already had the weather gage, in the manner enjoined by this signal.

(The *Victory*'s signal log has a further entry of this signal at 2.15 p.m. addressed not to the fleet but to a single ship, the *Excellent*. This was recorded in the *Excellent*'s log, but nowhere else. Neither at the time or in anything that was written subsequently is it mentioned. Perhaps it was made by mistake, and anyway it was rendered nugatory ten minutes later by a signal to the *Excellent* to bear up.)

This matter of the 'passing through the enemy's line' signal has taken us ahead of the narrative, for within half an hour of her first broadside the *Culloden* had passed the last ship of the main body of the enemy. There were no ships to windward on her starboard beam and the eight ships (now that one had made off) to leeward were well separated from their commander-in-chief. At 12.08 p.m., therefore, Jervis ordered the fleet to tack in succession and as soon as this expected signal was seen on its way aloft Troubridge immediately put his helm down and came round to renew the action with the ships he had already engaged. It may be said that it would have been better if Jervis had ordered this manoeuvre somewhat earlier or if he had decided to tack together instead of in succession, for as things were it was more than half an hour before the *Culloden* could overtake the main body of the enemy—and now that both were on the same tack overtaking might have been impossible if the Spaniards had carried on under full sail and had been as well handled as the British. But tacking together would have been a hazardous manoeuvre with some of the ships still engaged with a more numerous fleet to windward. In addition it so happened that the vice-admiral in the leading three-decker of the Spanish leeward body did make an attempt, soon after the British van ships had come round, to come to windward, hoping perhaps that his division would be able to join the main body if the latter sailed more large. In this he was unsuccessful for he found himself heading for the *Victory* just before the latter had reached the turning point and was repulsed by a broadside from ahead and then raked from astern as his ship fell off.

The subsequent moves of these eight Spanish ships during the next few hours are uncertain. One seventy-four is said to have made her way to the northward and entered the main battle; the others were partially engaged with the British rear on opposite courses but did not rejoin their commander-in-chief until the battle was over.

Whatever might have happened had Jervis tacked his fleet earlier or together, the situation that in fact developed was now to bring about what has always been considered the most brilliant event of the battle. The nub of the matter was that while the place at which each succeeding British ship was tacking remained a fixed point, the Spanish fleet was sailing to the northward away from it. One does not know how far past the rear of the main body the *Culloden* had gone before Jervis made the signal to tack, but although she put her helm down immediately and had her foresail and mainsail set it was, as already stated, more than half an hour before she had made enough ground on the enemy to enable her to open fire again. That was the case with the leading ship: every succeeding ship, starting later from the same turning point, would of course have farther to go, however slowly the enemy sailed. So it came about that Nelson in the *Captain*, the thirteenth ship in the line, had already passed the enemy's main body on his starboard hand while there were still several ships ahead of him who had not yet reached the tacking point.

From this position it appeared to him that Cordova had now put his helm up with the aim of steering round the head of the British fleet so that the ships to leeward with his vice-admiral should be able to rejoin him. If this was so, it was evident that he could achieve his aim before the *Culloden* and the ships astern of her could overtake the bulk of his force. Nelson having so decided immediately ordered the *Captain* to be wore.

Why he wore instead of tacking has never been made clear and in logs of several ships including the *Victory* Nelson, when seen to have come round, is said to have tacked, as being the rational manoeuvre. The Spanish fleet was still to windward of him and wearing inevitably lost ground to leeward as well

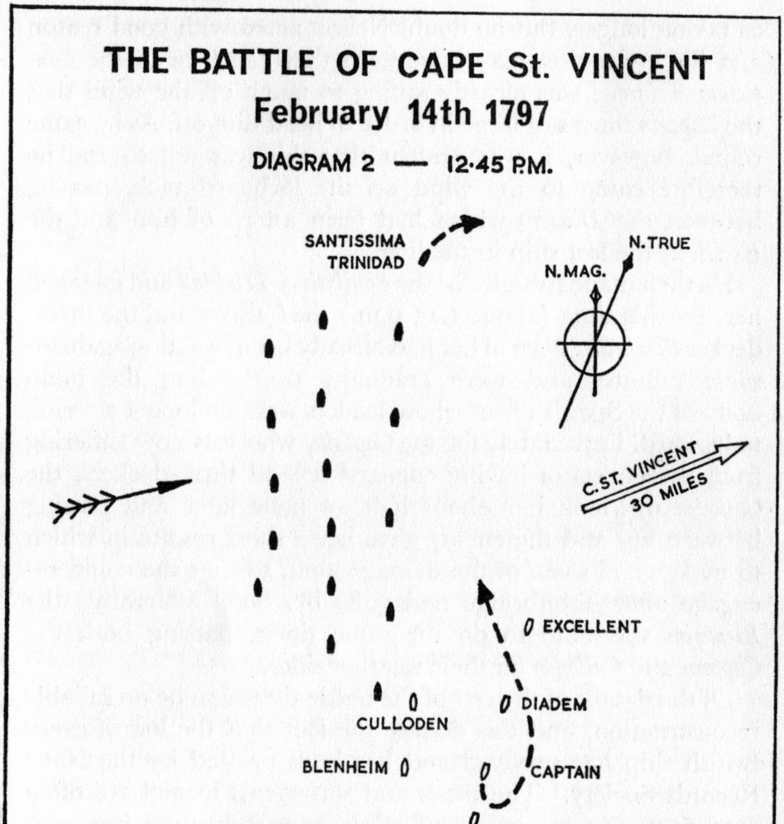

THE BATTLE OF CAPE St. VINCENT
February 14th 1797

DIAGRAM 2 —— 12·45 P.M.

SANTISSIMA
TRINIDAD

N. TRUE

N. MAG.

C. ST. VINCENT
30 MILES

○ EXCELLENT

CULLODEN ○   ○ DIADEM

BLENHEIM ○   ○ CAPTAIN

PRINCE GEORGE ○   ○

LEE DIVISION
OF SPANISH FLEET
HEREABOUTS

○

○

○   ○

○   ○

○ VICTORY

0   1   2

SEA MILES

as taking longer. But no doubt Nelson acted with good reason and his impression may have been that Cordova in the *Santissma Trinidad* was already sailing so much off the wind that the *Captain* must sail large in order to head him off. As he came round, however, it was evident that this was not so and he therefore came to the wind on the larboard tack, passing between the *Diadem* which had been astern of him and the *Excellent*, the last ship in the line.

He then made straight for the *Santissima Trinidad* and engaged her. By this time (about 1.15 p.m.) the *Culloden* and the three-decker *Blenheim* astern of her had already been in action again for some minutes and were gradually overhauling the main body of the Spanish fleet whose leaders were no longer steering to leeward. Fortunately for the *Captain*, who was now suffering from the effects of having engaged several three-deckers, the *Culloden* overtook her about half an hour later and passing between her and the enemy gave her a short respite in which to make good some of the damage aloft, so that she could re-engage after Troubridge had gone by. Soon afterwards the *Blenheim* was able to do the same thing, passing both the *Captain* and *Culloden* on their weather sides.

Of the details of the rest of the battle there can be no reliable reconstruction, and this despite the fact that the log of every British ship has survived and has been printed by the Navy Records Society.[1] The times and statements logged are often confusing and sometimes conflicting. As an indication, however, of where the brunt of the fighting fell it may be noted that the only heavy casualities were suffered by the *Captain*, *Blenheim*, *Excellent*, *Prince George* (next astern of the *Blenheim*) and *Culloden*, in that order, who had between them sixty-five killed against a total of eight for the other ten ships of the fleet. This brings us to the exploits of the *Excellent*, Captain Collingwood, which are even more difficult to follow than some of the others. In a letter to one of his regular correspondents he says: 'a skilful manoeuvre, which was led by Commodore Nelson, turned most of our force to the greater part where their admiral was. Nelson and the *Culloden* were the first in this assault. I was not

[1] *Logs of the Great Sea Fights, 1794–1805.*

long after them'.[1] This might be taken to mean that the *Excellent*, the last ship in the line, followed the *Captain*'s example in turning out of the line (in this case tacking) without waiting for orders. It seems, however, that he did not tack till about half an hour later, when Jervis made the general signal 'to come to the wind on the larboard tack', though neither the *Excellent*'s log nor Collingwood's letters give any indication of what influenced him in putting his helm down when he did. Thereafter he lost no time in getting into close action with the greatest possible vigour, and the impression one gets, not merely from Collingwood's own account, is that the way the *Excellent* was handled and the way her guns were served and aimed were more effective than those of any other ship. It seems that she did at one time penetrate the enemy's disorderly formation, perhaps in response to Jervis's unusual signal (when addressed to a single ship) to pass through the enemy's line, but she didn't remain there long, probably because of her subsequent signal to bear up, which has been mentioned above. It was soon after this, when once more to leeward of the enemy, that she battered two of the fleet's eventual prizes so heavily as to make them strike their colours to their next assailants. Still gaining ground ahead she passed between the now severely shattered *Captain* and the latter's even more decrepit opponent the *San Nicolas*, giving the Spaniard a terrific hammering as she passed, while some of her gunfire also reached the *San Josef*, severely damaged by previous British ships, who was just to windward of her consort and was soon to become entangled with the *San Nicolas*'s larboard bow. Collingwood then drew ahead to the best of the *Excellent*'s ability, aiming to engage Cordova in the *Santissima Trinidad*, already in action with the *Blenheim* and two seventy-fours. But this he was unable to do at close range.

It was at 3.30 p.m. or so, just after the *Excellent* had drawn clear of the *San Nicolas*, that occurred the most renowned and spectacular episode of the battle. The *Captain* had by that time been in close action, off and on, for more than two hours and was now barely manoeuvrable, but with two of the enemy

[1] *The Private Correspondence of Admiral Lord Collingwood* (Navy Records Society), p. 80.

locked together and immobile it was just possible to put her larboard bow in contact with the *San Nicolas*'s starboard quarter and to board. With Nelson among the foremost of the boarding parties she soon surrendered and the boarders then passed forward to her larboard bow and clambered aboard the *San Josef*, who also struck her colours. Whether her surrender was due to the boarding party or to the gunfire of the *Prince George* who had also been engaging her up to now is uncertain, but it was on the quarter deck of this three-decker that Nelson received the swords of all her officers.

With these two ships made prize, added to the two surrendered previously and now in tow of frigates, the height of the British victory had been reached. The *Orion* and *Egmont*, fourth and eighth in the original line, had forged ahead and engaged the *Santissima Trinidad* closely enough to have brought down her foremast and mizzen-mast and she had acknowledged defeat by hoisting either British colours or a white flag—accounts vary. But just then many uninjured consorts, probably including the two ships which had chased Nelson's frigate in the Straits of Gibraltar three days earlier, were crowding sail from to windward to protect their commander-in-chief and forced the British ships to haul off. By this time, too, about 4 p.m., Jervis had already made a general signal to bring-to, followed soon afterwards by one to form line ahead in close order. As far as he knew, the enemy, including those that had previously been to leeward and were now rejoining, still had twenty-three ships of the line against his fifteen. It is true that some of the Spanish ships had been severely damaged but so had some of his, particularly the *Captain* who had now to be taken in tow by a frigate. Though the seamanship of the Spaniards had evidently been found wanting, a proportion of their crews were styled artillerists and seem to have known how to serve their guns when given the opportunity.

Jervis therefore lay to during the night in close order with his prizes just to leeward of him and with the enemy away to the north-west. There they were sighted again in the morning, but they showed no sign of wishing to renew the contest. At noon Cape St Vincent bore north-north-east (that is north, true) distant six miles from the *Victory* and the fleet was gradually making its way towards Lagos Bay, twenty miles to the east-ward, where it anchored the following afternoon. The Spaniards were now heading for Cadiz, keeping to the westward and southward of their victorious enemy, and in a few days all those remaining to them had reassembled there—all, that is, except the crippled *Santissima Trinidad* who was nearly three weeks at sea under a jury rig and even then had to put in to Algeciras for repairs before finally reaching Cadiz.

As already mentioned, the battle of Cape St Vincent differed drastically in its setting from any of the encounters between British and French fleets and therefore differed in the tactics needed to deal with the siuation. Jervis, a strict disciplinarian in his handling both of his men and his ships, was firmly grounded in the view that if the enemy were sailing in a well-drilled line of battle the British must also be well drilled unless and until the enemy commander-in-chief misconducted his line in such a way as to give the British admiral an opportunity to concentrate on a part of the enemy's force while remaining untroubled by the rest of it. But here the Spanish fleet was in such disorder that it could not even be described as a line, even though when first sighted its disarray could not be fully comprehended and the wide separation of two parts of it was assumed to be merely a gap in a line. Connected with this aspect was the great preponderance in the numerical strength of the Spanish fleet over the British, a preponderance that not even Nelson would have accepted against a French fleet, and few if any admirals besides the dauntless Jervis would have been prepared to face against a Spanish fleet whose quality was as yet untried.[1] It was for this reason that he saw that his first duty was to keep the two clumps of enemy ships from getting together and, following this, that he continued for a while after passing the enemy's weather division on opposite tacks, so as

[1] It has often been recorded (though the original authority is unknown) that Nelson, when chasing Villeneuve and his Franco-Spanish fleet back from the West Indies in 1805, told his captains that he would face almost exactly the same odds, twenty (six of them Spaniards) to his eleven, if he encountered his enemy before reaching European waters and there were no British reinforcements to be expected. But this was on the principle that: 'By the time the enemy has beat our fleet soundly, they will do us no harm [i.e. Napoleon's projected invasion] this year.'

to make sure that the lee division would not work up to windward to the south of him and so tail on to their main body. This in fact they tried to do and, as related, were severely repulsed by the *Victory* herself and some of the ships astern of her.

That he might have tacked his line together once the van was well through the wide gap between the two parts of the enemy fleet and thus hastened re-engagement with the main body of the Spaniards has already been noted, but he thought it best to tack in succession; and without viewing the exact situation as he saw it from the quarterdeck of the *Victory* it cannot be said whether he was right or wrong. Only on one aspect of the matter can it be supposed that he may have been troubled by afterthoughts. That evening, when discussing the events of the day with Calder, his first captain, the latter suggested that wearing the *Captain* out of the line was an unauthorized departure by Nelson from the prescribed mode of attack. 'It certainly was so', replied Jervis, 'and if ever you commit such a breach of your orders I will forgive you also'.[1] Was he perhaps thinking that he might himself have given orders for this manoeuvre to the four or five ships of his rear without waiting half an hour after Nelson had shown the way before making the general signal to come to the wind on the larboard tack? On that one cannot expect any further evidence. It was indeed a glorious victory, physically and morally. Any enthusiasm the Spaniards may have felt for joining their allies in the English Channel had been severely damped, probably extinguished. Enthusiasm in England was unbounded and as a well-deserved honour Jervis now became the earl of St Vincent.

[1] Tucker, *Memoirs of the Earl of St Vincent*, vol. I, p. 262 n. Tucker's father was Jervis's secretary and may have been present at this conversation.

Chapter 17

TRAFALGAR

Though the immediate background of the battle of Trafalgar on 21 October 1805 was comparatively simple, this contrasted strongly with the incessantly fluctuating strategy and diverse movements of the spring and summer of that year. These arose from Napoleon's complex schemes for deceiving the British navy into dispersing its fleets and squadrons, what time French and Spanish ships concentrated in the West Indies prior to a united descent into the English Channel to protect his invasion of England from Boulogne. These plans had gone awry at almost every important point. The penultimate episode was the return of Admiral Villeneuve from the West Indies with a Franco-Spanish fleet of twenty of the line with Ferrol as his immediate destination. There he was to collect further French and Spanish ships and take them with him to join Admiral Ganteaume in Brest. Though all previous instructions from Napoleon had enjoined avoidance of battle before the final concentration had been effected when it came to this last lap, action might be accepted at need.

In fact a partial and inconclusive action was forced on Villeneuve on July 22nd, still 120 miles short of Cape Finisterre, by a British squadron of fourteen ships commanded by Sir Robert Calder which had been detached from the fleet off Ushant. This resulted in his anchoring in Vigo Bay before completing his voyage to Ferrol and it was not until August 2nd that he arrived in the latter harbour. Reinforced by the ships waiting for him he sailed again on August 13th, ostensibly for Brest though it had already been indicated to him that if that was impossible the only alternative was Cadiz. Two days later, being then 140 miles west of Cape Finisterre, this was the alternative he decided on. It was this decision, when the news reached France, that rang the death knell on Napoleon's existing invasion plans.

During Villeneuve's return voyage from the West Indies Vice-Admiral Viscount Nelson had been pursuing him with eleven sail of the line. Nelson, as commander-in-chief of the Mediterranean station, felt that his first duty was to prevent Villeneuve returning to those waters. He had therefore steered for Gibraltar and arrived there on July 20th (two days before Villeneuve's battle off Cape Finisterre) to revictual and take in much needed fresh provisions. And there he put foot ashore for the first time in twenty-three months. But there was no news of Villeneuve, and although there was no proof that Nelson had not passed *en route* a lagging opponent who was still making for the Mediterranean, he soon decided that the greater probability was a northward destination of the Franco-Spanish fleet. He therefore sailed again on July 23rd and joined Cornwallis off Ushant on August 15th. Leaving the bulk of his squadron there he took the *Victory* to Portsmouth for a short spell of relaxation, while his flagship was refitted. Twenty-five days were all he could be spared for, and on September 16th he was once more under sail and bound for Cadiz, which was now known to hold the bulk of the Franco-Spanish fleet—save only the Brest squadron, still held in check by Cornwallis. Collingwood, who had been watching Cadiz with a few ships for several months and had escaped being entrapped by Villeneuve's fleet as it approached, had recently been reinforced with sufficient ships to enable him to establish a close blockade.

It was at this point that strategy was at its simplest. When Nelson arrived on September 28th as commander-in-chief, with Collingwood now his second-in-command, the British aim remained the same, to engage any Franco-Spanish fleet that put to sea; but the disposition of the British ships was changed and so was their spirit. Only half-a-dozen of the thirty or so captains had served under Nelson previously but the acquaintance of all was soon made and as soon as made so was their enthusiasm aroused. Through this a spirit of optimism and zest, not easily engendered by the austere Collingwood, quickly permeated the whole fleet.

It was one of Nelson's most strongly held principles that brought about the change of the fleet's cruising ground. In his view everything must be aimed at a decisive defeat of the enemy's fleet and in this case it must be such a defeat as would sicken Napoleon of any idea of a naval revival, quite possible from the material aspect, aimed once more at an invasion of England. And Nelson knew that no French fleet with a British fleet blockading its harbour mouth had ever yet dared to sail straight into battle. From this it followed that his fleet must be kept out of sight of the blockaded port, with only frigates to watch it closely, but with some single ships disposed as signal links between them and the *Victory*. That this entailed a risk of missing an emerging enemy was apparent, for he had more than once been subjected to the heart-stressing anxiety that such a mishap engendered. But this risk must be accepted and it may well be that his self-confidence, ever buoyed up by the prospect of a victory, accepted it without hesitation.

At the same time optimism was also needed to envisage the Franco-Spanish fleet emerging even if the coast seemed clear, as he knew well from his previous two-years watch for the Toulon fleet. But here, unknown to him, the Fates had cast a die in his favour. Villeneuve, still a young man, five years younger than Nelson, had lost much of such enterprise as he possessed and had no difficulty in finding genuine reasons for postponing obedience to his orders to take his fleet into the Mediterranean—orders given by Napoleon now that he had transferred his activities to central Europe. Equipping for sea with only such resources as Cadiz could provide was a slow process, and not unnaturally little zest was displayed by his Spanish allies. But it gradually dawned on him that there was one compelling reason for making a move. News filtered through that there was a senior admiral on his way from Paris to Cadiz where, as Villeneuve at first supposed, he would help to speed up Spanish assistance. But this optimistic view gradually faded and instead he realized the probability that the newcomer was being sent to relieve him and that he was to return to France in disgrace. Sooner than face this he must make an early attempt to pass through the Straits of Gibraltar if conditions seemed to offer some chance of success, despite the known high standard of the British fleet and the already almost mystical reputation of Nelson.

By mid-October the British strength had been gradually increased to thirty-three ships of the line, but as there was no possibility of predicting how many months or years might elapse before the enemy put to sea, however open the blockade, it was clearly advisable that detachments should be sent in rotation to Gibraltar and Tetuan to renew provisions, water and fresh beef. When, therefore, the Franco-Spanish fleet emerged somewhat sooner than experience could have led Nelson to hope, he had with him only twenty-seven of the line—seven three-deckers, one eighty, sixteen seventy-fours and three sixty-fours. The fleet he was now to find ranged against him was also smaller than he had expected: eighteen French— four eighties and fourteen seventy-fours; and fifteen Spanish— four three-deckers, two eighties, eight seventy-fours and one sixty-four.

It was on the afternoon of October 19th that the enemy started to move, closely watched by Captain Blackwood of the *Euryalus*, the senior frigate captain, and the ships under his orders. But only a few ships had cleared the harbour by dark and it was not till the next morning that Villeneuve was at sea with the bulk of his fleet and started to form his line, steering to the northward on a westerly wind. During the night Nelson had been steering south-east (magnetic—the variation was 21° west) so that he might forestall his opponent whose destination he believed to be the Mediterranean. But at dawn being then some fourteen miles south-west (true) from Cape Trafalgar with nothing in sight and no further news, he retraced his steps to the westward, and during the following night he cruised in the vicinity of a position roughly thirty or forty miles south-west of Cadiz, relying on his frigates to keep in touch with the enemy. (Nelson recorded in his private diary that 'the Frigates and look-out ships kept sight of the Enemy most admirably all night, and told me by signals which tack they were on'. The signals were: Enemy standing to the southward, two blue lights together every hour; Enemy standing to the westward, three guns, quick, every hour.)

When on October 21st day at last dawned it disclosed the whole of the enemy fleet about ten miles east of the *Victory*, steering to the southward. The British fleet should already have been sailing in two columns as on the previous day, but as it had worn, rear ships first, twice during the night it was in fact in somewhat irregular formation.[1] Now, however, the signal was again made to form the order of sailing in two columns followed by the signal to steer east-north-east and about the meaning of this there were no doubts. The two columns were the two divisions led respectively by Nelson, with twelve ships, and Collingwood, with fifteen. The columns were to be in line ahead and Collingwood's *Royal Sovereign* leading the so-called rear or lee division was to be one mile on the lee beam of the *Victory*. As the course ordered was east-north-east and the light breeze was coming from the west-north-west, this was the starboard beam (to the southward), and to this position Collingwood immediately steered. (Of his previous position relative to the *Victory* there is no record. At midnight, six hours earlier, he had been half a mile east of her.) The remaining ships had then to take up their assigned positions as best they could, for both flagships were soon under a full spread of canvas, including studding sails and royals, to make sure that no time should be lost in closing the enemy.

It is here that varying and sometimes conflicting views on the subject of Nelson's tactical handling of his fleet have their start: views which were to continue to be discussed for a hundred years or more. Soon after he had assumed command at the end of September he had summoned all his flag officers and captains on board to give them his general ideas on the way he would join battle, and a few days later, on October 9th, he had issued a memorandum in which he had sought to embody his intentions. After his great victory had been won and he himself was dead it was not unnatural that there should be some discussion as to whether his achievement had resulted

[1] The *Africa* (sixty-four) had completely lost touch and was now out of sight to the northward. She was unable to rejoin Nelson's column until after the latter was already engaged and suffered some damage from the enemy's van on her way to do so.

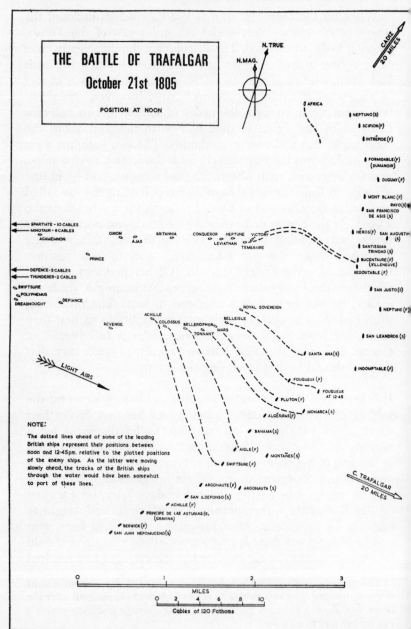

THE BATTLE OF TRAFALGAR
October 21st 1805

POSITION AT NOON

N. TRUE
N. MAG.

CADIZ 20 MILES

AFRICA

NEPTUNO (s)
SCIPION (f)
INTRÉPIDE (f)

FORMIDABLE (f)
(DUMANOIR)

DUGUAY (f)

MONT BLANC (f)
RAYO (s)
SAN FRANCISCO
DE ASIS (s)

HÉROS (f)   SAN AUGUSTIN
(s)

SANTISSIMA
TRINIDAD (s)

BUCENTAURE (f)
(VILLENEUVE)

REDOUTABLE (f)

SAN JUSTO (s)

NEPTUNE (f)

SAN LEANDROS (s)

SANTA ANA (s)

INDOMPTABLE (f)

FOUGUEUX (f)

FOUGUEUX
AT 12·45

PLUTON (f)

ALGÉSIRAS (f)   MONARCA (s)

BAHAMA (s)

MONTAÑES (s)

ARGONAUTE (f)   ARGONAUTA (s)

SAN ILDEFONSO (s)

ACHILLE (f)

PRINCIPE DE LAS ASTURIAS (s,
(GRAVINA)

BERWICK (f)

SAN JUAN NEPOMUCENO (s)

ROYAL SOVEREIGN

BELLEISLE

BELLEROPHON
MARS
TONNANT

ACHILLE
COLOSSUS

REVENGE

AIGLE (f)

SWIFTSURE (f)

SPARTIATE - IO CABLES
MINOTAUR - 8 CABLES
AGAMEMNON

ORION   BRITANNIA   CONQUEROR NEPTUNE VICTORY
        AJAX   LEVIATHAN
                                             TEMERAIRE

PRINCE

DEFENCE-5 CABLES
THUNDERER-2 CABLES

SWIFTSURE
POLYPHEMUS
DREADNOUGHT   DEFIANCE

LIGHT AIRS

NOTE:

The dotted lines ahead of some of the leading
British ships represent their positions between
noon and 12·45pm. relative to the plotted positions
of the enemy ships. As the latter were moving
slowly ahead, the tracks of the British ships
through the water would have been somewhat
to port of these lines.

C. TRAFALGAR
20 MILES

0   1   2   3
MILES

0   2   4   6   8   10
Cables of 120 Fathoms

from the tactics he had outlined therein or whether, as many thought, he had attacked pell-mell, regardless of risk and of all normal tactical principles, relying on the superiority of his ships in the way they fought their guns, and on his own prestige both in his own fleet and in the enemy's. There was something to be said on each side and a century later there were still some doubts on the details of the positions and movements of the British ship during the approach. In 1912, therefore, the Admiralty appointed a committee of two admirals who had given much time to the study of history (Sir Cyprian Bridge and Sir Reginald Custance) and the Regius Professor of Modern History at Oxford (Charles Firth) to go into these questions. Their report was published in July 1913. Because of the absence of some of the ships' logs and the inaccuracy of others it was not fully conclusive and a further investigation of the subject by Rear-Admiral A. H. Taylor in 1936 has justified some alterations in their narrative.[1] There are now few unknown factors, therefore, and it seems best to set out first what happened from the time of sighting the enemy up to the point when the fleets were well engaged and to follow this with a detailed examination of the memorandum in which England's last and greatest admiral of a sailing fleet in battle embodied his tactical ideas, comparing each aspect with the decisions he took when the enemy at last came within his reach.

At 6.45 a.m., half an hour after ordering the fleet to form in two columns steering east-north-east, Nelson decided to alter course two points to starboard, that is to east, so as to make sure of preventing the whole of the allied fleet from getting ahead of him if, as at first appeared, they were making for the Straits of Gibraltar. This was the last manoeuvring signal he made to his fleet as a whole. A quarter of an hour later he believed that the enemy were wearing in succession, presumably to make their way back to Cadiz, but he stood on on the same course, which was still suitable if Villeneuve was bringing his fleet round *in succession*. In fact he was not doing

[1] Admiral Taylor's narrative, which included the details of the battle as well as the approach, was not published till 1950—in the *Mariner's Mirror*, vol. 36.

so. What Nelson had seen was one or two of the French ships, whose position in the order of battle was in the centre but who had found themselves sailing to the head of the line during the night and were now turning back to resume their proper stations. At 8.15, however, Villeneuve signalled his fleet to wear together, fearing, so he stated, that his original rear would be engaged before it could follow the van when the latter bore up for the Straits. At this time the *Victory*, according to her own log as well as that of the *Euryalus* who was close on her beam, was eight or nine miles from the enemy, only a mile or two nearer than she had been two hours before. But these distances could only be approximate, particularly the longer ones, and the Allied fleet sorting itself out, close-hauled but making very little headway, would have been making considerable leeway.[1] It is recorded that in the early morning the wind in their vicinity was so light that some of them could hardly steer and that even later, when they were at last heading to the northward, they were only making half a knot headway.

Because of these conditions it was not till about ten o'clock that all the French and Spanish ships had worn, but even then they were not in a line ahead. With the wind west-north-west the close-hauled line before wearing would have been from south-west to north east. After wearing together and coming to the wind on the other tack the line would have been on the same slant, but as the ships would now be steering north this would not have been a line ahead but a bow-and-quarter line, each ship being on the larboard quarter of her next ahead. This, however, was not the formation in which Villeneuve wanted to join battle and he therefore ordered a line ahead, and this made it necessary for every ship except the leader to fall down to leeward so as to get in the leader's wake. Those most to the southward would have a long way to go before they got into station, and during this process it was natural that the line should be crescent-shaped. It was in fact still in such shape when the battle opened.

Nelson's main tactical aim now was to ensure that his enemy

[1] 'When a ship is close-hauled in a very light wind and scarcely having steerage-way, the lee-way is considerable even in smooth water' (Falconer, *Marine Dictionary*).

could not get back to Cadiz. To achieve this there was no need
to alter his fleet's course but only to press on. As things were
going, with the allies only under their topsails and not making
much headway, he could judge that Collingwood's division
could engage a substantial part of the enemy's rear, and
Collingwood knew that his instructions were to engage a body
of ships there somewhat less in number than his own. But it
was speed that mattered and it was this fact that prevented
the second-in-command from engaging in the manner that had
been intended, which was that his division should come down
in a line parallel to his opponents so as to engage them simultaneously, each ship cutting through the enemy's line astern of
her opponent and engaging her from the lee side—as had been
Howe's plan for his whole fleet on the First of June. With his
division much strung out this was impossible unless he, and
what ships there were close astern of him, shortened sail to
allow the laggards to come up. This he had no intention of
doing, realizing that it was the last thing Nelson would have
expected of him. He did, however, go through the drill, so to
speak, by making the signal to his division at 8.50 a.m. to
'form the larboard line of bearing'. This implied that they should
be in such a formation as would bring them into line ahead
when they hauled to the wind on the larboard tack, that is
steering north, and that they should therefore now strive to
make ground to the south of him. Though they could not in
fact achieve this while the *Royal Sovereign* was booming along,
if one can apply such an expression to a speed of three knots,
the four or five ships astern of her did their best by steering
slightly to starboard instead of following in her wake.

The speed of sailing of the British fleet in the light breeze
now blowing is a matter on which opinions have differed and
it is certainly a point of importance, for by this time it was
clear that Nelson was going to engage with his two leading
ships, the *Victory* and the *Royal Sovereign*, virtually head-on to
the expectant enemy's line. This meant that if the enemy did
as he should these two flagships would have to pass through a
zone of fire from the broadsides of many ships before they were
able to reply, and the length of time during which they were
thus exposed would, of course, depend on their speeds. On the

available evidence it seems that this was about two and a half knots; but had the breeze, already easing, failed still further at this time the risks to which the British leaders were to be exposed would have been substantially increased.[1]

Whatever the actual speeds, however, there was no doubt that the two flagships were doing as well or better than their followers, with the possible exception of the *Temeraire*, next astern of the *Victory*. By about 10 a.m. the *Royal Sovereign* had seven ships astern of her or slightly on her starboard quarter but their average distance apart was about three cables. The *Victory* had four astern of her in close order, one cable apart or less, but the remainder of this division were trailing well behind. It was at this time that there was a revealing view of Nelson's demeanour on going into action. His important decisions were made instantly and adhered to so long as there was no alteration of circumstances calling for a change. But there is nothing to suggest that he was in a state of frigid and unnatural calm. On this occasion he knew quite well that in the dangerous form of attack on which he was now intent it was wrong that he and his second-in-command should put themselves in the forefront of the battle at the most hazardous moment, the initial collision. He therefore signalled the *Mars*

[1] Admiral Taylor in his detailed narrative of the battle, mentioned above, says at the end of appendix IV: 'A comparison of the logs of the British fleet shows that the *Victory* was overlogging her speed. This is confirmed by the fact that the enemy's distance when sighted at 6 a.m. is given as 9 or 10 miles, whereas the distance run by the *Victory* from 6 to noon is given as $17\frac{1}{2}$ miles.' It is true that the speeds recorded in the sixteen log books that had entered them were all less than the *Victory*'s (3 knots up to and including 11 a.m. and $2\frac{1}{2}$ knots at noon), but nearly all of them logged 2 knots or more at noon. With regard to the distance run, assuming that the enemy were 8 or 9 miles ahead of the *Victory* at 8 a.m., as already noted, she would have neared the enemy by only 8 miles by noon (when the latter were still one mile ahead) instead of the $11\frac{1}{2}$ miles she had logged. It is not impossible, however, that the allies had drifted $3\frac{1}{2}$ miles to leeward during those 4 hours, what with excessive leeway when making so little headway and the sweep to leeward when wearing in such a light breeze. But it may be that the heaving of the log in the British flagship had not been as accurate as it should have been, a matter which usually depended on frequent checks of the half-minute glass and discarding a faulty one. Unfortunately there is no check from the *Royal Sovereign*. Her master was killed early in the battle and no log book has survived.

to lead the lee division, that is ahead of the *Royal Sovereign* and her assigned position in the order of battle—as distinct from the order of sailing, the last formation signalled. As the *Mars* was then some three or four cables on the *Royal Sovereign*'s starboard quarter she had no hope of getting there unless the latter shortened sail—which Collingwood had no intention of doing. About this time, also, the same point was discussed by some of the *Victory*'s officers on her quarterdeck and Blackwood, who was on board while the *Euryalus* lay off, was persuaded to approach the Admiral with the suggestion that the *Temeraire*, who was close astern and would have been ahead of the *Victory* in the order of battle, should be ordered to pass her. This he did, and Nelson (smiling significantly at Captain Hardy, his flag captain, so it is said) replied, 'Oh! yes, let her go ahead'. The *Temeraire* was accordingly hailed and told to lead the line. It so happened that soon afterwards the lieutenant in charge of the forecastle, seeing that the starboard lower studding sail was improperly set, had taken it in, so as to set it afresh. Nelson, seeing this and assuming that sail was being shortened to let the *Temeraire* pass, at once ran forward and rated the lieutenant soundly for what he was mistakenly thought to have done. No doubt this hastened the resetting of the sail. When shortly afterwards the *Temeraire* ranged up on the *Victory*'s quarter she was hailed by Nelson himself with: 'I'll thank you, Captain Harvey, to keep in your proper station which is *astern* of the *Victory*.' It is evident that in the intense exhilaration of approaching battle the logic of tactical theory had little appeal to the commander-in-chief when it conflicted with his eagerness to lead his fleet physically as well as in spirit.

The climax of the approach was reached at noon. Because of the curve in the allied line the *Royal Sovereign* was then about a mile closer to the enemy than was the *Victory* and it was at this point that Collingwood says in his journal that 'the *Royal Sovereign* opened a fire on the 12th, 13th, 14th and 15th ships from the enemy's rear and stood on with all sail to break the enemy's line'. At the same time one French ship fired a full broadside and soon afterwards seven ships in all, French and Spanish, were firing at Collingwood's flagship and the three ships on her starboard quarter. Just how the *Royal Sovereign* fired at four of the enemy in succession before reaching their line is not clear; whether she gave them one broadside each or divided her fire. It seems possible that she may have yawed a point or two to port before firing each broadside. As against any such proceeding it has sometimes been suggested that the enemy fired first and that the *Royal Sovereign* only fired a few guns to provide herself with a smoke screen during this critical period; but this view is contradicted by Collingwood in a letter to his old patron, Sir Peter Parker, dated November 1st, in which he says: 'They formed their line with nicety, and waited our attack with great composure, nor did they fire a gun until we were close to them and we began first.'[1] However that may be, there is no doubt that ten or fifteen minutes later the *Royal Sovereign* passed through the enemy's line astern of the *Santa Ana* and rounded up alongside her. A few minutes later her closest supporters, the *Bellisle*, *Mars* and *Tonnant*, were well into or beyond the enemy's line and within half an hour four more ships were similarly engaged.

About twenty minutes before the *Royal Sovereign* opened fire Nelson had signalled to Collingwood: 'I intend to push or go through the enemy's line to prevent them from getting into Cadiz', and then or shortly afterwards it seems that he altered two points to port, to east-north-east, either to make sure of being able to prevent them doing so or to confuse them as to where the blow from his division would fall. He had always had it in mind that this should encompass Villeneuve's flagship, the eighty-gun *Bucentaure*, but although several admirals' flags were flying, both French and Spanish, the commander-in-chief's flag had not yet been seen and it can only have been conjecture that he was near the centre. In fact the *Bucentaure* was twelfth ship from the van.

The ships in the allied van opened fire on the *Victory* at longer range than had those in the rear on the *Royal Sovereign*, but what with the distance and the beam swell in which they were rolling their fire was ineffectual until the *Victory* had closed to within about five hundred yards of the *Santissima Trinidad*, the Spanish four-decker next ahead of the *Bucentaure*.

[1] *The Private Correspondence of Admiral Lord Collingwood* (Navy Records Society), p. 165.

Just how the *Victory* was manoeuvred during the last quarter of an hour of the approach has never been clear. Her log says: 'At 4 minutes past 12 [12.24 p.m. when adjusted to the mean time adopted by the Admiralty committee of 1912] opened our fire on the enemy's van in passing down their line.' This seems to mean passing on opposite courses and firing her larboard broadside. But some historians have related that her first target was the *Santissima Trinidad* and that she engaged her with her starboard broadside, heading well to the northward of east.[1] This would account for the quarter of an hour which was to elapse before she cut under the stern of the *Bucentaure*, next astern of the *Santissima Trinidad*, and it has some backing from the log of the *Temeraire* who was only a ship's length astern of the *Victory*. In this it is noted: 'Quarter past noon, cut away the [larboard] studding sails and hauled to the wind. At 18 minutes past noon the enemy began to fire. At 25 minutes past noon the *Victory* opened her fire. Immediately put our helm aport to steer clear of the *Victory*, and opened our fire on the *Santissima Trinidad* and two ships ahead of her when the action became general.'[2] The masters' logs, presumably written up subsequently with a fierce battle intervening, cannot be relied on for details, but there seems no doubt that the *Victory* did haul to the northward for a while before turning and cutting into the enemy's line, but whether she gave the *Santissima Trinidad* her starboard broadside first must remain uncertain.[3]

The *Victory's* thrust into the French line was under the stern of the *Bucentaure*, still not knowing, it seems, that this was Villeneuve's flagship. She just got through, though in the process her starboard side became locked with the *Redoutable*'s larboard, the latter ship, an ably commanded seventy-four,

[1] The earliest detailed narrative of the battle (W. James, *The Naval History of Great Britain*) says that only one gun was fired to starboard at this time and that was by mistake.

[2] 'Two ships ahead of her' evidently means ahead from the *Temeraire*'s point of view, i.e. farther down the enemy's line. The *Temeraire*'s times seem to be the same as those of the Admiralty committee of 1912.

[3] James notes: 'We know also that, owing to the death early in the action of the two persons whose places (in succession) it was to take minutes, the [*Victory*'s] log entries were written up next day.'

having done her best to close her flagship so as to prevent the British break-through. It was now 12.45 p.m., just over half an hour since Collingwood had first come to close action. The *Victory* was quickly followed by the *Temeraire*, but it was nearly an hour later before more than six of the twelve ships of the weather column were in action, so strung out had they been during the approach.

When Villeneuve realized where Nelson's blow would fall he had made a signal which he thought would have the effect of bringing the seven ships of his van squadron (commanded by Dumanoir) to join in the battle by immediately tacking. But either because the meaning of the signal was not clear enough or because it could not be distinguished through the smoke which was now beginning to shroud the scene, Dumanoir did nothing as yet but sail on, away to the northward and away from the fighting.

With the heads of the two British divisions now heavily engaged and the remainder following into action as fast and as well placed as they were able to, the organized tactics of the battle, which some supposed had been outlined in Nelson's memorandum of October 9th and some did not, had come to an end. The rest depended on individual initiative and hard fighting. His memorandum therefore warrants examination in detail. But there are at first two general aspects on which some remarks are justified; one on Nelson's underlying views and one on the cogent judgment of an officer who took part in the battle and who summed up his considered views in a paper written twenty years later.

The first of these derives from a conversation which Nelson had with his trusted counsellor Keats shortly before he sailed for Cadiz in September. (Keats's *Superb* had been with him to the West Indies and back but was now undergoing such extensive repairs that she was unable to rejoin the fleet before the coming battle.) To Keats he outlined his subsequent memorandum, adding: 'I think it will surprise and confound the enemy. They won't know what I am about. It will bring on a pell-mell battle and that is what I want.' It is this last sentence that seems to indicate Nelson's innate view on tactics. If one thinks that the best way of winning a battle is through the superiority of one's tactical planning the last thing one wants is a pell-mell battle, a mêlée, the very negative of tactical science. If, on the other hand, one is prepared to rely on the inspiration that leadership can instil into the whole fleet and a superiority in the way captains, officers and men handle their ships and their guns, then, considering the severe limitations of tactical planning with a fleet of sailing ships and the fact that it was only by taking advantage of the enemy's blunders and doing so instantly that tactics had had any notable effect, it was no doubt best to 'go at them at once', as Nelson had expressed it to Keats. Looked at in that light it may be that the original and unusually intricate plan of attack expounded to his captains when he joined the fleet off Cadiz had its value more in the enthusiasm and zeal which its novelty roused in his listeners than in its tactical merits. And it may also be that, with that at the back of his mind, he paid no attention when the time came to what seemed the niceties of his plan.

The second general point by way of preface to a detailed examination of Nelson's memorandum is the view expressed by Humphrey Senhouse, who had been a lieutenant in the *Conqueror* (fifth in Nelson's line) at Trafalgar and who twenty years later, then a captain, wrote an extensive paper on the subject of Nelson's tactics.[1] This included the following paragraphs.

The mode of attack adopted with such success in the Trafalgar action appears to me to have succeeded from the enthusiasm inspired throughout the British fleet from their being commanded by their beloved Nelson, from the gallant conduct of the leaders of the two divisions, from the individual exertions of each ship after the attack commenced, and the superior practice of the guns in the English vessels. It succeeded also because the enemy's Admiral was determined to fight the threatened battle and to give his followers an opportunity of trying their strength fairly, encouraged by what had happened in Sir Robert Calder's action. Admiral

[1] First printed in *Macmillan's Magazine* for April 1900. Senhouse was later knighted. He died during the Canton operations of the First China War.

Villeneuve, therefore, waived certain advantages that a skilful manoeuvre might have insured him.

It was successful also from the consternation it spread throughout the combined fleet on finding the British so much stronger than was expected, from the astonishing and rapid destruction which followed the attack of the leaders, witnessed by the whole hostile fleets, inspiring one and dispiriting the other, and from the loss of their Admiral's ship early in the action. The disadvantages of this mode of attack appear to consist in bringing forward the attacking zone so leisurely and alternately, that an enemy of equal spirit and equal ability in the practice of gunnery would have annihilated the ships, one after another in detail, carried slowly on as they were in this instance by a heavy swell and light airs.[1]

This was a considered opinion on the queries raised by a comparison of the memorandum with the events of the battle and only on one point is it clearly at fault. Senhouse states that 'the enemy's Admiral was determined to fight the threatened battle and give his followers an opportunity of trying their strength fairly. . . . Admiral Villeneuve, therefore, waived certain advantages that a skilful manoeuvre might have afforded him'—one supposes that he was unaware of the fact that Napoleon was standing behind Villeneuve with a pistol at his head.

With the above prefatory comments the memorandum of October 9th, 1805, can be considered in detail.

Thinking it almost impossible to bring a Fleet of forty Sail of the Line into a Line of Battle with variable winds, thick weather, and other circumstances which must occur, without such a loss of time that the opportunity would probably be lost of bringing the Enemy to Battle in such a

[1] The statement that a heavy swell carries a ship along is an interesting one. It is generally supposed that an ocean swell merely lifts a ship up and down; but with the water gradually shallowing to the eastward a westerly swell might have had that effect. When the battle started the fleets were in 50 fathoms, but the 100-fathom line was only twelve miles to the westward, and by the late afternoon the *Victory* found herself in 32 fathoms, and before midnight in 13 fathoms.

manner as to make the business decisive I have therefore made up my mind to keep the fleet in that position of sailing (with the exception of the First and Second in Command) that the Order of Sailing is to be the Order of Battle, placing the Fleet in two Lines of sixteen ships each, with an Advanced Squadron of eight of the fastest Two-decked Ships, which will always make, if wanted, a line of twenty-four Sail, on whichever Line the Commander-in-Chief may direct.

It is this first paragraph that contains the essence of Nelson's tactical thought, from which he never deviated—apart, that is, from deletion of the Advanced Squadron when he found that he had only twenty-seven ships against the thirty-three of the enemy, not the forty against forty-six that he had originally calculated on. 'Without such a loss of time that the opportunity would probably be lost of bringing the Enemy to Battle in such a manner as to make the business decisive' was the key sentence. 'Time is everything,' he had remarked on a previous occasion, 'five minutes may make the difference between a victory and a defeat.' It was for this reason that he decreed that 'the Order of Sailing is to the Order of Battle'. He deferred to the generally accepted doctrine that the admiral should not lead the line in battle by inserting 'with the exception of the First and Second in Command', and not long after October 9th he issued an Order of Battle which put the *Temeraire* (ninety-eight) and the *Superb* (seventy-four) ahead of the *Victory* (though Keats did not in fact arrive in time for the battle), and the *Prince* (ninety-eight) and *Mars* (seventy-four) ahead of the *Royal Sovereign*. But, as we have seen, all he signalled was to form the order of sailing, in which admirals always led their divisions.[1] He refrained from making any signal for the

---

[1] In some diagrams and lists of orders of sailing the flag officers of each of the two or three or more columns are shown in the centres of their respective lines, so as to be in their orthodox positions when a single line of battle was formed. But it is evident from the instructions respecting the Orders of Sailing included in the Signal Book that they were expected to lead their columns in the first instance, perhaps, moving into central positions just before deploying. But in fact there was no instance in all the battles related above of a British deployment being preceded by an elaborate

order of battle, and his show of going through the motions by putting at least one private ship at the head of each line was nullified by his refusal to let the *Temeraire* go ahead of him and Collingwood's determination to allow no such thing if Nelson didn't.

> The Second in Command will, after my intentions are made known to him, have the entire direction of his line to make the attack upon the Enemy, and to follow up the blow until they are captured or destroyed.

The 'after my intentions are made known to him' appears to have referred to the signals (which are given in full below and on p. 249) 'to lead through' (if to leeward), and if to windward, as was the case on October 21st, 'the lee line to bear up together'. This signal was never made because the intended disposition of squadrons had never been taken up. But this did not worry Collingwood, who no doubt assumed that Nelson's intentions had been made clear enough in previous conversations, and he had no hesitation in ordering his divisions to form a line of bearing when he thought it appropriate—even though the prevailing situation and the *Royal Sovereign*'s speed made his orders only partially effective.

> If the Enemy's Fleet should be seen to windward in Line of Battle and the two Lines and the Advanced Squadron can fetch them, they will probably be so extended that their Van could not succour their Rear.

This assumption seems at first sight to rest on the idea that the enemy were less efficient in station-keeping than the British; but it may, on the other hand, have been based on the near certainty that a single line of forty-six ships could not be so well closed up throughout as could three shorter lines acting separately.

> I should therefore probably make the Second-in-Command's signal to lead through, about their twelfth ship from their

order of sailing followed by the manoeuvres prescribed in detail in the Instructions for forming the Line of Battle from the Orders of Sailing—which in the 1799 Signal Book were much the same as those that Hoste had proposed a century earlier.

Rear (or wherever he could fetch if not so far advanced); my line would lead through about their Centre, and the Advanced Squadron to cut two or three or four Ships ahead of their Centre, so as to ensure getting at their Commander-in-Chief on whom every effort must be made to capture.

The whole impression of the British Fleet must be to overpower from two or three Ships a-head of their Commander-in-Chief, supposed to be in the Centre, to the Rear of their Fleet. I will suppose twenty Sail of the Enemy's line to be untouched, it must be some time before they could perform a manoeuvre to bring their force compact to attack any part of the British Fleet engaged, or to succour their own Ships, which indeed would be impossible without mixing with Ships engaged.

This gives only a sketch of what he intended to do if he attacked from the lee side of the enemy—which he would only do if there seemed no probability of being able to attack from windward. As it stands it gives no guidance to the fleet as a whole, only to the leaders of divisions, though no doubt he had discussed the matter with his admirals and captains. The two fleets would, of course, have been on opposite courses, with the enemy close-hauled and probably the British, and in that case the angle of impact would have been four points. The signal (27, with a blue pendant) would have been addressed to the divisions separately and, in the words of Article XXXI of the Instructions for the Conduct of a Fleet in Action in the 1799 Signal Book, '. . . the fleet [in this case each division] is to preserve the line of battle as it passes through the enemy's line, and to preserve it in very close order, that such of the enemy's ships as may be cut off may not find an opportunity of passing through it to rejoin their fleet'. But as to how the ships that had passed through were then to be manoeuvred there is no indication. Evidently the twelve ships of the enemy's rear that Collingwood would have cut off, if there was no hitch, were the ones that he was to engage, but presumably he would not want to do this on opposite courses, for that would be passing them too quickly. Perhaps it was reckoned that the leading ships of the enemy's twelve would be so shattered while the British division was passing through that the latter could then wear and impinge on the remainder of the enemy's line, possibly repassing the enemy's formation individually as they came round, so that each enemy ship could be engaged on her lee side. On only two previous occasions had there been any resemblance to this form of attack—at The Saints, when Rodney went through by chance because of a shift of wind, and on 29 May 1794, when Howe took his flagship through the tail of the enemy's line and then tacked so as to follow their main body. But on the latter occasion the ships ahead of him had not been able to get through and his next astern had not been able to follow through the same gap, though she succeeded further on. There is little doubt that Nelson would have been victorious had this plan been forced on him by the direction of the wind, but it is improbable that the tactics enjoined would have had any other advantage than that of bringing the enemy to action at the earliest opportunity.

Something must be left to chance; nothing is sure in a Sea Fight beyond all others. Shot will carry away masts and yards of friends as well as foes; but I look with confidence to a Victory before the Van of the Enemy could succour their Rear, and that the British Fleet would most of them be ready to receive their twenty Sail of the Line, or to pursue them, should they endeavour to make off.

If the Van of the Enemy tacks, the Captured Ships must run to leeward of the British Fleet; if the Enemy wears, the British must place themselves between the Enemy and the Captured, and the disabled British Ships; and should the Enemy close, I have no fears as to the result.

The Second-in-Command will in all possible things direct the movements of his Line, by keeping them as compact as the nature of the circumstances will admit. Captains are to look to their particular Line as their rallying point. But, in case signals can neither be seen or perfectly understood, no Captain can do very wrong if he places his Ship alongside that of an Enemy.

This seems to confirm the comments given above on the previous paragraph: that the details of his tactical plan for the approach, complete success in which he realized was chancy, would have been comparatively of far less importance than the initiative of individual captains in deciding how to manoeuvre their ships once battle was joined and on the prowess of their ships' companies in fighting.

That completed the memorandum as far as an attack on the enemy from their lee side is concerned. All the rest concerned the *intended* attack.

Of the intended attack from to windward, the Enemy in Line of Battle ready to receive an attack.

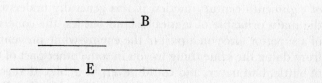

The divisions of the British Fleet will be brought nearly within gunshot of the Enemy's Centre. The signal will probably be made for the Lee Line to bear up together, to set all their sails, even steering [studding] sails, in order to get as quickly as possible to the Enemy's Line, and cut through beginning with the 12 Ships of the Enemy's Rear. Some Ships may not get through their exact place, but they will always be at hand to assist their friends; and if any are thrown round the Rear of the Enemy, they will effectually complete the business of twelve Sail of the Enemy.

Should the Enemy wear together, or bear up and sail large, still the twelve Ships composing, in the first position, the Enemy's Rear are to be the object of attack of the Lee Line, unless otherwise directed by the Commander-in-Chief, which is scarcely expected, as the entire management of the Lee Line, after the intentions of the Commander-in-Chief is signified, is intended to be left to the judgment of the Admiral commanding that Line.

The remainder of the Enemy's Fleet, 34 Sail, are to be left to the management of the Commander-in-Chief, who will endeavour to take care that the movements of the Second-in-Command are as little interrupted as is possible.

NELSON and BRONTË.

From the narrative of the British fleet's approach, already related, it is clear that the only thing it had in common with the memorandum was Collingwood's attack on the enemy's rear, though in the event he did not succeed in concentrating a superior force there. The question still arises, however, whether the tactics that Nelson expounded therein would have been sound for the generality of commanders-in-chief—however successful they might have been for Nelson himself. As has been suggested previously throughout this examination of eighteenth century tactics, it was generally understood that the main principle of tactics in land battles, the concentration of a superior force on a part of the enemy while preventing him from doing the same thing to you in some other part of the field of battle, had never, and could never, be achieved at sea unless the enemy commander-in-chief misconducted his line. Evidently Nelson did not admit that limitation. He believed that his plan would have completely conquered the enemy's centre and rear, basing his belief partly on his prestige in enemy eyes, partly 'because it must be some time before they [the enemy van] could bring a force compact to attack any part of the British Fleet engaged', and partly because, as he had said to Keats a few weeks earlier, 'I shall go at them at once, if I can, about one-third of their line from their leading ship . . . I think it will surprise and confound the enemy. They won't know what I am about.' No doubt the plan in his memorandum would have been as successful as was his battle under the far less advantageous conditions that prevailed on October 21st, when his fleet was never in such a position as to make it feasible to signal the lee line to bear up together and cut through the line of the enemy's twelve rear ships simultaneously—signal 27: 'Break through the enemy's line in all parts where it is practicable, and engage on the other side.' Though the ships in Collingwood's line did their best, without any need of a signal, to comply with the underlying idea, it is clear that Nelson had no compunction in jettisoning the principle of a simultaneous blow on the enemy's rear when it was found to conflict with his desire to 'go at them at once'. In fact, far from Collingwood being able to impose a superior concentration on the enemy's rear, it was not till an hour after he had driven through astern of the *Santa Ana* that he had even eight ships out of his fifteen in action. They were opposed by thirteen of the enemy and there were three of the latter at the tail of their line not engaged. Six of his division were now approaching and would before long be hammering at the last five of the enemy, but his last ship of all was still a mile and a half away.

This was the situation at 1.15 p.m., ten minutes before Nelson was to be struck down by a musket ball fired from the mizzen top of the *Redoutable*. At this time there were only three of his division in close action and a concentration of eight enemy ships should have opposed them, though in fact four of these had fallen so far to leeward as to be out of the battle. Of the remaining nine of the British weather division, seven would be joining within the next hour and a half but the other two not till later still.

The long interval, however, between the start of the battle and the British fleet being fully engaged was partially balanced by the fact that until 1.45 p.m. eight of the enemy's van stood on to the northward and were now more than a mile away. At that time Dumanoir ordered these ships to tack and stand to the southward, but with little wind and a heavy swell this took a long time and it was not till an hour later that he was coming down to windward of the battle with four ships. After a brief engagement with the last two ships of Nelson's division he escaped to the southward, only to surrender after an action with a British squadron of equal strength in the Bay of Biscay a fortnight later.

About 4 p.m. Nelson died of his wound and by five o'clock all firing had ceased. Eighteen of the enemy (nine French, including the *Bucentaure*, and nine Spanish) had struck their colours and Villeneuve was now a prisoner in a ship of the *Victory's* line. In addition to Dumanoir's four who had got away to the southward and westward, five French and six Spanish ships had escaped to leeward and thence to Cadiz.

So overwhelming a defeat of his fleet by a lesser number of

British ships must, one supposes, have made it clear to Napoleon that however many and however well equipped the ships he might be able to provide for his seamen in the future, he had no real hope of reviving a feasible plan for the invasion of England, whatever the success of his Continental campaigns.

As regards the influence on the British navy's views of this most famous of its victories Senhouse's opinion again merits quotation.

The mode of attack used on the 21st may be recorded for our admiration as having led on that day to such magnificent results, and as one that may be used against an enemy when the boundary of caution may be outstepped for the purpose of throwing the die to try the chance of skill and an impetuous headlong courage against numbers; but it can only be in cases like this in question where a passive courage [on the enemy's side] occupies the place of spirited ability. Our heroic and lamented Chief knew his means, and knew the power he had to deal with. He knew the means he adopted were sufficient for the occasion, and that sufficed.

He planned and circulated that mode of attack commited to writing as one of his last legacies to the British Navy, which may be hereafter used under the mantle his spirit may have left behind. This plan appears to be perfect in its operation. Having so done he reserved the right of deviating from its stricter rules under his personal discrimination, and like a skilful artist employed the precise impulse to obtain his object without any unnecessary waste of exertion. At some future period someone less discriminating might attempt to follow in his footsteps and might fail.

Chapter 18

CONCLUSION

It may seem paradoxical that the way in which the British fleet was handled under sail in its last and most famous victory over French and Spanish adversaries was not, in its tactical aspects, the outcome of battle experience of the previous century. Nowadays, and for the past hundred and fifty years or more, 'progress' has seemed to dominate the affairs of mankind and this progress has been based on inspiration or on theory, followed by experiment and experience. But during the era in which the sailing ship of the line of battle dominated sea warfare there was no change in the underlying doctrine on which fleet tactics were based. Only in the fanciful ideas of Clerk of Eldin, which no admiral had attempted to implement, and in the memorandum that Nelson had promulgated in October 1805, to which he had paid no attention once the enemy were in sight, were there any signs of basic changes, and in neither instance were they followed up. Against a disciplined enemy there could be no sound plan of attack that could ensure a concentration on part of the enemy's line while preventing him from turning the tables on you elsewhere. Nelson's confidence that an unmolested Franco-Spanish van would not be handled with the promptitude needed to frustrate his plan was justified in the event but would have lacked a logical background against a well-drilled enemy attacked by a British fleet commanded by an admiral, however competent, if he had lacked Nelson's genius and the prestige that had sprung from it. Apart from hard fighting there could only be the hope that the enemy's commander-in-chief would so misconduct his line as to give you an opportunity of bringing such a concentration to bear. For this there must be instant readiness to take advantage of the resulting situation.

This apparent stagnation has sometimes been thought to reflect on the intelligence of admirals and captains, French, Spanish and Dutch as well as British, for all were of the opinion that against an enemy fleet of equal fighting and manoeuvring ability there could be no sound tactical basis other than a single close-hauled line ahead, a basis which was still included in Admiralty instructions after all the experience of the Napoleonic wars had been digested. There was not, of course, any stagnation in the art with which this underlying principle should be applied, an art which included taking advantage of any shifts of wind, if such could be derived from them, as well as profiting by the enemy's mistakes; and this takes one back to Hoste's dictum of a century earlier: 'It is the genius of a hero, possessing talent and experience, that is necessary to constitute a great admiral'. Here, in respect of experience, British admirals usually had advantages over their enemies. In the fifty years up to Trafalgar the British and French had been at war during twenty-three of them and during those years British fleets had often been at sea for long periods while the enemy remained in Brest or Toulon even when they were more numerous than their blockaders. Not every British admiral had the genius of a hero, but neither Rooke, Hawke, Howe, St Vincent, Duncan or Nelson could have been faulted in the handling of their fleets, and to these one could add Keppel and Byron, had not luck been against them in one way and another.

There is, however, nothing strange in the absence of change in tactical theory during the period covered here. Unless the doctrines generally accepted at the beginning of the century were unsound, which they were not, how could there be any progress in theory when there were not, and could not be in those days, any substantial changes in the materials of the tactician's trade—his ships and his guns? The ships must still be built of wood and the more intricate parts of their hulls must depend on the natural-grown bends of the trees which provided them. There was as yet little scope for the gun-founder's art. And the winds, on whose vagaries all tactics depended, could not be tamed by man.

Although the main aspect of fleet tactics is that which concerns

the formation and movements of the ships, this cannot be altogether divorced from questions of their gunfire, on which
victory or defeat ultimately depended. Some aspects of this
have been mentioned in previous chapters, but one may be
left wondering why it was that British fleets so often overcame
their French opponents, when the latter were of roughly equal
strength both in numbers and in weight of broadsides. The guns
of each fleet were of much the same pattern and there is no
reason to suppose that the French were in any way less skilled
in handling them than were their rivals. But there seems to
have been some lack of stamina in the way they were served if
an action was prolonged. This is a matter on which one can
hardly expect convincing evidence, but there is one source
which throws some light on the subject: the reminiscences of a
Swedish lieutenant who served in the French navy throughout
the Seven Years War.[1] In summing up his experiences he
remarks: 'The crew's discipline is based on the ground that
each man is driven to do his duty more by ambition than by
fear of punishment, which—except for mutiny or serious crime
—is very mild. A man who fails in any way is either put in
irons under the half-deck or is deprived of his daily issue of
wine and this is sufficient punishment'. This view of an almost
idyllic state of affairs was derived not merely from a limited
experience in one ship, for during those seven years he had
served in three ships of the line (in one of them at the battle
of Quiberon Bay) and one frigate; but it certainly contrasts
strongly with the generally accepted view of the harsh and
sometimes brutal discipline of the British navy in those days.
It is not to be supposed that harshness had any direct impact
on British guns' crews in action, but it may be that it contributed to a toughness and resolution which the French seaman's
ambition could not sustain when hard pressed.

The above is a view of the question at the working end, so to
speak. But there is also to be considered the influence on the
guns' crews which stemmed from the admirals, captains and
lieutenants above them, and here one can refer to Senhouse's
remarks already quoted at the end of the previous chapter,

[1] 'The Reminiscences of Lieutenant Malmsköld', translated and edited
by R. C. Anderson, in the *Naval Miscellany*, vol. IV (Navy Records Society).

where he speaks of a passive courage (on the enemy's side) occupying the place of spirited ability—on one's own side. French admirals seldom wanted to fight fleet actions; they looked to other means of achieving their strategical aims. And mere passive courage did not, it seems, inspire their fleets to the same high level of resolution as their British adversaries so often achieved.

Although, as has already been emphasized, there was no basic change in the tactical theory of fleets under sail, there was the one original manoeuvre in implementing an attack from to windward which Howe had introduced before the end of the eighteenth century with a view to countering the French tendency to break off action by falling to leeward. This was that each ship should pass through the enemy's line under the stern of her immediate opponent and engage the latter from to leeward. As already related, it had been partially successful at the battle of the Glorious First of June 1794 despite its difficulties and its risks, of which Howe was well aware. A similar manoeuvre, though in very rough form, was adopted successfully by Duncan at the battle of Camperdown, where it gave the only possibility of victory, for he was fighting a Dutch fleet off a steadily shoaling lee shore and the Dutch ships drew less water than the British. And at Trafalgar, although there was no regularity of attack, Nelson's captains well knew that they were expected to pass, if they could, through any part of the enemy's line that confronted them and to hold their enemies under fire until they surrendered. In this most of them succeeded despite the general drift of both fleets towards the Trafalgar shoals.

BIBLIOGRAPHY

PUBLICATIONS OF THE NAVY RECORDS SOCIETY

Barham, Letters and Papers of Charles, Lord (3 vols, ed. J. K. Laughton, 1907–11)
Barrington, Letters and Papers of Admiral the Honourable Samuel (2 vols, ed. D. Bonner-Smith, 1937–41)
Collingwood, The Private Correspondence of Admiral Lord (ed. E. Hughes, 1957)
Fighting Instructions 1530–1860 (ed. J. S. Corbett, 1905)
Hood, Lord, Letters of, 1781–3 (ed. D. Hannay, 1895)
Leake, The Life of Admiral Sir John (by Stephen Martin-Leake, 2 vols, ed. G. A. R. Callender, 1920)
Logs of the Great Sea Fights 1794–1805 (2 vols, ed. T. S. Jackson, 1899–1900)
Sandwich, The Private Papers of John, Earl of (4 vols, ed. G. R. Barnes and J. H. Owen, 1932–8)
Signals and Instructions 1776–94 (ed. J. S. Corbett, 1908)
Spencer, The Private Papers of George, second Earl, vols I and II (ed. J. S. Corbett, 1913–14); vols III and IV (ed. H. W. Richmond, 1924)

SELECTED BOOKS

Admiralty,	Report of a Committee appointed to examine and consider the evidence relating to the Tactics employed by Nelson at the Battle of Trafalgar (London, 1913)
Barrow, J.,	*The Life of Richard, Earl Howe* (London, 1838)
Beatson, R.,	*Naval and Military Memoirs of Great Britain from 1727 to 1783* (London, 1804)
Burrows, M.,	*The Life of Edward, Lord Hawke* (London, 1883)
Camperdown, Earl of,	*Admiral Duncan* (London, 1898)
Chadwick, F. E. (ed.),	*The Graves Papers* (Naval History Society U.S.A., New York, 1916)
Clerk, J.,	*Naval Tactics* (3rd edition, Edinburgh, 1827)
Corbett, J. S.	*England in the Mediterranean* 1603–1713 (London, 1904)
	England in the Seven Years War (London, 1901)
	The Campaign of Trafalgar (London, 1910)
Cornwallis-West, G.,	*The Life and Letters of Admiral Cornwallis* (London, 1927)
Douglas, H.,	*Naval Evolutions* (London, 1832)
Drinkwater, J.,	*Narrative of Proceedings of the British Fleet comamanded by Admiral Sir J. Jervis, 14th February 1797* (London, 1797)

Ekins, C.,	*The Naval Battles of Great Britain* (2nd edition, London, 1828)
Falconer, W.,	*Marine Dictionary*, originally published in 1769, extensively revised and enlarged by Burney W. (London, 1815)
Grenfell, R.,	*Nelson the Sailor* (2nd edition, London, 1952)
Hoste, P.,	*Naval Evolutions*, translated by J. D. Boswall (Edinburgh, 1834)
Howarth, D.,	*Trafalgar The Nelson Touch* (London 1969)
James, W.,	*The Naval History of Great Britain* (new edition, London, 1859)
James, W. M.,	*The British Navy in Adversity* (London, 1926)
Keppel, T.,	*The Life of Augustus, Viscount Keppel* (London, 1842)
Laughton, J. K. (ed).,	*Memoirs Relating to Lord Torrington* (Camden Society, London, 1889)
	Biographies of many British admirals of the 18th Century in the *Dictionary of National Biography* (London, 1885–1900)
Laughton, L. G. C.,	'The Battle of Velez Malaga, 1704' in the *Royal United Service Institution Journal* (1923)
Lloyd, C.,	*Battles of St Vincent and Camperdown* (London, 1963)
Mackay, R. F.,	*Admiral Hawke* (Oxford, 1965)
Mahan, A. T.,	*The Influence of Sea Power upon History* 1660–1783 (Boston, 1890)
	The Influence of Sea Power upon the French Revolution and Empire 1793–1812 (Boston, 1892)
	The Life of Nelson (revised edition, Boston, 1897)
	Types of Naval Officers, Drawn from the History of the British Navy (Boston, 1901)
	From Sail to Steam (New York, 1907)
	Major Operations of the Navies in the War of American Independence (Boston, 1913)
Marcus, G.,	*Quiberon Bay* (London, 1960)
	A Naval History of England, I, The Formative Centuries (London, 1961)
	A Naval History of England, II, the Age of Nelson (London, 1971)
Mundy, G. B.,	*The Life and Correspondence of the late Admiral Lord Rodney* (London, 1830)
Nicolas, N. H.,	*The Despatches and Letters of Vice-Admiral Lord Viscount Nelson* (London, 1846)
Owen, J. H.,	*War at Sea under Queen Anne 1702–8* (Cambridge, 1938)
Pack, S. W. C.,	*Admiral Lord Anson* (London, 1960)
Puleston, W. D.,	*Life and Works of Captain Alfred Thayer Mahan* (New Haven, Conn., 1939)

Richmond, H. W.,	*The Navy in the War of 1739–48* (Cambridge, 1920)
Robertson, L. F.,	*The Evolution of Naval Armament* (London, 1921)
Spinney, D.,	*Rodney* (London, 1969)
Taylor, A. H.,	'The Battle of Trafalgar' in the *Mariner's Mirror*, vol. 23
Tucker, J. S.,	*Memoirs of Admiral the Earl of St Vincent* (London, 1844)
Tunstall, B.,	*Admiral Byng and the Loss of Minorca* (London, 1928)
Warner, O.,	*The Glorious First of June* (London, 1961)
	Nelson's Battles (London, 1965)
	The Life and Letters of Vice-Admiral Lord Collingwood (Oxford, 1968)
White, T.,	*Naval Researches* (London, 1830)

Index